This Book was presented to

Mayor Allan Kauffman

In appreciation of his support

Of The Sister City Committee.

Our Sincere Thanks ...

Producing and publishing a book to capture the first half-century of Sister Cities International's extraordinary history was no small task, but it was well worth the effort.

We want to thank historian/archivist Sharon Receveur and book publishers Carol and Bill Butler, longtime Sister Cities International supporters from Louisville, Kentucky, for offering two years ago to help us publish this 50th Anniversary volume.

Thanks to Executive Director Tim Honey and the dedicated members of the Sister Cities International Board of Directors for believing in this book project and for providing the staff support, archival materials and historical photos needed to produce this book.

Special thanks to all the members of Sister Cities International worldwide who combed through their own sister city archives and submitted the inspiring stories and heartwarming photographs that are the core of this 50th anniversary salute. Through their personal stories and photos, readers can trace the rich history and understand the true spirit of the people-to-people/sister cities movement and its impact on global diplomacy.

Special recognition must be given to Dick Oakland, who kept a camera with him at all times for more than thirty years to record sister city memories. Although Dick is no longer with us, his photo and history files were essential to the creation of this book. Special thanks to Development Director Phyllis Warren-Briggs for keeping the renowned "Dick Oakland files" intact through office moves and filing reorganizations.

We want to thank the dedicated staff members who worked so hard to make this book – and Sister Cities International's 50th Anniversary – a huge success.

Special thanks to the diligent book team members who scavenged through archives, edited submissions, then wrote, designed and poured their hearts and souls into the creation of this book: Carol Butler, Emily Carter, Ami Neiberger-Miller and Sharon Receveur. We are also grateful to the interns who worked tirelessly to help them put this book together – Mariam Alkazemi, Julie Riouallon, Amanda Straub and Sheryl Thomas – and to Scott Stortz and Heather Jones of Louisville who designed this beautiful book.

It "takes a village" to produce a volume of this magnitude, complexity and historical importance. We are grateful to all who believed in this project and helped make it a reality, and to all who support the worldwide mission of Sister Cities International.

Published by Butler Books
P.O. Box 7311
Louisville, KY 40207
(502) 897-9393
www.butlerbooks.com

Book Design by Scott Stortz and Heather Jones
Book Jacket Design by Scott Stortz

Printed in Canada

Table of Contents

SOWING SEEDS OF FRIENDSHIP

This parade of "Amigos de San Antonio, Texas" marks the beginning of a beautiful friendship, as Guadalajara, Mexico celebrated its new sister city relationship with San Antonio, Texas. This sister city relationship has generated decades of goodwill, industry, trade and technical exchanges.

BEFORE 1956: THE SISTER CITY MOVEMENT'S EARLY SEEDS ARE SOWN

From the earliest days, communities have forged ties in other parts of the world. Relationships fostered by immigrants traveling to a new land enabled them to retain their culture, language, and understanding of themselves. New citizens developed towns they named for their ancestral homes or in honor of patrons in the Old World – in the United States names like New York, Williamsburg, Lafayette and St. Louis are just a few examples.

For some communities, these early names hearkening back to another time would become a starting point to a sister city relationship – and within the fledgling sister city movement they became known as "nametowns." New Bern, North Carolina and Bern, Switzerland trace their relationship to 1710, although formal papers officially linking the communities weren't signed by both mayors until the 1960s. In some cases, few records remain of these early relationships.

The lengthy conflicts and carnage of World War II devastated entire cities in Europe, Asia, Eurasia and the Pacific, leaving millions dead, wounded or displaced. Reduced to rubble, cities prized by western civilization for centuries lay in ruin, and thousands ached in hunger, need and want.

The war's destructive power tore asunder the barriers and assumptions many held – and made some more open to the idea of reaching out in brotherhood and generosity – not fear and hatred. Ironically, it was an ideal environment – both socially and technologically – for communities to come together.

International travel and communication were more readily accessible. A number of war relief and humanitarian aid organizations emerged during and after the Second World War that catalyzed the movement to forge linkages. Historian Wilbur Zelinsky noted that projects like Bundles for Britain, Russian War Relief and American Aid to France sent goods overseas and laid the early groundwork for post-war humanitarian aid efforts.

In Europe, former enemies began the job of healing and reconciliation – setting up twinning relationships between pairs of municipalities in Germany and France, and later reaching out to other countries. And the goodwill between former enemies expanded, with U.S. communities reaching out to Japan and Germany. In 1951, Arlington, Texas mounted a large-scale humanitarian aid project for Königshofen, Germany that would kindle a relationship stretching across the decades.

On the heels of the Second World War, the Nuclear Age dawned, and it wasn't long before a Cold War would rumble thunderously in the distance. Preventing the horrors of war from engulfing our nations again was not far from the minds of many people – including Dwight D. Eisenhower.

As commander of the Allied Expeditionary Forces in Europe and leader of the occupying forces in Germany, General Eisenhower saw firsthand the devastation and ruin the war's hostilities brought. Although he had been a soldier for all his adult life, it was soon evident that Eisenhower had a gift for bringing together people of diverse backgrounds to plan and work toward common peaceful goals. With the majority of the world's people living in cities, Eisenhower dreamed of a program that would facilitate the creation of links between people of one city to another, so friendships could be established. By becoming friends, he reasoned that people of different cultures could celebrate and appreciate their differences, instead of deriding them, fostering suspicion, and sowing new seeds for war.

While many methods could be used to develop greater international understanding, Eisenhower said, "Yet none can be more effective than direct, close, and abiding communications between cities, where indeed most of our people now live."

After he became president in 1953, Eisenhower continued to work for peace. And communities all over the United States, continued to forge new "town affiliation" links. In 1955, Hagerstown, Maryland and Wesel, Germany forged a sister city relationship.

On September 11-12, 1956, Eisenhower brought Americans representing all walks of life to Washington, D.C. to attend a White House Conference on Citizen Diplomacy. The meeting had been postponed earlier in his administration and the President was eager to hear their ideas for implementing his people-to-people concept – otherwise known as citizen diplomacy.

He told delegates attending the conference that, "Two deeply held convictions unite us in common purpose. First, is our belief in effective and responsive local government as a principal bulwark of freedom. Second, is our faith in the great promise of people-to-people and sister city affiliations in helping build the solid structure of world peace."

And this was only the beginning…

Toledo, Ohio and Toledo, Spain have the oldest documented sister city relationship recognized by Sister Cities International. In honor of the 50th anniversary of their sister city relationship in 1981, the mayor of Toledo, Spain delivered a speech about their friendship through the years.

When Making Friends

"....sincere but overly-enthusiastic approaches by American community groups steeped in the pragmatic tradition that in an age of salesmanship tends to get deafened by the sound of its own voice, may frighten and put on their guard overseas communities used to more formal and low-keyed approaches."

- Dr. George C. Wynne

Did You Know?

So, Who Really Has The Oldest Sister City Relationship?
Although many communities cite evidence of exchanges or other activities, Sister Cities International has verified that officials from Toledo, Ohio and Toledo, Spain signed a twinning document in 1931 linking their communities.

Germans and Americans Forge Life-Long Friendship in Aftermath of Second World War

"We began sharing our love with the world in 1948. Pasadena decided to "adopt" a heavily bombed town in Germany, and Ludwigshafen was chosen because the Pasadena Friends Service Committee already had a clothing depot there. Pasadenans were asked to send warm clothing and blankets and Ludwigshafen became our first sister city. It was suggested that if anyone would be interested in corresponding with the recipients, addresses could be slipped into a pocket.

Our family of four children started a wonderful life-long relationship writing to a German family with five children. In 1965 when my parents visited them, Frau Clemons showed them a shoe box filled with letters and pictures.

We began hosting exchange students in 1986, and have been so blessed by the 85 Germans that we have hosted and learned to love. Our entire family has been touched by this program. Two of our sons' families housed German exchange visitors and visited Ludwigshafen. Three of our grandchildren have been to our German sister city, the youngest flying there to stay with a family at the age of 12.

In 2003 we visited Ludwigshafen and saw all of our "grandchildren" who had moved away. When we go to Germany we feel like we are coming home. In another month, we are "expecting" our 20th German great-grandchild!"

By Laura Hallinger
Pasadena, California

Operation Town Affiliations, Inc.
The Forerunner of the Civic Committee

Formed in New York City in the 1950s, Operation Town Affiliations, Inc. served as a clearinghouse to help communities link together. The organization distributed a newsletter and even held a training conference. Services were provided for free and through donations. Any town affiliation could belong to a list of "contributing town affiliations" by sending in $10 per year.

Town affiliation was defined as "an affiliation or cultural tie between a town in the United States and a town in another country, where two-way correspondence is possible. Your organizations correspond with their counterparts."

Kathleen Sparkman served as the organization's president and director and built a list of more than 200 town-to-town affiliations. Sparkman corresponded with the Civic Committee and the American Municipal Association, as well as People-to-People.

Operation Town Affiliation, Inc. eventually faded and ceased operations some time in the early 1960s. Some of the pioneering sister city relationships benefited from the work of Operation Town Affiliations, Inc.

Rebuilding a Nation: Americans Reach Out to Former Battlefield Enemies

As these photos show, after World War II, Japan needed significant help rebuilding its communities and economy. Dozens of U.S. communities reached out to Japanese communities in friendship and initiated sister city relationships. Considering that only a decade earlier, Japanese-Americans in the United States were incarcerated in camps and anti-Japanese fervor was patriotic in war-time America, their friendly embrace of an enemy in the post-war years was remarkable.

Friendship Blossoms From Cold War Aid to Bavarian Town

In 1951 Kurt Zühlke, city manager of a German town, then called Königshofen, visited Arlington, Texas. He was near the end of a study tour of the United States and stopped in Arlington with fellow tour participant Irene von Falkenried, who had a pen pal there.

Theda Howell, the Arlington pen pal, and her parents invited them into their home and learned about the difficulties Königshofen was facing due to its location just a few miles west of what had become the border between West and East Germany. Hundreds of refugees from the East were overwhelming the small town. There was a shortage of food and clothing.

Arlington citizens immediately wanted to help the Bavarian town. The city and the Arlington Chamber of Commerce began to collect clothing, food and gifts. On September 17, 1951, Mayor Vandergriff wrote to Königshofen's Mayor Kaspar Lurz about Arlington's decision to provide assistance and said that the people of Arlington were anxious to strengthen the bonds between the United States and Germany, and especially the bonds between the two cities.

A railroad boxcar filled with items for Königshofen was readied for shipment from Arlington in February 1952. It was the first of four shipments. In June 1954, Königshofen named its city park "Arlington-Park" as an expression of thanks and honor to the Texas community which helped its citizens so generously.

Much has changed since the 1950s and the early days of the Cold War, but the friendship between the two cities has continued. In 1991 a group of Arlington citizens traveled to Bad Königshofen to celebrate the German city's 1250th Anniversary and the 40th Anniversary of their sister city friendship. In 1992 a large delegation from Bad Königshofen came to Arlington for the dedication of the new picnic pavilion in the Bad Königshofen Recreation Area.

In 2006, the cities continue to share deep friendships forged out of a visit by two people to Arlington in 1951.

Tucson Renders Aid…and Finds a Sister

In 1950, Tucson, Arizona came to the aid of Trikkala, Greece, a war-torn city ravaged by guerrilla forces. Food, medicine and other supplies were followed by reciprocal student and cultural exchanges when the rehabilitation needs of the Greek community had been met. This "adoption" of a community in the theaters of war was a method embraced by many U.S. communities trying to help reconstruction efforts.

Town Affiliations As Distant Neighbors

A SIMPLE PROCESS

(A) What you do in your own town:

1) Contact your Mayor, your City Council and the heads of all your municipal and social organizations.

2) Call a meeting of these people, or their representatives.

3) Decide at this meeting the foreign country in which you want to establish your own direct community contact.

4) Form an executive committee to represent your town; this is important.

5) Write to: Operation Town Affiliations, Inc., 104 East 40th St., New York 16, New York. giving: the country you have chosen; a description of your own town, population, organizations, industries, etc., the names of your Mayor and your executive committee.

(B) What Operation Town Affiliations, Inc., does:

Volunteers, with no charge, to do its best to:

1) Find, for you, a town similar to yours, in the country you have chosen;

2) Give you details of this town;

3) Arrange to have the foreign town establish a representative committee similar to yours;

4) Put your committees in touch with one another.

At this point, your two communities are "on your own" in your relationship. For, as one American community puts it, "We like this program because it lets us do things in our own way. It credits us with initiative and intelligence."

Ask O. T. A., for any further information you may need.

(a) Cultural Exchange—

This is the important aspect of your town affiliation program—

1) Contact and correspondence—

In order to put your affiliation on the widest possible basis, officials, organizations, groups and individuals in each town should be put in touch with one another and urged to correspond—
City Officials, City Departments (Fire, Police, etc.)

Post Offices, Schools, Universities, other educational institutions; Churches, Doctors, Hospitals, Lawyers, Boy and Girl Scouts, Campfire Girls, Hobby Groups, Red Cross, Chambers of Commerce or other business groups; libraries, Clubs or Societies — Women's, Men's, Garden, Photographic, Stamp, Chess, Historical, Sports or others; National Organizations—Rotary, Lions, Kiwanis and others; Farm Organizations, Newspapers, Language Groups, Banks.

2) Besides general and individual correspondence, the above groups can exchange:

Scrapbooks—on— schools, local history, hobbies, home life in either community. Books—technical, educational, any literature of special or general interest. Magazines, Newspapers, News items of interest or special columns about the other town can be carried in the local paper.

Motion pictures, still pictures and snapshots. Paintings, Exhibits, of different kinds; Handicrafts, Stamps and stamp albums, Gardening information and seeds, Natural history information, Recipes, Costumes, Greeting cards for various special occasions—Christmas, Easter, etc.

Music, records, sheet music, scores. instruments. General information on the functioning and operation of similar organizations in each town. Gifts of any kind; Information on local customs, traditions and ways of living.

3) Personal Exchange—

Any town affiliation may arrange to send visitors from one town to the other as good-will ambassadors, Mayors, committee heads, students, teachers, professional people, educational leaders, business people.

(b) Material Aid—

If you choose to make your affiliation in a country where economic conditions are poor, you may be able to provide some needed material aid:
Clothing, Household equipment, Food packages, Medical supplies, School materials, Athletic equipment, Tools—gardening and carpentry, Special aid for orphanages and old people, Toys.

It is important to remember that a town affiliation is primarily a cultural relationship. It should be as much as possible a "two-way street," with each town contributing what it can to the program to the end that each comes to know the other better, as neighbors, and as friends.

This 1955 article in *The American City*, published by the American Municipal Association, highlighted the activities of Operation Town Affiliations, Inc. and the many U.S. communities seeking partners around the globe.

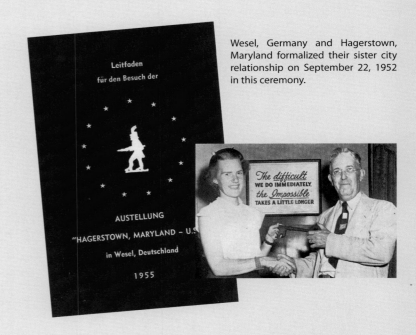

Wesel, Germany and Hagerstown, Maryland formalized their sister city relationship on September 22, 1952 in this ceremony.

Early Beginnings
Hagerstown, Maryland – Wesel, Germany

This 1955 guide, published in both German and English, walked visitors through an exhibition in Wesel about sister city Hagerstown. The authors wrote, "As a means of better understanding, this booklet is presented to the citizens of Wesel and Rees County by the people of Hagerstown and Washington County, in the hope of strengthening the bonds of an already established friendship." A year earlier, Hagerstown had hosted an exhibit from Wesel. The two communities signed a sister city affiliation agreement three years earlier on September 22, 1952. The sister city relationship emerged from a visit to Hagerstown in 1951 by a delegation of 25 people from Germany and a friendship forged during that trip between Hagerstown's mayor Dr. Rolf von Bonninghausen, chief administrator of Rees County in Germany. The project organizers reported enthusiastic support from Operation Town Affiliation in New York.

The devastation of the Second World War left large swaths of Europe and Asia in ruin. Many U.S. communities reached out to communities in war-torn areas to offer aid and hope.

Profound Gratitude

"The personal contact with your new friends will be a delightful experience. Its overwhelming effect will become evident at your parting with them. Your own and their eyes, be not surprised, will be "glistening with heavenly tears." You will be overtaken by a feeling of profound gratitude for having been instrumental in bringing an entire community to a consciousness of an ideal movement – Town Affiliation."
- excerpted from "The ABC's of Town Affiliation: A Guide for Beginners," by Moses N. Friedman, York-Arles Twinning Committee

A Peek Inside an Early Town Affiliation

Distant Neighbors:

What can we, as individual citizens, do to improve world understanding and good will?

By cooperating with the mayor, a neighborly acquaintance has been established between Garden City, New York and Coburg, Germany. This acquaintance was started by the Mayor of Garden City sending greetings and a letter of inquiry to the Mayor of Coburg to ask if he would be interested in the exchange of letters to start an acquaintance between his town and Garden City. Our Mayor received a most cordial reply.

The exchange of letters has led to personal visits in both directions.

There was a student in the Garden City High School for one year, from Coburg. This was the straw in the wind which led the committee to select Coburg.

Garden City has sent Christmas tree decorations and small gifts to decorate a tree in the Town Hall at Coburg, and Coburg has sent decorations for a Christmas tree in the Town Hall at Garden City.

Under the supervision of the U.S. State Department, eight Coburg citizens came to this country to see how our local groups operate to get things done. The following illustrates their need for seeing local group cooperation in action:

At a luncheon meeting of about 80 persons, the chairman asked if one of our guests would favor us with a few comments. Dr. Frederick Trueheit, who was Headmaster of the Teachers' Training College in Coburg, responded. He apologized for his English and his comments for, as he said, "You know it has been twenty years since we have been permitted to freely express ourselves publicly – either at home or in other countries." Consequently, free group activities and local democratic procedures were still theoretical to them.

They were taken to a Property Owners' Association meeting, a PTA meeting, school board meeting, etc. and were given some general information about our form of Town government and education systems. They were told something about our exchange of letters program which we had started.

They were very much interested and made a tape recording of some of their thoughts and constructive suggestions.

Tape recordings of a Christmas greeting message and group songs were sent by air mail to a French town, where contacts had previously been established. The message was translated into French by the French Department of the High School and was read into the record by a high school French student.

The above projects indicate some of the wide range of friendly activities which are made possible by a neighborly Town Affiliation. Establishing acquaintance with distant towns can relieve a lot of tension and develop good will.

It is not enough that we give our youth training here and abroad with the hope that they will be able to solve the problems they inherit. It is our sacred obligation to those who have sacrificed, fought and died for our Country, that we do our very best to minimize the strife, contentions and misunderstandings we pass on to future generations.

France gave us the Statue of Liberty. We gave Germany the Freedom Bell and Freedom Scrolls. Now, with our quick communication and transportation, is the time when citizens in all countries need to energetically translate the spirit of those wonderful gifts into neighborly understanding and good will, as communities, and as citizens.

As our town meetings have been the source of the very life blood of our country's democracy, so Town Affiliations can be the means of expressing neighborly interest and good will to the peoples of various countries who have contributed so much to the development of our country and the principles for which it stands.

If we get acquainted with a neighbor, it is not long before we come to understand him and in many cases become good friends.

The discovery of distant good neighbors and friends can be a great pleasure and service.

Establishing a Town Affiliation does not require constant work, but continued mutual understanding and a readiness to cooperate to improve neighborly good will. The same as good neighbors here at home.

By close local cooperation, we can effectively improve world understanding and good will both here and abroad.

Written by Frank Warner
Board member of Operation Town Affiliations, Inc.

The First U.S. – Japan Sister City Connection

The first sister city linkage between the United States and Japan joined St. Paul, Minnesota with Nagasaki. Their relationship began December 7, 1955, on the anniversary of the attack on Pearl Harbor that initiated hostilities between the two countries. While touring Peace Park in Nagasaki in 1990, Mayor Jim Scheibel of St. Paul paid tribute to the victims of the atomic bomb and said, "It is important that we honor the memory of war victims, in our country as well as Japan. The best way to do that is to work to make sure that this kind of war and destruction never happen again. That's what sister city relationships and people-to-people diplomacy are all about."

PRESIDENT DWIGHT D. EISENHOWER

President Eisenhower announces the creation of the People-to-People program to a group of reporters on September 11, 1956.

The Cold War was getting colder, saber rattling was heard around the world, and bomb shelters were the rage in America. President Dwight D. Eisenhower tried to kindle a thaw by starting an extraordinary program called People-to-People.

Eisenhower's goal was revolutionary at the time when he stated, "If we are going to take advantage of the assumption that all people want peace, then the problem is for people to get together and to leap governments – if necessary to evade governments – to work out not one method, but thousands of methods by which people can gradually learn a little bit more of each other."

This unique concept to enlist hundreds of thousands of volunteer citizen diplomats in a quest for peace was initiated at a White House Conference on Citizen Diplomacy called by President Eisenhower and held September 11-12, 1956. Leading business people, civic organizers and Americans from every walk of life attended the event to undertake the monumental task.

The President told the assembled delegates that "…in the opinion of this administration there is no more important work than that in which we are asking you to participate." He summarized the goal as "…the most worthwhile purpose there is in the world today."

1956

The White House Conference
September 11-12, 1956

The White House Conference formed the capstone of the people-to-people program. It represented the coming together of government specialists – who had been working continuously on the program for almost a year and who had fairly definite ideas on how it should proceed – with private individuals who were to carry the program into action but who had only a superficial knowledge of what they were expected to accomplish and how they might do it.

During the two-day conference, the appointed delegates drafted action plans and 42 People-to-People committees were organized. The conference was called by the White House, with coordination provided by the U.S. Information Agency. By September 12, it was evident that each committee would be autonomous and would have to be responsible for its own funding and direction.

Some of the committees incorporated and set forth their own plans for program development and fundraising. Some worked through organizations whose membership they represented and some never functioned, or for only a short period.

Finally, 33 committees were settled on to carry out Eisenhower's dream. The sister cities idea originally came under the charge of the Civic Committee of People-to-People that Eisenhower had envisioned as a main cog in the mechanism of citizen diplomacy. This belief was to prove prophetic.

Actually, an announcement of the fledgling citizen diplomacy program was planned a year earlier, but it was postponed when the President fell into ill health. At that time, the original program was to have been named "The President's People-to-People Program for World Understanding," then "The President's Program for People-to-People Diplomacy," until the final shorter name stuck.

September 11, 1956

Ladies and Gentlemen:

I appear before such an audience with mixed emotions. There are so many of my friends among you that on the personal side I feel like I am coming to sort of a family gathering with all of the enjoyments we normally accord on such occasions.

When I look at the cross-section of American brains and ability here – some of you experienced widely in the fields in which I expect to talk – I must say I am very diffident if not embarrassed.

But I am emboldened to talk to you because the purpose of this meeting is the most worthwhile purpose there is in the world today: to help build the road to peace, to help build the road to an enduring peace.

A particular part of the work that we expect to do is based upon the assumption that no people, as such, want war – that all people want peace.

We know this to be a true assumption, but we know also that in certain portions of the world it is not understood as such. Some people are taught – and they are captive audiences – that others, including ourselves, want war: that we are warlike, that we are materialistic, that we are, in fact, hoping for cataclysms of that kind so that a few may profit, they say, out of the misery of the world.

For my part, and I have been around a long time and therefore am more or less acquainted with all of the wars the United States has fought, to the glory of American businessmen I have never heard one single one – ever – refer to war in any terms except those of regret and hope that war will never occur again.

If we are going to take advantage of the assumption that all people want peace, then the problem is for people to get together and to leap governments – if necessary to evade governments – to work out not one method but thousands of methods by which people can gradually learn a little bit more of each other.

The problems are: How do we dispel ignorance? How do we present our own case? How do we strengthen friendships? How do we learn of others? These are the problems.

The communist way, of course, is to subject everything to the control of the state and to start out with a very great propaganda program all laid out in its details – and everybody conforms. They do this in every walk of life, in everything they do; and for a while it seems to score spectacular successes.

Presented at the White House Conference on a Program for People-to-People Partnership Washington, D.C. on September 11, 1956

"...I am tremendously enthusiastic about this new project which you ladies and gentlemen here symbolize, in that its purpose is to continue, to intensify what we have been doing, to try to demonstrate to the world that our kind of free society produces that which all people most want. If we can get that idea across then, as I say, the rest of our problems will become relatively easy. So I greet you with enthusiasm and I hope with all sincerity that you will be able to make, as I believe you will be able to make, an important contribution to this essential basic task."

— John Foster Dulles, Secretary of State

Of course, its great weakness is that in times of stress, whenever the love of freedom, for example, grows greater in a population than the fear of the gun at their backs, then the dictatorships fall. Indeed, in war, when the fear of the machine gun in front grows greater than that of the machine gun behind, the dictatorships' armies begin to disintegrate.

Our way is a different one. We marshal the forces of initiative, independent action, and independent thinking of 168 million people. Sometimes it appears slow and awkward – weak. But the fact is that since all crises are met and action taken according to the will of the great majority, the tougher the going gets, the tighter is bound the whole: the more effective becomes the whole.

Today, we have this problem that I have stated: that of creating understanding between peoples. Here are people that we hope will lead us. Governments can do no more than point the way and cooperate and assist in mechanical details. They can publish certain official documents.

But I am talking about the exchange of professors and students and executives, the providing of technical assistance, and of the ordinary traveler abroad. I am talking about doctors helping in the conquering of disease, of our free labor unions showing other peoples how they work, what they earn, how they achieve their pay and the real take-home pay that they get.

In short, what we must do is to widen every possible chink in the Iron Curtain and bring the family of Russia, or of any other country behind that Iron Curtain, that is laboring to better the lot of their children – as humans do the world over closer into our circle, to show how we do it, and then to sit down between us to say, "Now, how do we improve the lot of both of us?"

In this way, I believe, is the truest path to peace. All of the other things that we do are mere palliatives or they are holding the line while constructive forces of this kind take effect.

Every bomb we can manufacture, every plane, every ship, every gun, in the long run has no purpose other than negative: to give us time to prevent the other fellow from starting a war, since we know we won't.

The billions we pour into that ought to be supported by a great American effort, a positive constructive effort that leads directly toward what we all want: a true and lasting peace.

So, in calling upon a group like this, I wanted to come before you, in spite of the diffidence of which I spoke, to tell you that in the opinion of this Administration there is no more important work than that in which we are asking you to participate. There is no problem before the American people – indeed, before the world – that so colors everything we do, so colors our thinking, our actions as does the problem of preserving the peace and providing for our own security.

Whether it be the Suez problem of today or another one of tomorrow, there is nothing else that so affects our daily lives. It dictates, almost, the level of our taxes. It colors every problem with which we deal at home.

So, as you start this work, as you have before you the government officials who will be the ones cooperating with you, you will understand that this is something that lies very close to the hearts of the Administration and to every man, woman and child in America – and indeed, we believe, the world – except for those few who want unjustly and improperly to rule others.

Thank you very much for your attention.

NOTE: On May 31, 1956, the White House announced that the President had asked a group of Americans representing many fields of activity to meet with him to explore the possibilities of a program for better people-to-people contacts throughout the world. In his letter of invitation, sent to 34 representative leaders and quoted in part in the release, the President said "there will never be enough diplomats and information officers...to get the job done without help from the rest of us. Indeed, if our American ideology is eventually to win out in the great struggle being waged between the two opposing ways of life, it must have the active support of thousands of independent private groups...and of millions of individual Americans acting through person-to-person communication in foreign lands."

On September 7 a further announcement listed the names of the chairmen of the 40 committees who were scheduled to meet with the President and other government officials on September 11.

The President spoke at the District Red Cross Building at 10:00 a.m.

Mark Bortman, president of Bortman Plastics, Boston, Massachusetts, was appointed by President Eisenhower to chair the Civic Committee. The Civic Committee works to link U.S. communities with others around the globe.

In 1966, Mark Bortman (right) had a decade of progress in forging town affiliations to discuss with President Dwight D. Eisenhower.

In his role as chair of the Civic Committee, Mark Bortman presents an award to Ruth Hendricksen.

A Sister City Leader: Mark Bortman

Mark Bortman, a Bostonian industrialist appointed by President Eisenhower to chair the Civic Committee, proved to be a tireless and irrepressibly enthusiastic leader. He came to be known to his associates as the 'Johnny Appleseed of international good will' through his sowing of some 4,000 mint condition U.S. Peace Dollars among the leaders and distinguished citizens of the 100 countries he visited in his 40 trips around the world. He saw the sister cities movement grow from some forty affiliations shortly after the Civic Committee was formed in 1956, to over 350 U.S. communities linked with communities in 57 countries. He served the program for eleven years until his death in 1967.

"…I know in talking about this program with leaders in United States communities that it is their desire to further expand their programs so that they will truly represent all the people of their communities, thus, each person would have an opportunity to participate in these international programs on his own level of interest, whether it be educational, cultural, technical, business, professional or in another area.

"An encouraging aspect in examining the programs carried out by communities that have been affiliated for longer periods of time, is the development of literally scores of different types of projects and exchanges on a cultural, social and economic basis that have enlisted the support of municipal officials, community organizations and vast members of the people in each community."

— Mark Bortman, Chairman,
Civic Committee People-to-People Program, 1959

Baseball Brings People Together
In the 1950s, more than 10,000 people in Downey, California turned out to watch their Little League baseball team play their sister city Guadalajara, Mexico. This photograph is from a publication produced in 1960.

A Warm Welcome
Huge crowds turned out in Montebellow, California in the 1950s to welcome these trans-Pacific sister city visitors from Ashita, Japan.

A Melody for Peace
Children from sister cities San Francisco, California and Osaka, Japan harmonize well together.

1957

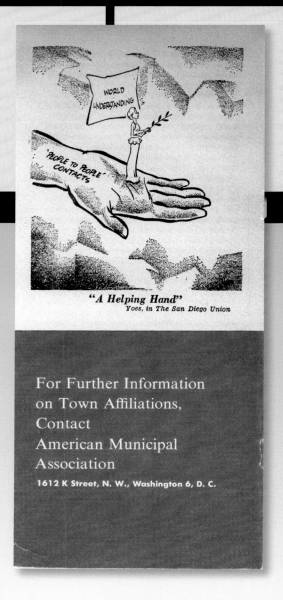

"A Helping Hand"
Yoes, in The San Diego Union

WORLD UNDERSTANDING

'PEOPLE TO PEOPLE' CONTACTS

For Further Information on Town Affiliations, Contact American Municipal Association

1612 K Street, N. W., Washington 6, D. C.

The Civic Committee Finds a Home: the American Municipal Association

Early in 1957, it became evident that the Civic Committee, representing the local private voluntary sector of the community, needed to expand its outreach to America's cities. The National League of Cities, then the American Municipal Association, with headquarters in Washington, D.C., was invited to serve as a clearinghouse and to manage and develop the program among the League's membership of over 14,500 municipal governments.

The association's executive committee approved the request for cooperation on July 24, 1957. It created a Committee on International Municipal Cooperation to work with the Civic Committee to establish policy and guidelines and provide a liaison with municipal organizations in other countries.

Robert E. McLaughlin, president of the Board of Commissioners of the District of Columbia, was named as the first chair of the Committee on International Municipal Cooperation.

The early successes of the program were accomplished on a shoestring budget. The Civic Committee operated primarily on donated funds, and the National League of Cities provided office space, a staff person titled director of Town Affiliations, office equipment, and other support funding through a small grant from the U.S. Information Agency.

Alan Beals was to become the first director of Town Affiliations for the League until he left to become the director of the Maryland Municipal League. John Slayton then became the second director. He was followed by Richard Oakland in 1960.

Momentum for a National Association Builds

As the creation of sister city relationships were promoted by United States Information Agency, the U. S. Foreign Service and the Civic Committee, it soon became apparent that a more formal structure was needed to handle the volume of requests. In 1965 the Executive Committee of the National League of Cities recommended the establishment of a national nonprofit voluntary association.

July 24, 1957
The Executive Committee of the American Municipal Association [now the National League of Cities] approves participation in a joint cooperative program with the Civic Committee of People-to-People to further the U.S. Sister Cities program.

A Sister City Relationship Is Born...and Lasts Through the Ages
Many of these early sister city relationships lasted to the present day. In 1957, Lexington, Kentucky and Deauville, France became sister cities, beginning a forty-plus-year journey together. Their mayors are pictured above after signing a sister city agreement.

Forty years later, in 1997, Mayor Anne d'Ornano of Deauville, France (left) and Mayor Pam Miller of Lexington, Kentucky (right) celebrated four decades of friendship.

A Salute to a Far-Off Sister City
Part of a week-long celebration in the 1950s, this float in Littleton, Colorado honored its sister city Bega, Australia.

Shoes for a Sister City
A monument showing a pair of comfortable shoes is dedicated in a park in Coral Gables, Florida replicating a famous statue in their sister city Cartagena, Colombia.

A Salute To A Bright Future
This float celebrating the People-to-People program was in the Inaugural Parade in Washington, D.C. for President Dwight D. Eisenhower on January 21, 1957. The photograph is from one of the first sister city publications ever produced.

Sharing Cultures, Sharing Lives
Below: India days were held annually in Darien, Connecticut to educate the community about their sister city, Mercara, India.

Left: Delegates from Darien are shown in 1964 when their partnership received an annual award for best overall sister city program for a community of under 25,000 in population.

February 27-28, 1958
The first Joint Conference of the Civic Committee, People-to-People program and the Committee on International Municipal Cooperation of the National League of Cities is held.

THE FIRST DECADE 1956-1965

1958

Mark Bortman announces to delegates at the first conference, "It is my belief this vital movement will make many significant contributions toward the creation of a world that one day must make peace workable. It is you, the chairpeople, committee members, municipal officials and the tens of thousands of individuals both here and abroad, that are working together to create this common goal for your children and posterity."

The First Conference

The First Conference: Washington, D.C.
The very first national sister cities conference was held in Washington D.C., February 27-28, 1958, and helped to point the way to the future growth the program would enjoy. The goal of the conference was to develop guidelines for cities joining the program and to publish helpful material and regular publications.

Mark Bortman, chair of the Civic Committee, outlined his vision for the program in an address to delegates stating:

> *"The experience that our committee members are gaining in carrying out affiliation projects has created an American more knowledgeable in foreign affairs than their parents or grandparents. Their visitations and personal experiences overseas have given them first hand knowledge in a practical and wise manner. The sister city program is a reciprocal exchange — not a one-way program. It is mutually beneficial to us and to our overseas counterparts who have worked so diligently to make it so successful and meaningful. Another magnificent aspect of this program has been the universal teamwork in our communities, which emphasizes the diverse activities of our people in a unified manner."*

Patrick Healy, director of the National League of Cities seconded Bortman saying, "We recognize the potential of the affiliation program, while having to be initiated by the chief municipal official, is absolutely dependent upon civic participation and wide-spread community support." The cooperative effort between the Civic Committee and the National League of Cities was to become a remarkable joining of two disparate entities — the first representing private volunteer citizens and the second the municipal official. At the time, because the program was new, there were no guidelines to follow and many of the early affiliations were established by trial and error. In addition, many other countries had no record of local voluntary organizations and the cities themselves provided the staff and funds to make the sister city program work. This was to lead to confusion and many false expectations of how the program would work in another country, how to formally affiliate, and exactly what kinds of projects to initiate. That it worked at all was a real tribute to the tenacious spirit of the thousands of local volunteers and their municipal leadership.

How fitting indeed, to hold the 50th anniversary conference in 2006 in Washington, D.C.

The first conference program was a mere one-page trifold flier – a far cry from today's Annual Conference programs – which typically run more than 60 pages long and are chock-full of information.

Student Exchange: New Ulm, Minnesota and Ulm, Germany
Exchange student Susanne Zoller of Ulm, Germany, points out to Mayor A.J. Eckstein of New Ulm, Minnesota, that in no matter what language, a town affiliation can basically carry out three types of exchanges – things, ideas, and people. Susanne spent the school term in New Ulm before returning to Germany.

International Partners in Peace
Members of the Chinju, Korea sister cities program take a photo on the anniversary of their linkage with Eugene, Oregon in the 1950s.

A Channel for Action

"Many people wring their hands over the bad situation the world is in. They complain about how badly the foreign relations of the United States are conducted. The same thing happens in all nations. The world is in a terrible turmoil and people often think, 'If there were only something I could do about it.' The People-to-People movement offers them a channel for action. Some amazing things have developed already in connection with this program."

— Ambassador George V. Allen, 1958

The Pasadenan

OPEN HOUSE, 1958

IN AFFILIATION WITH OUR
SISTER CITY -- MISHIMA, JAPAN

Putting Your Best Foot Forward
This 1958 publication highlighted Pasadena's charms for its sister city, Mishima, Japan.

Baseball Brings People Together
French youngsters from Arles learn to play baseball with their U.S. counterparts from York, Pennsylvania in this 2,000-year-old Roman coliseum in the 1950s. Pictured with some of the ball players are Jean Laurin, an exchange teacher from Arles who lived in York; Mrs. Charles Privat, wife of the Mayor of Arles; and Susan Boyd, York exchange teacher to Arles.

Help Scouting Potential Partners Overseas

"Following the White House conference, all American embassies and consulates general were informed of the sister city program, and U.S. Information Service posts in the free world were urged to offer suggestions of likely cities and towns abroad and to provide demographic and cultural information to assist U.S. cities and towns in choosing overseas partners. Such affiliations were to be a people-to-people activity completely dissociated from official U.S. foreign policy, and the American Foreign Service was to confine its participation to advising the Civic Committee."

—Hummel

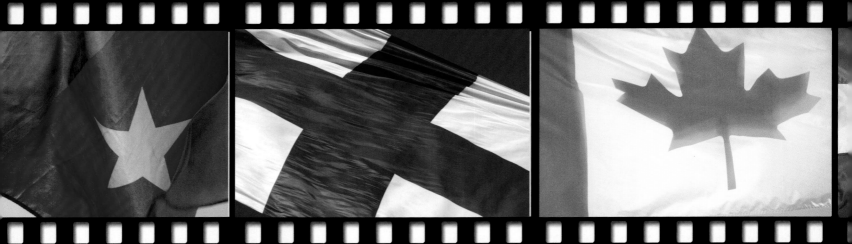

Civic Committee

People-to-People Program
Members 1958

Chairperson – Mark Bortman
Boston, Massachusetts

Orson Adams
Vice President, First National Bank of Boston
Boston, Massachusetts

Edwin H. Armstrong
Attorney at Law
Santa Ana, California

Catherine L. Beachley
Board of Education
Hagerstown, Maryland

Kenneth D. Benne
Director, Human Relations Center
Boston University
Boston, Massachusetts

Leonard Bernstein
Conductor-Composer
New York, New York

Warren Blackman
Director, Chamber of Commerce
Coral Gables, Florida

Daniel Bloomfield
Director, Boston Conference on Distribution
Boston, Massachusetts

James E. Boyce
President
Associates for International Research
Cambridge, Massachusetts

Frederick W. Brittan
Vice President
International Latex Corporation
Dover, Delaware

Dr. George Brodschi
Director, International Center
University of Louisville
Louisville, Kentucky

Joel I. Brooke
Elmo Roper and Associates
New York, New York

John D. Brown
Massachusetts House of Representatives
Boston, Massachusetts

Edward R. Carr
Realtor
Washington, D.C.

Thomas J. Carty
Stone's Express
Cambridge, Massachusetts

Phyllis Case
Boston University
Boston, Massachusetts

Theodora H. Coshel
Worthington, Minnesota

H. Walton Cloke
Coordinator of Public Relations
Kaiser Industries Corporation
Washington, D.C.

Erie Cocke, Jr.
Vice President, Delta Air Lines, Inc.
Atlanta, Georgia

William G. Colbern
Manager, Chamber of Commerce
Riverside, California

Phillips Davies
Attorney at Law
San Francisco, California

William F. Devin
Seattle, Washington

Edward Donnelly
President, John Donnelly and Sons
Roxbury, Massachusetts

Frederick Dumaine
President, Avis Rent-A-Car System, Inc.
Boston, Massachusetts

The Reverend Edward L.R. Elson
National Presbyterian Church
Washington, D.C.

Sterling Fisher
Director of Public Relations, "Readers Digest"
Pleasantville, New York

Dr. Leon H. Franklin
Montclair, New Jersey

Rabbi Moses N. Friedman
York, Pennsylvania

Pauline Goddard
Boston, Massachusetts

Thomas Y. Gorman
Manager, WEEI
Boston, Massachusetts

H. DeForest Hardinge
Hardinge Company, Inc.
York, Pennsylvania

Ellen Harris
Denver, Colorado

Mrs. George Harvill
University of Arizona
Tucson, Arizona

Patrick Healy, Jr.
Executive Director
American Municipal Association
Washington, D.C.

Ernest Henderson
President, Sheraton Corporation of America
Boston, Massachusetts

H.H. Hillyer
President, South Atlantic Gas Company
Savannah, Georgia

Judge Jacob J. Kaplan
Trustee
Boston, Massachusetts

Roger Kennedy
Director, Dallas Council on World Affairs
Dallas, Texas

Dr. Owen B. Kiernan
Commissioner
State Department of Education
Boston, Massachusetts

The Very Reverend Monsignor Francis J. Lolly
Editor, "The Pilot"
Boston, Massachusetts

Harry Lindquist
Chairperson, Hobbies Committee
People-to-People Program
New York, New York

Dr. Milton Lord
Director, Boston Public Library
Boston, Massachusetts

Ralph Lowell
President, Board of Overseers
Harvard University
Boston, Massachusetts

Edna McDonough
Executive Secretary
International Friendship League
Boston, Massachusetts

Dr. Thomas H.D. Mahoney
Department of Humanities,
Massachusetts Institute of Technology
Cambridge, Massachusetts

Frank Maria
Consultant
Lowell, Massachusetts

J.P. Marto
Boston, Massachusetts

William P. McCahill
Committee for the Handicapped
Washington, D.C.

Robert E. McLaughlin
President, Board of Commissioners
Washington, D.C.

Norris Nash
Director, Community Relations
Kaiser Corporation
Oakland, California

Ambassador Thomas Pappas
Belmont, Massachusetts

A.H. Parker
President, Old Colony Trust Company
Boston, Massachusetts

Mrs. John E. Peters
Pasadena, California

Mary D. Poog
Director, City Beautiful Commission
Nashville, Tennessee

Joseph Prendergast
Executive Director
National Recreation Association
New York, New York

Frank Reynolds
Chamber of Commerce
San Diego, California

Irwin Sanders
Associates for International Research
Cambridge, Massachusetts

J. Benjamin Schmoker
General Secretary, Committee on Friendly
Relations Among Foreign Students
New York, New York

Lee Schooler
President, Public Relations Board
Chicago, Illinois

Dr. Elmer L. Severinghaus
Essex Falls, New Jersey

Mrs. O.J. Sharpe
Vice President
International Friendship Council
Fresno, California

The Honorable Robert G. Simmons
Chief Justice, Supreme Court of Nebraska
Lincoln, Nebraska

Dr. Frank W. Snowden, Jr.
Dean, School of Liberal Arts
Howard University
Washington, D.C.

Charles H. Sorter
International Friendship Council
Fresno, California

Robert G. Sproul
President, University of California
Berkeley, California

Delmar G. Starkey
General Manager, Chamber of Commerce
Columbus, Ohio

Ruth E. Stevens
Director, Office of International Relations
Detroit, Michigan

Woodrow W. Strickler
Vice President, University of Louisville
Louisville, Kentucky

Charles L. Todd
President
International Advisory Council, Inc.
New York, New York

Muriel Tolle
Chairperson
San Diego–Yokohama Friendship Committee
San Diego, California

Jennie Vimmerstedt
Jamestown Post-Journal
Jamestown, New York

John A. Volpe
President, Volpe Construction Company
Molden, Massachusetts

Charles von Loewenfeldt
Public Relations
San Francisco, California

Mrs. Lyman Wagers
Lexington – Deauville Committee
Lexington, Kentucky

Griffith Way
Attorney at Law
Seattle, Washington

H. Price Webb
Director, Department of Adult Education
San Jose, California

Charles H. Williston
President, Rosenheim Club
Port Angeles, Washington

Elmer Wilson
Pasadena, California

James P. Wilson
Manager
San Francisco Chamber of Commerce
San Francisco, California

The Jumelage Luncheon at the Cosmopolitan Hotel on September 4, 1959 celebrating the sister city relationship between Brest, France and Denver, Colorado. The two mayors exchanged speeches and gifts.

The Gala de Paris on September 5, 1959 with Mayor G. Lombard, Mrs. Stapleton and Mr. Will F. Nicholson.

Celebrating Ten Years As Sister Cities – in 1958: Denver, Colorado – Brest, France

In 1947, a high school teacher named Amanda Knecht visited Brest, France. The city had been bombed extensively during a six-week period in the Second World War. More than 5,000 sorties flew over the city before the occupying Germans finally surrendered.

When she returned to Denver, Knecht told the stories of the devastation done by the war. Over the next year, Denver students raised more than $32,000 in nickels, pennies and dimes. The funds were presented to the City of Brest to be used to re-build the children's wing of the Brest City Hospital.

The City of Denver and the City of Brest became "twinned" in 1948. Since that time, the people of Brest and Denver have enjoyed many exchanges of city officials, educators, and business people. In addition, there have been high school student exchanges and email pen-pals between the two cities. In 2004, Denver hosted a French delegation from the City of Brest affiliated with hospitals, engineering, technology and education.

The airport reception on September 2, 1959 with Mr. Stapleton at the microphone.

September 21, 1958 – Attendees at a reception in Brest, France for the inauguration of the Academic and Medical School. The reception was held in honor of Mr. and Mrs. Stapleton from the city of Denver. Their sister city relationship was already 10 years old when this photo was taken!

Ruth Hashimoto

Ruth Hashimoto with Richard Neuheisel (left) and Ray Schultz in the 1980s.

A Sister City Leader: Ruth Hashimoto

The diminutive Ruth Hashimoto of Albuquerque, New Mexico first emerged on the national sister city scene in 1958. For more than forty years, she has traveled around the world bringing a message of peace and understanding through the sister cities program. Old-timers have many fond memories of Ruth efficiently running the registration desk at national meetings. Getting John Denver to write a song for the sister cities program was only one of her many accomplishments. She helped raise funds for the national program and served on the Board of Directors with distinction. But it is her special touch with people that has been so helpful to the growth and development of Sister Cities International.

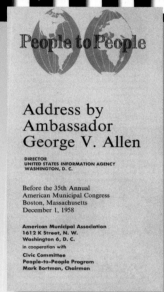

People to People

Address by Ambassador George V. Allen

DIRECTOR
UNITED STATES INFORMATION AGENCY
WASHINGTON, D. C.

Before the 35th Annual
American Municipal Congress
Boston, Massachusetts
December 1, 1958

American Municipal Association
1612 K Street, N. W.
Washington 6, D. C.
in cooperation with

Civic Committee
People-to-People Program
Mark Bortman, Chairman

Ruth chuckles as Board President Glenn Gray offers her a bow while presenting her with the President's Award in 2004 at the Annual Conference in Fort Worth, Texas. Executive Director Tim Honey (left), Sherman Banks (right) and Mary Jean Eisenhower are as thrilled as Ruth is. After accepting her award, Ruth humbly bowed before the audience, which offered thundering applause to honor her contributions over the decades.

A Call to Diplomacy: For Every Citizen

Ambassador George V. Allen delivered an exemplary address to the 35th Annual American Municipal Congress in Boston, Massachusetts on December 1, 1958. He noted that 70 American cities were affiliated with communities overseas, mostly in Europe, but that interest in Japan was on the rise with a dozen west coast U.S. cities already linked with Japanese communities. He closed saying, "If I can leave one message with you today, it is the hope that the American Municipal Association will carry on this affiliation program until we have, not 70 as we have today, but 3,000 city affiliations. Such a development could have an irresistible impact on the projection of America overseas and the building of understanding among the people of the world."

1959

This exhibit about Stockton, California was displayed at ceremonies commemorating the founding of their sister city, Shimizu, Japan.

"The idea of affiliation is based on the premise that the cities, towns, or incorporated municipalities represent the grass roots base of our respective nations. In our desire to know and understand other peoples, it is felt that the municipality has common characteristics the world over. Therefore they represent our way of life as they do in other nations of the world. Cities represent a natural unit for affiliating with a counterpart overseas to build new roads to international understanding based on our common interest."

— Mark Bortman, Chairman, Civic Committee, People-to-People Program, 1959

Riverside Mayor E. V. Dales shows Susan Vaught and Craig Kessler examples of Japanese artwork sent by children from their sister city, Sendai, Japan. The artwork was part of a gift exchange between the two communities.

Sister city ceremonies marking the twinning of Los Angeles, California and Nagoya, Japan. (L to R): Bernard Caughlin, manager of Port of Los Angeles; Shirley Mizufuka; Mayor Kissen Kobayashi of Nagoya, Japan; Councilman Edward Roybal (in back); Los Angeles Mayor Norris Paulson and Lloyd Menveg, president of the Board of Harbor Commissioners.

A Linkage at the 350 Mark
Hampton, Virginia, when it celebrated in 1959 its 350th anniversary as the oldest continuous English-speaking settlement in America, marked the occasion with an affiliation with Southampton, England, the departure port of the *Mayflower* in 1620.

It is heartening to see the continuing contacts that have been established, expanded and extended as a result of affiliations between cities."

— Mark Bortman, Chairman, Civic Committee, People-to-People Program, 1959

Mayor Nabuo Hayashi, Kokura, Japan welcomes Tacoma, Washington Mayor Ben Hanson for sister city festivities. At left is Genji Mihara with the Japanese Community Service of Seattle, Washington.

In November 1959, "Western City" highlighted town affiliation programs, including San Jose, California and Okayama, Japan, as well as Sendai, Japan and Riverside, California.

"What can you be sure of in a town affiliation? The only thing that you can be sure of is that your understanding of the attitudes, customs and ways of life of peoples in other parts of the world will increase, and you will be making a significant contribution toward easing of world tensions and improving the chances of peace in a people-to-people way."

— Mark Bortman, Chairman, Civic Committee, People-to-People Program, 1959

WESTERN CITY

NOVEMBER • 1959

Official Publication

League of Alaskan Cities
League of Arizona Cities and Towns
League of California Cities
Nevada Municipal Association
League of Oregon Cities
Association of Washington Cities

Members, American Municipal Association

Town Affiliation Programs

Sendai, Japan, sister city of Riverside, Calif., in Star Festival celebration. Inset photo shows San Jose Attorney Wayne Kanemoto (with package) and David L. MacKaye, president of the sponsoring San Jose-Okayama, Japan affiliation presenting signs to be sent to sister city for display.
(See Page 22)

A fabulous sister city gift – In the 1950s, San Francisco, California presented Osaka, Japan with this cable car. Osaka Mayor Mitsuji Nakai and his wife; Mayor George Christopher; Public Utilities Commissioner Stuart Greenberg and Lester Goodman affiliation chair, take a ride in the 50-year old car.

Dr. Edward Teller, Director of the Lawrence Radiation Laboratory at the University of California, talks about People-to-People at a luncheon of the Third Annual Joint Meeting of the Civic Committee of the People-to-People Program and the Committee on International Municipal Cooperation, American Municipal Association, Washington, D.C. To his left is Mark Bortman, Chairperson of the Civic Committee.

1960

Organizational Structure of the Civic Committee

The Civic Committee is part of the general People-to-People program organized at the White House in 1956 by the President. The purpose of the Civic Committee is to encourage American communities to join hands with overseas communities and to carry out programs of mutual interest in international friendship and understanding. Such present programs generally take the form of town affiliations, community salutes and international friendship groups. The Civic Committee is composed of civic leaders in the various stats of the community. This would include such people as university presidents, Chamber of Commerce presidents, women's club members, veterans' groups and other people representing all facets of community life.

The mayor is usually appointed as the honorary chairman of any particular affiliation and he usually names the committee as the university groups, the commercial groups, the cultural groups, fraternal groups, children, etc. This means that the city is fully represented in every facet of its organization and of its life. There is then a parallel community overseas and the two groups can then correspond. The Civic Committee, then, is the organizational structure which represents the various civic leaders and organizations within the community who, in turn, represent the mayor and, therefore, the entire community in this People-to-People program.

— By Mark Bortman, chair, Civic Committee and Chair pro-tem, People-to-People Program, excerpted from "Condensed Proceedings, Third Annual Joint Meeting, Civic Committee, People-to-People Program and Committee on International Municipal Cooperation, Washington, D.C." 1960.

This Bay City, Michigan beauty queen was selected to carry goodwill greetings to Ansbach, Germany.

Jamestown, New York and Jakobstad, Finland became sister cities in 1960.

One thing many "old-timers" recall about the sister city movement is that it was inclusive at the very start. In 1960, America did not always see people of different races breaking bread together.

Mark Bortman, Chairperson of the Civic Committee, talks to attendees about town affiliations and hopes for world peace.

YOUR COMMUNITY IN WORLD AFFAIRS

Your Community in World Affairs
Created to offer guidance in forming city-to-city linkages, this publication was printed in 1960 by the American Municipal Association and the Civic Committee of the People-to-People program. It is one of the first sister city publications ever produced.

Did You Know?
Pasadena, California entered the first float honoring a sister city in the Tournament of Roses Parade in 1960. The float honored Yokohama, Japan.

What is a Town Affiliation?

When an American community of whatever size or character joins with a community in a foreign land for the purpose of communicating, of learning more about each other, of knowing each other better, the two may propose a formal affiliation. The ideal affiliation is a sister city arrangement which involves a large number of citizens and organizations in both communities which engage in continuing projects.

Why Have a Town Affiliation?

A Town Affiliation helps you make friends for your country and help it promote world peace:

1. You help demonstrate how your ideals are reflected in your way of life;

2. You help bring about a better understanding of what your country is doing to bring peace and understanding in the world today;

3. You help combat the distortions of Communistic propaganda.

Peoples of other nations want peace as much as we do. A Town Affiliation gives your community an avenue to dramatically explain on a people-to-people basis the truth of our way of life, our firm belief in the brotherhood of man, and the efforts we sincerely exert in helping strengthen international amity. Your community has the opportunity to take an active role in world affairs.

A Town Affiliation helps you and your overseas neighbors know each other better. When you exchange ideas with your sister-city, the news of the day has a new meaning.

In any language, as in the story which appeared in the Reader's Digest, a town affiliation results in a double advantage to both cities.

PROJECTS OF SOME COMMUNITIES

PEOPLE -to- PEOPLE

EXCHANGE OF IDEAS | ORGANIZED TOURS | EXCHANGE OF PUBLICATION

LETTER WRITING | EXCHANGE OF TEACHERS | YOUTH EXCHANGES

EXCHANGE OF SPORTS | EXCHANGE OF CULTURE | COMMUNICATIONS EXCHAN

Le double avantage des jumelages

par Marianne Bezier & Joseph Alvarez

リーダーズ

CIUDADES HERMANAS EN CUATRO CONTINENTES

Por Marianne Bezier y Joseph Alvarez

Numbers Don't Lie
A 1960 questionnaire found that 79% of sister city programs had visited their sister city in person within the past year. Most respondents reported that 10 or more other organizations in their local community helped them with the sister city program. Seventy-five percent felt the sister city program improved their community locally and economically.

This historic photo from Burbank, California chronicles their 40+ years relationship with Incheon in the Republic of Korea. They signed their sister city agreement on October 1, 1961.

World Conference of Local Government Sparks Interest

In June 1961, more than one thousand mayors and municipal officials attended the World Conference of Local Government in Washington D.C. The event was convened by the International Union of Local Authorities (IULA), based at The Hague, Netherlands. Two plenary sessions at the conference encouraged officials to form sister city affiliations. Pictured: U.S. Secretary of State Dean Rusk, General Dwight D. Eisenhower and Mark Bortman discuss the sister city program at the conference. Fifty years later, IULA still collaborates with Sister Cities International and encourages communities to build peace through affiliations.

Calling Up Not Just a Friend, But a Sister

Creative promotion has been part of the sister city movement from its early days. This 1961 phone directory for Lodi, California featured its sister city relationship with Kofu, Japan on the cover. The cover was created as part of a high school art contest sponsored by the Pacific Telephone and Telegraph Company. The winning artist was 17-year-old Judy Michiko Kosaka of Lodi, who won a trip to San Francisco to watch the first copies roll off the presses. San Diego did this in 1962 with its phone directory –ensuring that thousands of citizens would know about the sister city program!

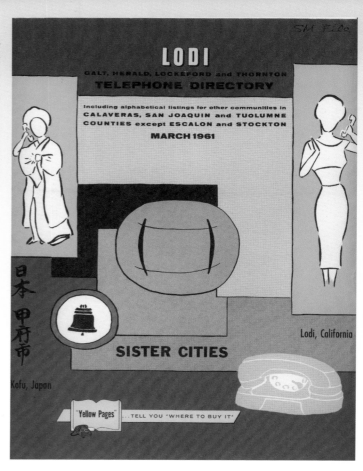

Size Does Not Matter

"It matters not that these two towns are small and unheard of, and that they are not in the orbit of world politics nor the arteries of international trade and commerce. What matters is that the peoples of Forest Heights and Villaviciosa are willing and ready and are doing their share in the promotion of peace and friendship among nations because in the context of today's world, anything that can help to banish fear and hatred, suspicion and intrigue from the atmosphere in which we live is highly important."

— Minister Plenipotentiary Mauro Calingo of the Embassy of the Philippines upon the signing of a sister city agreement between Forest Heights, Maryland and Villaviviciosa, Philippines in 1961.

President John F. Kennedy

"No impersonal representation of a culture can fully communicate its reality to others who have never known its living substance. Through personal relations – our curiosity can be fulfilled by a sense of knowledge, cynicism can give way to trust and the warmth of human friendship to be kindled."

"The Town Affiliation Program is making a real contribution throughout the United States and with many communities abroad. I hope that you will work to spread its effectiveness to other communities in your part of the country."

— U.S. President John F. Kennedy,
served as Honorary Chairman
of the Town Affiliation program

JFK Asks Eisenhower to Head People-to-People Program

President John F. Kennedy tapped Dwight D. Eisenhower's services for the first time in 1961, asking the former president to head the People-to-People program. President Kennedy said at a November 8th news conference, "I am delighted to announce that General Eisenhower has agreed to serve as the first Chairman of the Board of Trustees of a new People-to-People organization. The purpose of the new organization will be, and I quote, "To foster contacts between citizens of the United States and people of other lands in every way possible." The original People-to-People Organization was formed in September of 1956 by a group of leading citizens at a White House conference. The new organization will provide private centralized coordination and fundraising leadership for the activities and projects of the People-to-People program, which has been of great interest to General Eisenhower. I consider it a great honor to be able to serve as Honorary Chairman of this outstanding citizens' organization."

In addition to the Board of Trustees, which included about 100 distinguished citizens, a nine-person Executive Committee was named. It included:

Mark Bortman, Chairman, Civic Committee, People-to-People Program
Walt Disney
Dr. Alfred Frankfurter, Editor of Art News
Alfred Gruenther, President, American Red Cross
Joyce C. Hall, President, Hallmark Foundation
A. Hillex, lawyer, Kansas City, Missouri
Dr. Franklin Murphy, President, University of California at Los Angeles
Anna Rosenberg, former Assistant Secretary of Defense
DeWitt Wallace, Publisher, Reader's Digest

Mansfield, Ohio – Dar Es Salaam, Tanzania
This photo shows the mayor of Mansfield, Ohio and Mayor Kaluta Amri Abedi of Dar Es Salaam, Tanzania in 1961. Their sister city relationship was featured in the popular *Look* magazine. Mayor Abedi spoke on a panel in 1961 about their sister city relationship at the World Conference of Local Governments, convened by the International Union of Local Authorities. The panel also included General Dwight D. Eisenhower, Commissioner McLaughlin and Mark Bortman. The event brought together more than 1,000 mayors and local government officials from 55 nations.

William Mitchell of Modesto, California has been active with the sister city program since 1961 and was listed as one of the original incorporators for the Town Affiliation Association of the United States, Inc., when it formed in 1967.

Sister Cities Leaders: William Mitchell

Building Cross-Cultural Understanding Over the Decades

Elected to the city council in Modesto, California in April 1961, Bill Mitchell accepted an invitation from the city manager to drive to the American Municipal Association annual meeting, which was being held in Seattle, Washington. He recalled that "both the city manager and myself were quite enthused by meeting Mark Bortman, who had a little stand and display about sister cities." They also met Gordon Clinton, the mayor of Seattle, who was very active with the sister city program, and returned to Modesto determined to start a sister city project. Today, Modesto has five sister cities: Aguascalientes, Mexico; Khmelnytskyi, Ukraine; Kurume, Japan; Vernon, Canada; and Vijayawada, India.

Mitchell remained active with the sister city program, and attended the 10th anniversary luncheon held at the U.S. Department of State in 1966, where he recalled that Mark Bortman presented President Eisenhower with a beautiful "Paul Revere" silver teapot and the former President delivered an outstanding speech. In 1967, Mitchell was one of the original incorporators listed on the incorporation papers filed to establish the Town Affiliation Association of the United States, Inc.

In 1973, Mitchell drove across the United States to Atlanta to attend the Annual Conference. While there, he met two mayors from the Soviet Union. Mitchell invited them to visit Modesto and much to his surprise, they accepted his offer and made immediate plans to visit in only a few days. After the conference's final banquet and dance, Mitchell loaded up his wife and two children and raced home in their Volkswagen bus, arriving in 2 days and 4 hours. They organized a reception for their Soviet guests, who stayed for three days and enjoyed a warm welcome. The *Modesto Bee* ran a headline proclaiming, "The Russians Are Coming" and Mitchell noted that the mayors were escorted by a KGB official.

Mitchell noted that President Eisenhower "realized that people the world over have the same needs – they are organized into families and have children." He felt that building relationships between people and communities "would further world peace and understanding….It's very hard to make enemies of your trading partners or your children's friends."

Excerpted from a 2004 interview with Tim Honey in Washington, D.C. at the offices for Sister Cities International.

A Voice for Peace

"For our travels this summer and last spring that we were privileged to make, we realize more than ever what personal contact means that knowing people, knowing cities – and how much difference that makes in situations. You can't have diplomacy based on anything better than friendship and knowledge."

— Mrs. William P. Rogers

The enthusiasm of Gordon Clinton, Mayor of Seattle, for the sister city program, inspired William Mitchell to get involved. Clinton was one of the original incorporators for the Town Affiliation Association of the United States, Inc., in 1967, along with William Mitchell.

U Pe Than, of Moulmein, and James Bradshaw, former assisant cultural affairs officer of the U.S. Information Agency-Rangoon carry an image of the Buddha to a pagoda in Moulmein where it will be blessed before Bradshaw makes the presentation in the United States. The wife and daughter of U Pe Than are also pictured.

1962

Barry Bingham and Andrew Broaddus were instrumental in twinning Louisville, Kentucky with Montpellier, France, in 1962. Photo by the Courier-Journal.

Buddha presented to Fresno Center

When Vice Mayor U Pe Than of Moulmein, Burma visited Fresno, California he was deeply impressed by the city's hospitality and its stately Buddhist temple. Upon his return to Burma, to acknowledge the courtesy extended to him, he decided to present a Buddhist statue as a lasting tribute to the People-to-People program. Out of his gesture grew the idea of a formal affiliation between the two cities, and it became the first city-to-city affiliation between the United States and Burma. He established 26 committees in Moulmein to support their affiliation.

Celebrating Ten Years of Friendship
In 1962, Rudolf Stams (left) and Christa Guenther of Wesel, Germany, celebrated their community's ten-year sister city relationship with Hagerstown, Maryland alongside Winslow Burhans and Walter Peitsch.

Kudos From President Kennedy

Upon hearing that the 39th American Municipal Congress voted to make the Town Affiliation program a continuing part of the overall activities for the American Municipal Association, U.S. President John F. Kennedy lauded the decision and wrote to Mayor Clinton of Seattle, Washington: "The expanding program of affiliations between American and overseas cities offers to municipal officials and private citizens an opportunity to assist the United States materially in carrying out its peaceful objective abroad…Please give my congratulations to the members of your Association and to the many individuals who are improving the climate of international understanding through the sister-city program."

The French Are Coming!
A 1962 press release announced that 80 French delegates from Arles were arriving just in time to mark Bastille Day in York, Pennsylvania. Their sister city affiliation was already 8 years old and because of their close relationship, more than 4,000 youngsters in York's elementary schools were already studying French. While on their trip, they visited with General Eisenhower in Gettysburg and a group of 168 people toured Washington, D.C. together and attended a reception at the Embassy of France.

August 26
National League of Cities
Conference Workshop Meeting,
Philadelphia, Pennsylvania.

Tadao Yamagishi (center) shows his
Japanese stamp collection to Jed (left) and
Bill Zelman (right). Yamagishi was visiting
San Bernardino, California from sister city
Tachikawa, Japan in 1962.

Children at the First Grammar School in Tachikawa,
Japan receive a gift of oranges from their sister city, San
Bernardino, California on June 8, 1962. Back row: Mrs.
Arthur Loving, sister city committee member; Mayor Mitsuo
Sokurai, Captain Lovering; Mr. Nuirano, school principal.
Front row: students of the school.

Exchange student Chizuko
Ohori from Tachikawa,
Japan, samples nectarines
at her host family's home in
San Bernardino, California
in 1962.

Chizuko Ohori plays piano at the Owens home in
San Bernardino, California in 1962 while visiting from
Tachikawa, Japan.

Bremerton, Washington was recognized for its work with Olongapo.

1963

Annual Awards Program

Through the Annual Awards program, the quality projects and activities conducted by sister cities throughout the world are recognized. Showcasing their outstanding efforts demonstrates to the world community that Sister Cities International fosters world peace through communication and exchange. The Reader's Digest Association, Inc. sponsored the awards program from their beginning in 1963 through the mid-1990s.

Mark Bortman, chair of the Civic Committee for People-to-People programs gets ready for the first Annual Awards ceremony.

Annual Awards

Sterling Fisher, executive director of the Reader's Digest Foundation, presents an award to San Jose California for its sister city programs with Okayama, Japan and San Jose, Costa Rica.

Sterling Fisher (standing), executive director of the Reader's Digest Foundation, which co-sponsored the Annual Awards Program, looks on as the judges for the awards make some difficult decisions. (L to R): General Alfred Gunther, president of the American Red Cross; Ambassador George V. Allen, former director of the U.S. Information Agency; and the Honorable Andrew Berding, former Assistant Secretary of State for Public Affairs.

Annual Awards 1963

Best Overall Town Affiliation Program
San Jose, California
York, Pennsylvania

Best Overall Town Affiliation Program From Abroad
Kobe, Japan (Seattle, Washington)
Bega, Australia (Littleton, Colorado)

Best Single Project
Toledo, Ohio
Bremerton, Washington
Kouderk-aan-den-Rijn, Netherlands (Artesia, California)
Honorable Mention – Sapporo, Japan

Sponsored by the Reader's Digest Foundation

Note: this was the first time the competition was held. Entries were collected in 1962 and the competition formally closed on December 31, 1962. The awards were presented in 1963.

Sterling Fisher of the Reader's Digest Foundation presents a certificate of merit to delegates from Riverside, California. He recognized all of the programs participating in the Town Affiliation awards program.

Delegates enjoy a quick break next to the exhibit showing the number of U.S. communities affiliated with communities abroad.

First Western Regional Conference, April 7-9, 1963
More than 250 people attended the First Western Regional Conference in Los Angeles, California for networking and workshops on how to strengthen their growing sister city programs. "People learning to know each other can do more than all the diplomats, all the summit conferences – all the government-to-government programs put together," said Senator Clair Engle as he called for 3,000 – 5,000 sister city affiliations around the globe.

A 17th Century Ship Builds Sister City Bonds That Thrive Today
Wilmington, Delaware – Kalmar, Sweden

The connection between Kalmar, Sweden and Wilmington, Delaware dates back almost 369 years. In 1637, 48 courageous soldiers and seamen began a journey across the Atlantic on a wooden ship, the Kalmar Nyckel, to the Delaware River on the mid-Atlantic coast of what would become the United States of America. They could not have imagined that their New Sweden would become the thriving city of Wilmington, Delaware. Formal exchanges between Kalmar, Sweden, and Wilmington were followed by a sister city relationship in 1963. In the decades since, hundreds of citizens have participated in exchanges of every kind: government, education, culture, music, art, business, and sports. The bonds of friendship are strong and continue to this day. Sister Cities of Wilmington has added four additional sister cities to the family. If you visit Wilmington today, you can sail on a replica of the Kalmar Nyckel (pictured below) – and envision how peace can truly be built through people.

Spreading the Word...Anyway We Can
Publicity in sister communities for their joint projects helps spread the word of the mission of the Sister Cities movement – to turn places into people. From 1960 to 1970, for example, 27 U.S. cities entered floats honoring their sister city relationships in the Rose Bowl Parade in Pasadena. Scores of columns about successful sister cities programs have appeared in every kind of written media – journals, newspapers, magazines, and even the *Congressional Record*.

Did You Know?
Honolulu, Hawaii, birthplace of many of the Japanese-American soldiers who in World War II fought and died at Bruyeres, is affiliated with that French city.

36

Did You Know?
The association of New Haven, Connecticut, with Madras, India, started with a request by Madras officials for information on town planning and solutions to municipal problems.

1964

Joint Conference
June 29-30,
Washington, D.C.

TOWN AFFILIATION

YOUR COMMUNITY IN WORLD AFFAIRS

Annual Awards 1964

Best Overall Program
Over 750,000: New York, New York – sister city to Tokyo, Japan
250,000 – 750,000: San Diego, California – sister city to Yokohama, Japan
150,000 – 250,000: Pensacola, Florida – sister city to Miraflores and Chimbote, Peru
75,000 – 150,000: Portsmouth, Virginia – sister city to Dunedin, New Zealand
25,000 – 75,000: Redondo Beach, California – sister city to La Paz, Mexico
Under 25,000: Darien, Connecticut – sister city to Mercara, India

Honorable Mention:
Los Angeles, California – sister city to Nagoya, Japan and Salvador, Brazil
Santa Monica, California – sister city to Mazatlan, Mexico
Santa Barbara, California – sister city to Curzco, Peru

Best Single Project
250,000 – 750,000: San Jose, California – sister city to Okayama, Japan
75,000 – 150,000: Norwalk, California – sister city to Hermosillo, Mexico
Under 25,000: Claremont, California – sister city to Guanajuato, Mexico

Honorable Mention:
Louisville, Kentucky – sister city to Montpellier, France and Quito, Ecuador
Portland, Oregon – sister city to Sapporo, Japan
Downey, California – sister city to Gadalajara, Mexico
Dover, Delaware – sister city to Lamia, Greece

Sponsored by the Reader's Digest Foundation
Source: Town Affiliation News, November 1964

Reader's Digest published this collection of inspiring people-to-people stories in the 1960s.

"People to People" in Action
ARTICLES FROM Reader's Digest

Greetings to a Sister
When a new telephone cable was laid 5,300 miles across the Pacific Ocean, one of the first calls it carried was warm greetings from Mayor Teery Schrunk of Portland, Oregon to Mayor Yosaku Harada of Sapporo, Japan.

Who Would Have Thought?
"If global television ever becomes reality, with programs and news coverage freely traded between TV stations around the world, it will have originated in Oakland, California and Fukuoka Japan, Oakland's sister city."

— excerpted from a 1964 town affiliation newsletter

● **1965 Leadership for the Town Affiliation Movement**
President Lyndon B. Johnson, Honorary Chairperson
General Dwight D. Eisenhower, Chairperson of the Board of Trustees, People-to-People, Inc.
Mark Bortman, National Chairperson, Civic Committee
Frederick Brittan, Associate Chairperson, Civic Committee

1965

Western Regional Meeting
August 29-31, Portland, Oregon

The first efforts are made to create an independent national organization to serve the U.S. sister cities program. Delegates unanimously recommended the establishment of a national association. Following the action, the League of California Cities and the League of Oregon Cities adopted resolutions supporting the idea during their respective annual conferences. The executive committee of the National League of Cities took identical action at their meeting late in 1965. An interim board of directors was named so that articles of incorporation and bylaws could be drafted and procedures outlined to complete the organization.

This April 1965 Colorado Municipalities magazine featured sister city relationships in a big way.

A Child Regains Her Sight

Eight-year-old Deisi Begazo of Arequipa, Peru underwent surgery to restore her sight after a terrible accident with a firecracker left her blind. Lions Club members in Arequipa and sister city Vancouver, Washington raised funds to bring her to the U.S. for treatment.

A Shipwreck Creates Lasting Bonds

Virginia Beach and Moss, Norway's Norwegian Ladies Foster Friendship

It all began in 1891 with a tragic shipwreck. The Dictator, a Norwegian bark, was bound to England from Florida. As it turned toward Hampton Roads, the ship ran aground. Captain Jordan Jorgesen sent his crew ashore because his wife, in a fit of hysteria, refused to leave the sinking ship. He tried to save his son and wife – but alas, the captain was the sole survivor.

Well there was one more survivor – a wooden figurehead that washed ashore in Virginia Beach and was erected as the "elegant Scandinavian Lady" on 16th Street in the community's downtown.

The figurehead fell into disrepair, and in 1960 a summer resident prevailed upon the City of Virginia Beach and the Norwegian Embassy to make the "beloved Norwegian Lady" a permanent memorial.

The "elegant Scandinavian Lady" on 16th Street in Virginia Beach gazes on the Norwegian flag and faces her counterpart across the sea.

His appeals on behalf of this shipwreck survivor stirred interest in building a permanent bronze memorial in Virginia Beach. The citizens of Moss, Norway raised funds to build a matching bronze "Norwegian Lady." Today the "ladies" stand facing each other across the ocean.

A close relationship with Norway was established in the 1960s and continues to thrive and even today, the sister cities continue to hold annual celebrations in their Norwegian Lady Parks.

Sister City Romance Blossoms

The December 1965 "Town Affiliation News" observed "perhaps the first romance to reach fulfillment through the Sister City Program between the U.S. and Japan occurred when a delegation of 16 Shimada friends, headed by Mayor and Mrs. Masaya Mori, arrived recently in their sister city of Richmond, California, to attend the wedding of the Mayor's daughter, Nagako Mori, to Douglas S. Quale, an East Bay reporter."

Annual Awards 1965

Best Overall Program

Over 750,000: Denver, Colorado – sister city to Takayama, Japan
250,000 – 750,000: Minneapolis, Minnesota – sister city to Santiago, Chile
150,000 – 250,000: Pensacola, Florida – sister city to Chimbote and Miraflores, Peru
75,000 – 150,000: Riverside, California – sister city to Sendai, Japan
25,000 – 75,000: Coral Gables, Florida – sister city to Cartagena, Colombia
Under 25,000: Claremont, California – sister city to Guanjuato, Mexico and Kumasi, Ghana

Honorable Mention:

Louisville, Kentucky – sister city to Montpellier, France and Quito, Ecuador
Portland, Oregon – sister city to Sapporo, Japan
Spokane, Washington – sister city to Nishinimoya, Japan
Pasadena, California – sister city to Ludwigshafen, Germany and Mishima, Japan
Palo Alto, California – sister city to Palo, Philippines and Oaxaca, Mexico
Bloomington, Illinois – sister city to Asahigawa, Japan
Redondo Beach, California – sister city to La Paz, Mexico and Ensenada, Mexico
El Segundo, California – sister city to Guayama, Mexico
Takoma Park, Maryland – sister city to Jequie, Brazil

Best Single Project

Over 750,000: No Award

250,000 – 750,000: San Diego, California – sister city to Yokohama, Japan
150,000 – 250,000: No Award
75,000 – 150,000: Richmond, California – sister city to Shimada, Japan
25,000 – 75,000: Santa Barbara, California – sister city to Cuzco, Peru
Under 25,000: No Award

Honorable Mention:

Hartford, Connecticut – sister city to Thessaloniki, Greece
Stockton, California – sister city to Shimizu, Japan

Sponsored by the Reader's Digest Foundation
Source: Town Affiliation News, October 1965

Visiting Government and Athletic Officials Receive the Key to the City of Culver City, California

Arranged through Sports International, Inc. and the U.S. Department of State, these exchange participants from all over the world lived and observed skills, colleges, government, and community life in Culver City and southern California from January 17-21, 1965. Left to right: Vasile Popescu, Romania; Pablo Porras, Columbia; Patricia Bielaski, interpreter; Carmen Caparroso, Colombia; Mukhtar Sayed, Morocco; Hector Canon, receiving key; Carlton Clarke, presenting key; Mary Moari, New Zealand; Efren Renteria, Columbia; Richard Castetterk official host; Robert Bailey, chief administrative officer, City of Culver City; Lazaro Soto, Columbia (foreground).

Carry the Spirit of America

In a 1965 speech to the National Legislative Conference of the National League of Cities, U.S. Vice President Hubert H. Humphrey urged the League to "continue your great efforts in the sister city program…I want you to know that this program means a great deal to our country because it is the way you carry the spirit of America and the diplomacy of America to the peoples of the world and place it in the hands of people who have aspirations similar to yours.

Laying the Groundwork

The first decade of the forming of the sister cities program could be characterized as one of great enthusiasm with thousands of dedicated and committed volunteers coming to the forefront to lead this new effort. Main streets were expanding to include new neighbors in dozens of other countries and the excitement for this massive citizen exchange effort grew faster than the management needed to give useful and thoughtful guidelines. In addition, the early efforts were almost exclusively devoted to raising the funds to keep the national office open and functioning. That would begin to change as the national program entered its second decade.

THE SECOND DECADE
1966-1975

CALLING HOME FROM A SISTER CITY

Hugo Martinez, 19, and Laura Castelli, 18, (from left), sister city exchange students from Bahia Blanca, Argentina make weekly calls home in the early 1970s to tell of their adventures in Jacksonville, Florida. William Black (right) is an amateur radio operator and made weekly calls to Jacksonville's sister city for two years to promote projects conducted by the Bahia Blanca – Jacksonville Sister Cities Association.

The Second Decade of the sister city movement may have opened auspiciously, but the rapidly expanding program soon faced new challenges. In late 1966, sister city leaders at the local level decided a national association was needed to assist the growing number of American cities entering the program and to service those already affiliated.

The new association, the Town Affiliation Association of the U.S., Inc., was finally incorporated on June 12, 1967, in the District of Columbia. Patrick Healy, executive director of the National League of Cities agreed to serve as "Interim President" until the organizational conference to be held in Los Angeles near the end of the year.

Just two weeks after the association was incorporated, the U.S. Information Agency abolished its Office of Private Cooperation, which had provided small grants to support the sister city program. The future looked bleak indeed. The association managed to survive until the conference in November on small donations and support from the National League of Cities, but there were few prospects for any kind of future at all.

New communities clamored to join the association, and requests for new linkages with U.S. communities poured in from abroad. The problems of an expanding association needing funds, energy and support were many. New leaders would rise to the challenge…

1966

United States Vice President Hubert Humphrey brought greetings to the delegates attending the 10th Anniversary Town Affiliation Conference. In his remarks to the delegates, the Vice President expressed his continuing strong interest in the sister city program, and said, "Get some more recruits. We need more of this. I want to thank you on behalf of a grateful government, a democratic government, a free government, and a free society for what you're doing."

I Remember...

How well I remember having the unique privilege and honor of sitting next to former President Dwight D. Eisenhower at the 10th anniversary Sister Cities International Conference luncheon in Washington, D.C. in 1966 at the State Department.

Ten years earlier, on September 11, 1956, President Eisenhower, known and respected for his military leadership in World War II, embarked on a program promoting a full-scale effort to involve millions of American citizens in the promotion of international peace and understanding.

Many cities became immediately involved. During this period I entered local elective office and began to learn of the President's call to promote international municipal cooperation. My city, Rochester, New York, became twinned with Rennes, France.

I remember the sister city bug biting me pretty hard. I got involved locally and nationally as a member of the Civic Committee of People-to-People, the National League of Cities' Committee of International Municipal Cooperation and Understanding, and the Town Affiliation Association of the U.S.

Then, to sit at lunch next to the founder and inspiration of this great organization, I can only say that I remember that moment as a thrill of a lifetime.

-Frank Lamb served as the mayor of Rochester, New York and on the Honorary Board of Directors for Sister Cities International.

Eisenhower Offers Gratitude and Inspiration

Sister City supporters were thrilled when General Dwight D. Eisenhower, father of the people-to-people concept, arrived. He told them, "I am here just to express to you my hope that you will let nothing deter you from following this effort to promote understanding. I think that you are engaging voluntarily and with your organization in the most valuable thing that any citizen of the United States can engage in, and I want to tell you that I, for one, am so appreciative of your work, your motives and efforts."

Did You Know?

A survey in 1966 of 39 sister city programs found 2,203 people traveled outside the United States within the previous year to visit a sister city, while 1,355 people traveled in-bound to the United States from abroad. The largest categories exchanged were business people and students.

Frank Lamb, member of the Board of Directors and then mayor of Rochester, New York (sister city to Rennes, France), greets President Eisenhower, who addressed the 10th anniversary conference in Washington, D.C. Mr. Lamb passed away in 2005, just short of Sister Citites International's 50th anniversary.

Delegates from Montclair, California accept an award for their work with Antigua, Guatemala.

TENTH ANNIVERSARY JOINT CONFERENCE
SEPTEMBER 12-14, WASHINGTON, D.C.
THEME: THE SEARCH FOR GREATER FRIENDSHIP AND UNDERSTANDING

10th Anniversary

Frank Curran is all smiles upon receiving a plaque for his hard work on behalf of the Sister City program.

Ensenada, Mexico and Redondo Beach, California are happy to receive an award from the Reader's Digest Foundation.

Award winners express their joy alongside Sterling Fisher, executive director of the Reader's Digest Foundation.

June 12, 1967
The Town Affiliation Association of the U.S., Inc. is incorporated in the District of Columbia.

1967

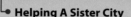

Helping A Sister City
Sister Frances Michaels, administrator of the Sacred Heart Hospital, hands a list of hospital equipment donations to Dr. Earl Wolf, president of the Escambia Medical Society, and Captain H.B. Grow, president of the Pensacola People-to-People Council. The donated equipment was used to set up a maternity hospital in Chimbote, Peru, sister city to Pensacola, Florida.

1966

A Sweet Memory

I was privileged to sit at the right of General Eisenhower at a special luncheon in 1966 commemorating the 10th anniversary of Sister Cities International and one of the things he said to me was, "If, for instance, you could ride a street car in any foreign city and could understand the language, you would learn that the mother sitting next to you does not want war – that people all over the world want peace."

President Eisenhower stated, "I believe that the people, in the long run, are going to do more to promote peace than governments. Indeed, I think that the people want peace so much that one of these days governments better get out of their way and let 'em have it…..I had great faith in the American people when we started this work. Now, ten years later, they have taken the initiative and marshaled their forces to fulfill the objectives of the People-to-People program."

I'm sure he is looking down on us on our 25th anniversary and is very happy with what we have done.

- Long-tine board member and president Betty Wilson pictured with President Eisenhower in 1966. Published in the Sister Cities International magazine for the 25th Anniversary in 1981.

A Sister City Leader: Ambassador George V. Allen
Ambassador George V. Allen was brought out of retirement by President Lyndon B. Johnson to head up and reorganize the Foreign Service Institute. He told the sister city membership during the Los Angeles conference when he was elected the first president of the new organization, "In assuming this honor of presidency of the Town Affiliation Association, I do so with pride and enthusiasm tempered by humility, and confident that with the help of all, we shall achieve the phenomenal success this splendid program deserves….As single individuals, we as sister city chairpersons and committee members, and we on the board of directors, cannot provide all the energy that is needed." Allen observed, "However, I am confident that together, we can create a groundswell that will inspire the people of hundreds of other American cities and towns to enrich themselves with this program and the rewards possible."

An Important Resource
"…the Town Affiliation Association's sister city program offers an important resource to the negotiations of governments by letting the people themselves give expression to their common desire for friendship, good will and cooperation for a better world for all." - Dwight D. Eisenhower

Aboard a train to Tokyo from Yokosuka, Japan, Corpus Christi, Texas exchange students Jane Trigg and Randy McManus discuss a snapshot camera with a Japanese friend in 1967.

Student Exchange Program

A reception in the Yoksuka, Japan Cultural Hall started the exchange program between Corpus Christi, Texas and Yokosuka, Japan in 1967. Four Japanese students traveled to Corpus Christi the day after four Texas students arrived in Yokosuka. Pictured with Mayor Masayashi Nagano (fifth from right) and his wife in kimono are (left to right) Kenichi Iwasaki, Osamu Kamata, Tomoko Suzuki, Yukiko Yirai, Jane Trigg, Bob Wesson, Randy McManus, and Mitzi Lytton.

Mitzi Lytton of Corpus Christi, Texas, tours the memorial ship Mikasa at Yokosuka in 1967. She was one of four students visiting Yokosuka, Japan as part of the sister city student exchange program.

Four students on a sister city exchange program from Corpus Christi, Texas, feed pigeons in the courtyard of the Buddhist temple in Yokosuka, Japan in 1967. Pictured (left to right): Shigeru Kanbayashi, president of the Yokosuka Junior Chamber of Commerce, an unidentified high school student, Jane Trigg, Mitzi Lytton, Randy McManus, and Bob Wesson.

Ambassador George V. Allen, director, Foreign Service Institute, is elected first president of the Town Affiliation Association.

First Annual Conference
Town Affiliation Association
of the United States

YOUR COMMUNITY IN A SMALL WORLD

November 30 - December 2, 1967
STATLER HILTON HOTEL
LOS ANGELES, CALIFORNIA

Hubert Humphrey sent this telegram to Patrick Healy to greet conference delegates. On a later page, he said that "it is a smaller, better world today because of the big men in the Town Affiliation Association."

WESTERN UNION TELEGRAM

904A PST NOV 27 67 LC154 CTA256
WJO55 WW NFAC24 GOVT NL PD NF WASHINGTON DC 27
MR PATRICK HEALY PRESIDENT TOWN AFFILIATION ASSOCIATION OF
THE US
CARE STATLER HILTON HOTEL LOSA
BY TAKING THE LEADERSHIP TO FOSTER BETTER UNDERSTANDING AMONG
THE PEOPLES OF THE WORLD THE TOWN AFFILIATION PROGRAM HAS BEEN
MOST REPRESENTATIVE OF THE SPIRIT OF THIS NATION. THAT YOU
HAVE SO SUCCESSFULLY PROMOTED IMPROVED RELATIONSHIPS ON A CITY
TO CITY AND PERSON TO PERSON BASIS DESERVES SPECIAL RECOGNITION
FOR A JOB "WELL DONE".

YOU HAVE DEMONSTRATED HOW VALUABLE AND HOW EXTENSIVE ARE THE
CONTRIBUTIONS OF YOUR PROGRAMS: IN STIMULATING CREATIVE INTERNATIONALISM
IN CREATING A REAL CLIMATE OF INTERNATIONAL UNITY; IN MOBILIZING
INDIVIDUAL AND PRIVATE RESOURCES; IN PROVIDING OUR YOUNGSTERS

FIRST ANNUAL CONFERENCE OF THE TOWN AFFILIATION ASSOCIATION OF THE U.S., INC.

NOVEMBER 30 – DECEMBER 3, LOS ANGELES, CALIFORNIA
THEME: YOUR COMMUNITY IN A SMALL WORLD

A Warm Welcome
Conference Chair Betty Wilson welcomes Jorge Rodriguez Pacheco and his son to the conference. Mr. Pacheco was president of the Committee of Mexican Sister Cities. The Bulletin of the Town Affiliation Association of the United States noted that "he has been of invaluable assistance to many U.S. cities wishing to affiliate with cities in Mexico."

Annual Award winners smile for the camera and rejoice in the promise sister city programs hold for world peace.

The Los Angeles conference was promoted using an "It's a Small World" Theme. Betty Wilson and Mayor Sam Yorty (left) encourage delegates to take part in the happiest little cruise to ever sail around the world.

Actor George Hamilton (far right) made an appearance.

A group of youth delegates get oriented at the conference.

Annual Awards 1967

Best Overall Program
Over 300,000: Portland, Oregon – sister city to Sapporo, Japan
150,000-300,000: Pensacola, Florida – sister city to Chimbote, Peru and Miraflores, Peru
75,000-150,000: Pasadena, California – sister city to Ludwigshafen, Germany and Mishima, Japan
25,000-75,000: Coral Gables, Florida – sister city to Cartagena, Colombia
Under 25,000: El Segundo, California – sister city to Guayamos, Mexico

Best Single Project
Over 300,000: Toledo, Ohio – sister city to Toledo, Spain
150,000-300,000: Dayton, Ohio – sister city to Augsburg, Germany
75,000-150,000: Portsmouth, Virginia – sister city to Dunedin, New Zealand
25,000-75,000: Beverly Hills, California – sister cityto Acapulco, Mexico
Under 25,000: Canisteo, New York – sister city to Wauchope, Australia

Sponsored by the Reader's Digest Foundation
Source: Bulletin, Town Affiliation Association of the United States, March 1968

How it is Done: A Town Affiliation
Historian G. Joseph Hummel noted in 1970 in the *International Educational and Cultural Exchange,* that, "An effective affiliation depends on careful study of the cultural profile, geographical and commercial nature, and social characteristics of hundreds of cities in the United States and abroad to insure the optimum matching of community interests essential for program continuity. Specialized groups are particularly important, since they can communicate in their vocational idioms unhampered by natural language barriers. When educators, professional athletes, stamp collectors, and gardeners meet, they communicate readily in the vernacular of their specialties, the Town Affiliation Association thus reaches deep into public attitudes of communities, however widely separated they may be by political predilections, language, and ethnic and national aspirations, to find the common denominators for successful vocational and avocational relations."

Town Affiliation Association of the U.S., Inc. Becomes Official - The articles of incorporation creating the Town Affiliation Association of the U.S., Inc., were signed June 12, 1967 in Washington, D.C., by Ambassador George V. Allen, director, Foreign Service Institute, Washington, D.C., seated; as Patrick Healy, executive director, National League of Cities, left, and John Garvey, deputy director, National League of Cities witness.

The Town Affiliation Association is Formed
The growing Town Affiliation Association became formalized in 1967. On June 12, when the incorporation papers were signed, Patrick Healy was named acting president. In November, Ambassador George Allen was named president.

Incorporators and Members Board of Directors

Ambassador George V. Allen
Director of the Foreign Service Institute
Washington, D.C.

Mayor Neal S. Blaisdell
Honolulu, Hawaii

F.W. Brittan
Vice President, International Latex Corporation
Dover, Delaware

Gordon S. Clinton
Clinton, Moats, Anderson & Fleck
Seattle, Washington
Mayor Frank Curran
San Diego, California

Mayor Frances Dias
Palo Alto, California

Richard Fitzgerald
Manager, Redondo Beach Chamber of Commerce
Redondo Beach, California

Howard Gardner
Associate Director, League of California Cities
Berkeley, California

Capt. H.B. Grow
U.S. Navy, retired
Pensacola, Florida

Patrick Healy
Executive Director
National League of Cities
Washington, DC

Mayor Frank T. Lamb
Rochester, New York
Mrs. May Ross McDowell
Johnson City, Tennessee

Mayor Roy B. Martin
Norfolk, Virginia

Stephen Matthews
Executive Director,
Texas Municipal League
Austin, Texas

Councilman William Mitchell
Modesto, California

Mayor Arthur Naftalin
Minneapolis, Minnesota

Mrs. Emma Rothblatt
Attorney at Law
New York, New York

Mayor Terry Schrunk
Portland, Oregon

Mrs. Gertrude Swanson
Minneapolis, Minnesota

Mayor Harold Tollefson
Tacoma, Washington

Frederick W. Brittan is elected second president of the Town Affiliation Association.

1968

Eisenhower Week Proclaimed by President Johnson
At the request of the U.S. Congress, President Lyndon B. Johnson signed the "Eisenhower Week Proclamation" in his office in the White House on July 18, 1968. About the sister cities program, President Johnson said, "Sister cities work outside government in a field vital to all: the promotion of friendship among citizens of every land so they will understand each other and want peace. I know of no other task more important for the people of every country."

The Real Impact of Sister City Programs

"I can think of no better or more appropriate way to share our heritage, on a People-to-People basis, throughout the world," said Mayor Robert Stoddard of Spartanburg, South Carolina during an address to the South Carolina Tri-Centennial Commission. "We have already reaped tangible benefits from the exchange of ideas and information. We have enjoyed a visit and performance by the Korean Little Angels, ages 6 to 16, choral and dance troupe. These youngsters visited in our homes and contributed more to future world understanding among our children and adults alike than we will ever see on television or read in books in a lifetime."

THE WHITE HOUSE SALUTE TO EISENHOWER WEEK BY THE PRESIDENT OF THE UNITED STATES OF AMERICA

A PROCLAMATION

Few men in history have contributed as much to their country and to the world as has General Dwight David Eisenhower.

As Supreme Commander of the Allied Expeditionary Forces in World War II, his leadership, resolution, and personal courage guided us to victory and to peace.

Following World War II, he served as the first Supreme Allied Commander of the North Atlantic Treaty Organization forces in Europe, and demonstrated an unrivaled capacity to create a united military organization.

During eight years as President of the United States, he enhanced his reputation as a leader of nations; a program of lasting international cooperation was inaugurated in his administration.

General Eisenhower is recognized as one of the most popular and respected living Americans – admired and loved by his fellow men not only as an outstanding military leader and statesman, but also as one whose character and high principles serve as a standard for all citizens.

It is fitting that on the occasion of General Eisenhower's 78th birthday on October 14, 1968, we pay tribute to this great American. To this end, the Congress, by a joint resolution approved July 18, 1968, as Salute to Eisenhower Week. It is my pleasure to do so.

NOW, THEREFORE, I, LYNDON B. JOHNSON, President of the United States of America, do hereby designate the week of October 13, 1968, as Salute to Eisenhower Week, and I call upon the people of the United States to observe that week with appropriate ceremonies and activities.

IN WITNESS WHEREOF, I have hereunto set my hand this eighteenth day of July, in the year of our Lord nineteen hundred and sixty-eight, and of the Independence of the United States of America the one hundred and ninety-third.

So, who's really a Sister City?

In 1968 the Town Affiliation Association of the United States, Inc. amended its bylaws to define an accredited sister city relationship as one that had formally been "recognized by the mayor and city council or the chief executive and legislative body of the area." Affiliations created before 1968 that had no documentation showing the date the relationships were formally created were "grandfathered" into the organization's national list.

A Sister City Leader: Frederick W. Brittan

Frederick W. Brittan was an advocate for the sister city program since its inception, and served as its president from 1968-1972. He was a charter member of the Civic Committee of People-to-People (the forerunner of Sister Cities International), and served as one of the original incorporators of the Town Affiliation Association of the U.S. Inc. He was an inexhaustible leader and traveled throughout the world inspiring volunteers to embrace the sister city mission and to raise funds. He set the stage in the early 1970s for stable financial support for the organization. Upon his death from cancer in 1982 at the age of 72, Dick Neuheisel sent condolences on behalf of the association and said, "He was a friend, confidante and pillar of strength in building a new national program of furthering world peace through the sister cities concept. We pray that his commitment to humanity will live on in understanding and friendship among people everywhere."

Do you know the way to San Jose?

Dionne Warwick smiles with representatives from San Jose, California and sister city San Jose, Costa Rica. Recorded in 1967, the now-famous song helped her win her first Grammy Award in 1968. She became the first African-American solo female artist of her generation to win the prestigious award for Best Contemporary Female Vocal Performance.

This 1968 congratulatory letter was mailed from Walter Reed Hospital, and was one of former President Eisenhower's last public acts.

Dear Mr. Brittan:

I have just learned of your election as president of the Town Affiliation Association of the United States. My warmest congratulations! I wish you all success in carrying on the "sister city" program which has brought United States cities and their hundreds of thousands of citizens into intimate contact with the citizens of a similar number of cities and towns in 56 countries.

You have accepted leadership in a mission for understanding and peace in the world of major significance to ourselves and the generations to come. Our most cogent diplomatists cannot achieve peace without understanding, and understanding can only be reached through the hearts of people. Thus the Town Affiliation Association's "sister city" program offers an important resource to the negotiations of governments by letting the people themselves give expression to their common desire for friendship, goodwill and cooperation for a better world for all.

You have a great opportunity for service to your countrymen.

Sincerely,

Dwight D. Eisenhower

Trade Activities Increase

According to Gorden S. Clinton, chair of the Seattle-Kobe-Japan Sister City Committee, in the ten years of affiliation between Seattle, Washington and Kobe, Japan, the dollar value of trade between the two communities increased more than 300 percent – going from a 1957 value of $8.3 million dollars to a 1967 value of $27.3 million dollars. The establishment of a trade information office in Seattle by Kobe helped open new doors for U.S. business and the exchange of professional staff. Their sister port affiliation and delegation visits enhanced commercial ties.

Dr. Louise Yim of Seoul, Korea, officiated at the presentation of awards by Chang-Ang University to General Eisenhower and leaders in the People-to-People program for outstanding contributions to international understanding and world peace. Ambassador George V. Allen accepted the degree presented to General Eisenhower. Dr. Yim was popularly known as the "Joan of Arc of Korea" for her devotion for 40 years to the cause of Korean independence.

1968

Delegates from Dover, Delaware receive an award from Sterling Fisher for their sister city efforts with Lamia, Greece.

OUR
CHANGING
WORLD

Where do we go
from here?

JOINT CONFERENCE

PEOPLE TO PEOPLE
TOWN AFFILIATION
ASSOCIATION

DECEMBER 4-6, 1968
HOLLYWOOD, FLORIDA
PROGRAM

At the time of the annual conference held December 4-6, 1968, in Hollywood, Florida, a serious move was made to consolidate the Town Affiliation Association with People-to-People Inc. - headquartered in Kansas City, Missouri. The effort did not materialize and a statement emerged from the conference: "As the sister cities program is specific in nature, a national association can best represent cities in the program and be more responsible to their needs than a combined organization."

Sterling Fisher, executive director of the Reader's Digest Foundation, presents the best overall program award for cities 25,000-50,000 in size to representatives of Coral Gables, Florida, sister city to Cartagena, Colombia.

"Let each affiliation committee first ask, "Are all our community groups — educational, cultural, business — doing all they can to reinforce our affiliation? This having been affirmatively resolved, the second question is: "Are our neighboring cities or towns that have no sister cities aware of the potentials the program may have for them?" It they are not, perhaps you who have savored the values of an overseas affiliate might whet the appetites of those who haven't."

- Ambassador George V. Allen

U.S. Senator Gale McGee and his wife enjoy a chat with Dr. Louise Yim of Seoul, Korea after the senator's opening address to conference delegates.

Announcing the . . .

THIRD ANNUAL
TOWN AFFILIATION AWARDS
COMPETITION

Sponsored by . . .

THE READER'S DIGEST FOUNDATION

Annual Awards 1968

Best Overall Program

Over 300,000: San Jose, California – sister city to San Jose, Costa Rica and Okayama, Japan
100,000-300,000: Hollywood, Florida – sister city to San Salvador, El Salvador
50,000-100,000: Redondo Beach, California – sister city to La Paz, Baja California and Ensenada, Mexico
Cities 25,000-50,000: Coral Gables, Florida – sister city to Cartajena, Colombia
Cities Under 25,000: Dover, Delaware – sister city to Lamia, Greece

Best Single Project

Pensacola, Florida – sister city to Chimbote and Miraflores, Peru
Redondo Beach, California– sister city to La Paz, Mexico
Modesto, California – sister city to Barranquilla, Colombia
Santa Fe Springs, California – sister city to Navajo, Mexico

Sponsored by the Reader's Digest Foundation
Source: Town Affiliation Conference Bulletin, January 1969

Board of Directors 1968-69

President - Frederick Brittan
Past President - Ambassador George Allen
Vice President - Mayor Frank Lamb
Treasurer - Honorable Gordon Clinton

Mayor J. R. Blackmon
Dr. Allan Crunden
Mayor Frank Curran
Mayor William Czuleger
Vice Mayor Frances Dias
Mayor Milton Graham
Captain Harold Grow
Ambassador Lloyd Hand

David F. Kelley
May Ross McDowell
William Mitchell
Sylvia Sass
Mayor Terry Schrunk
Ruth Stevens
Gertrude Swamson
Betty Wilson

Simon Russek was named March 30, 1969 to fill the term of Ambassador Lloyd Hand.

Robert Hildreth was named March 30, 1969 to fill the term of Captain Harold Grow.

1969

ANNUAL TOWN AFFILIATION CONFERENCE
SEPTEMBER 15-17, WASHINGTON, D.C.
THEME: THE 70S: A WORLD OF CITIES

(Left to right): Frank J. Shakespeare, Director, USIA observes as Charge d'Affaires Rafael Vazquez, Embassy of the Argentine Republic and Mayor Wade F. Lower, San Clemente, California exchange Town Affiliation Association charters during the conference. Standing behind Mayor Lower is F.W. Brittan, President of the Town Affiliation Association. San Clemente del Tuyu accepted the offer of affiliation in late August, joining the growing sister city movement.

Group-Session

Undersecretary of State Elliott Lee Richardson welcomed delegates to the Department of State auditorium for the opening general session. He told delegates, "We who labor in this building [the Department of State] are very much aware that our diplomatic activity represents only the very top of the large and growing iceberg of international exchanges, and among these we respect and value particularly the programs carried on by your Association. " He recalled many effective educational, cultural and business exchanges by sister city programs, and said, "Let me say then, for us at the State Department, we see the work you are doing as contributing in a most constructive kind of way in strengthening the bonds of relationship with other countries – forging a kind of channel of communication and understanding that can better endure the shocks of political circumstance and change that come along than we can do through diplomatic channels alone."

Hollywood, Florida's delegates receive an Annual Award for their work with San Salvador, El Salvador. Hollywood hosted 25 students and adults from their sister city for a week, sent a delegation of 67 to visit their sister city, conducted a project providing prosthetic devices, and created a 16 mm sound project for use in orphanages in San Salvador. The two communities co-hosted the national joint conference of the Town Affiliation Association and People-to-People.

"The dramatic past successes of the Sister Cities International program give you and your fellow members a dynamic role in the task of building a more peaceful and prosperous world community."

-U.S. President Richard M. Nixon

Keep Whittling At Stereotypes
"In this situation, it is essential for the peace of tomorrow that sister city contacts, people-to-people diplomacy, keep whittling away at the outmoded stereotypes we hold of each other."

- *George G. Wynne, Foreign Service Officer, U.S. Information Agency*

First Photographic Achievement Awards
Presented by Japan Air Lines

Program initiated in 1969

Over 500,000
First Place - San Jose, California
Second Place – Seattle, Washington
Third Place – none awarded

100,000-500,000
First Place – Albuquerque, New Mexico
Second Place – Portland, Oregon
Third Place – Omaha, Nebraska

Under 100,000
First Place – Bremerton, Washington
Second Place – Dover, Delaware
Third Place – Frankenmuth, Michigan

Source: Town Affiliation Conference Summary, 1969, within *Town Affiliation News*, December 1969

Annual Awards 1969

Best Overall Program
Over 300,000: Portland, Oregon – sister city to Sapporo, Japan
100,000-300,000: Hollywood, Florida – sister city to San Salvador, El Salvador
50,000-100,000: Coral Gables, Florida – sister city to Cartagena, Colombia
25,000-50,000: Johnson City, Tennessee – sister city to Guaranda, Ecuador

Best Single Project
Philadelphia, Pennsylvania– sister city to Florence, Italy
San Diego, California – sister city to Yokohama, Japan
Santa Fe Springs, California – sister city to Mersin, Turkey
South El Monte, California – sister city to Gomez Palacio, Mexico

Sponsored by Reader's Digest Foundation
Source: Town Affiliation Conference Summary, 1969, within Town Affiliation News, December 1969

Tournament of Roses Parade 1969

Title of the float was, "Hands Across the Sea," calling attention to the sister city relationship Santa Fe Springs has with Mersin, Turkey. Specifically designed to honor the sister city program, the colorful float depicted a flying carpet on which rested both traditional and modern Turkish buildings, the mosque and the skyscraper. Clasped hands on a globe at the front in sweet peas and vandal orchids symbolized the purpose of sister city relationships. Dr. Talat Kulay, consul general of Turkey, played a key role in the design and construction of the float.

Santa Fe Springs Princess Ann Milella, Miss Santa Fe Springs Cheryl Tiller, Miss Sema Poyraz, daughter of Governor Poyraz from Istanbul, Turkey, Princess Lucy Menchaka, and (standing) Miss Digdem Yeneriz, Santa Monica College student from Istanbul, Turkey are shown on the float.

President Eisenhower wanted for people to understand each other and for the world to truly know peace.

DWIGHT D. EISENHOWER
1890-1969

A Sad Passing

U.S. President Dwight D. Eisenhower passed away on March 28, 1969, a scant three years after the 10th anniversary of the fledgling People-to-People program. Cables carrying condolences arrived from around the world. In the *Town Affiliation News*, the editors encouraged readers, saying:

"Now is the time and the opportunity for all Americans as well as the citizens of the many friendly nations to join in the spirit of People-to-People and build in Eisenhower's remembrance not just an inert monument of stone, but a living memorial that will carry on his drive for universal understanding and peace."

Frederick W. Brittan, president of the Town Affiliation Association wrote, "Our best memorial to our departed leader will be the realization of Eisenhower's dream. So animated by his spirit and our nation's commitment to world peace, we can and we will enlist the people of the United States in a 'Sister City' crusade for peace."

Board of Directors 1969-70

President - Frederick Brittan
Mayor J. R. Blackmon
Honorable Gordon Clinton
Dr. Allan Crunden
Mayor Frank Curran

Mayor William Czuleger
Vice Mayor Frances Dias
Mayor Milton Graham
Mayor Frank Lamb
May Ross McDowell

William Mitchell
Simon Russek
Sylvia Sass
Ruth Stevens
Rhoda Stewart

Howard Traver
Betty Wilson
Louis Wozar

1970

Visitors from San Bernardino, California look at equipment in their Sister City Mexicali, Mexico in the 1970s.

Japan Airlines Photographic Competition 1970

Category I – Population Over 250,000

First Place – San Francisco, California – Osaka, Japan – Alfred T. Palmer

Second Place – Denver, Colorado – Best, France and Takayama, Japan – C.L. Barker

Third Place – Buffalo, New York – Kanazawa, Japan – Millard C. Browne

Category II – Population over 75,000 but less than 250,000

First Place – Glendale, California – Higashiosaka, Japan – Dennis Neufeld

Second Place – Fresno, California – Kochi, Japan – Lousander A. Markarian

Third Place – Hialeah, Florida – Managua, Nicaragua – Phil Donohue

Category III – Population Under 75,000

First Place – Bellevue, Washington – Yao, Japan – Mayor Kenneth Gates

Second Place – Horicon, Wisconsin – Senonches, France – Mayor Everett L. Myers

Third Place – Coral Gables, Florida – Cartagena, Colombia – Frank Kerdyck

Annual Awards 1970

Best Overall Program

Over 500,000: Seattle Washington – sister city to Bergen, Norway
100,000-500,000: Spokane, Washington – sister city to Nishinomiya, Japan
50,000-100,000: Redondo Beach, California – sister city to La Paz and Ensenada, Mexico
25,000-50,000: Coral Gables, Florida – sister city to Cartagena, Colombia
10,000-25,000: South El Monte, California – sister city to Gomez Palacio, Mexico
Under 10,000: Newport, Oregon – sister city to Mombetsu, Japan

Best Single Project

Over 500,000: Los Angeles, California – sister city to Nagoya, Japan
100,000-500,000: Portland, Oregon – sister city to Sapporo, Japan
50,000-100,000: Redondo Beach, California – sister city to La Paz and Ensenada, Mexico
25,000-50,000: Johnson City, Tennessee – sister city to Guaranda, Ecuador
10,000-25,000: South El Monte, California – sister city to Gomez Palacio, Mexico

Sponsored by Reader's Digest Foundation
Source: Town Affiliation News, September – October 1970

Amateur Radio: A Communications Line for Sister Cities

Beginning in 1974, a demonstration "ham radio" station was sponsored at the Annual Conference for several years to inform delegates about the communication benefits ham radio could provide to sister city programs. In many communities, amateur radio operators provided a vital link home for exchange students. Sister Cities International worked with the Amateur Radio League and the American Radio Relay League to set up the demonstration and to inform radio operators about sister city work. This oft-over-looked communications method helped many sister cities stay in touch.

Representatives of Newport, Oregon and sister city Mombetsu, Japan accept the award for Best Overall Program for communities under 10,000 in population.

These delegates are all decked out and ready to celebrate outstanding sister city programs.

The Best Overall Program and Best Single Project awards for the 50,000 – 100,000 population class were both won by Redondo Beach, California and its sister cities Ensenada and La Paz, Mexico. Almost a dozen delegates from both sides of the border were on hand to receive their plaques and certificates from John F. Maloney, Vice President of the Reader's Digest Foundation.

A dozen smiling delegates won the Japan Airlines Photographic Competition. The competition honored photos portraying the objectives, accomplishments and spirit of the international sister city movement.

A New Dedication, A New World

"In the decade of the '70s we will witness a new response – a new commitment to the solving of those human and technical problems which face man and society. We will see a new dedication among young and old alike to devote more of their time, their talent and their energy to volunteer programs striving to solve these problems. We will see more and more citizens throughout the world looking to the sister city concept as the vehicle through which they can serve as a volunteer of the '70s to help make this a better world and a peaceful world." - Tom Gittins, Executive Vice President, Sister Cities International

The George V. Allen National Youth Essay Contest is initiated.

Support for the National Office
In his speech to delegates attending the 1970 Annual Conference, President F.W. Brittan pointed out to members that of 349 communities utilizing services at the national office and logging Sister City affiliations, only 125 communities paid their membership dues. He urged members to get the number to at least 200 paying communities.

Straining for Support: Growing a National Association

The fledgling Town Affiliation Association struggled to make ends meet as it found itself caught in a conundrum. More U.S. cities were discovering the benefits of participating in the program and wanted to join. However, with each new community joining the program, the demands for services also increased. Revenue could not keep pace with the growth rate, and communities in other countries requested links in unprecedented numbers.

When the annual conference was held in San Diego, California, in August 1970, the service/growth dilemma was critical and had to be resolved by the association's board of directors. The need for outside funding and support for the program had to be met. John Richardson, Jr., assistant secretary of state for educational and cultural affairs, was the keynote speaker. He said, "We are deeply conscious that your sister city diplomacy is our invaluable private partner and support, able in innumerable ways, to strengthen and enlarge the opportunities for peace we all seek."

By the close of the conference, after numerous meetings with delegates and with the association's board, Secretary Richardson agreed in principle that the program should have government support and funding. Following subsequent meetings in Washington between the U.S. Information Agency and the U.S. Department of State's Bureau of Educational and Cultural Affairs, an official notice was sent to all concerned on January 19, 1971, that "the primary responsibility for U.S. government relations with the Town Affiliation Association of the U.S. government relations with the Town Affiliation Association of the U.S., Inc., (Sister Cities Program) has been transferred from USIA to State." Policy had been set and grant support found for the immediate future.

Eight task forces comprised of local sister city members were appointed in early 1971 to study and recommend ways and means by which the national organization could be more responsive to member needs and how to meet the challenge of future directions. To help improve member services, Thomas W. Gittins was hired to fill a new position created by the board of directors - that of executive vice president.

Board of Directors 1970-71

President - Frederick Brittan	Mayor J. R. Blackmon	Mayor James Hunter	Ruth Stevens
Vice President - Frank Lamb	Gordon Clinton	Vice Mayor William Mitchell	Rhoda Stewart
Vice President -	Dr. Allan Crunden	Vice Mayor Norman Mineta	Howard Traver
Mayor Milton Graham	Mayor Frank Curran	Simon Russek	Louis Wozar
Treasurer - May Ross McDowell	Mayor William Czuleger	Sylvia Sass	
Secretary - Councilman Betty Wilson	Vice Mayor Frances Dias	Robert Seipp	

Honoring Excellence ●
Gordon Clinton, chairperson of the Seattle-Kobe Committee, receives the award for
best single project for a community over 250,000 in size, from Japan Airlines official
Ken Sameda. Mary Warner, winner of another award, stands nearby.

1971

FIFTEENTH ANNIVERSARY ANNUAL TOWN AFFILIATION CONFERENCE
SEPTEMBER 15 – 17, WASHINGTON, D.C.
THEME: INTERNATIONAL RELATIONS AND CITIES: THE DECADE AHEAD

"First of all we are in a world where changing technology is making people-to-people communication more important than ever before in building toward a better, safer, more just world order," said the Honorable John Richardson, Jr., assistant secretary of state for educational and cultural affairs who opened the conference.

Representatives from Redondo Beach, California, Ensenada and La Paz, Mexico show their delight at winning the Best Overall program award in their category. Pictured at far right is General Paul Thompson, President of the Reader's Digest Foundation.

President Cites "Commendable Achievement"

President Nixon, in a letter to F.W. Brittan prior to the annual conference, expressed his strong backing for the important work of the Sister Cities program. He wrote:

"As Honorary Chairman of the Town Affiliation Association I am proud to express to all who are engaged in the important work of this organization not only my personal admiration but the deep gratitude of every citizen.

Through the Association's efforts nearly four hundred American communities now participate in a wide range of educational and cultural activities with cities in 60 foreign countries. This commendable achievement is in the best tradition of America's commitment to a peaceful, prospering world community.

Finding corrective solutions to the urban crisis that has become a priority on the agenda of so many nations makes it imperative that cities and their inhabitants around the world strengthen their ties of cooperation. In keeping with the spirit that has guided the People-to-People movement for so many successful years this kind of coordinated effort will surely help solve the common urban and environmental problems we face.

The dramatic past successes of the Town Affiliation Association give you and your fellow members a dynamic role in the task of building a more peaceful and prosperous community."

This photo contest entry from Seattle, Washington and Kobe, Japan celebrated the growth of understanding that comes with sister city relationships.

George V. Allen National Youth Essay Contest - 1971
Theme: "What does the sister city concept mean to you?"

Senior Division
First place – Barbara Leffler, Ralston, Nebraska
Second place – Paul Ried, Kent, Washington
Third place – Benjamin Gregg, Berkeley, California

Junior Division
First place – Sally Stanton, Bakersfield, California
Second place – Barbara Butler, Oakland, California
Third place – Elizabeth Cammerer, Oakland, California

Annual Awards 1971

Best Overall Program

Over 250,000: Jacksonville, Florida – sister city to Bahia Blanca, Argentina
75,000-250,000: Pensacola, Florida – sister city to Chimbote, Peru
25,000-75,000: Redondo Beach, California – sister city to La Paz and Ensenada, Mexico
Under 25,000: Millbrae, California – sister city to La Serena, Chile

Best Single Project

Over 250,000: Seattle, Washington – sister city to Kobe, Japan
75,000-250,000: Dayton, Ohio – sister city to Augsburg, Germany
25,000-75,000: Coral Gables, Florida – sister city to Cartagena, Colombia
Under 25,000: Luray, Virginia – sister city to Luray, France

Sponsored by Reader's Digest Foundation
Source: Town Affiliation Association Newsletter, published September-October 1971

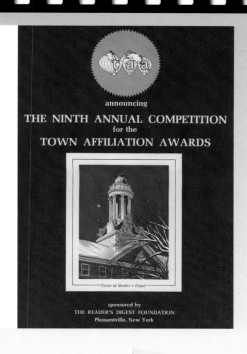

announcing
THE NINTH ANNUAL COMPETITION
for the
TOWN AFFILIATION AWARDS

Tower of Reader's Digest

sponsored by
THE READER'S DIGEST FOUNDATION
Pleasantville, New York

Board of Directors 1971-1972

President - Frederick Brittan
Vice President - Councilman Frank Lamb
Vice President - Mayor Milton Graham
Vice President - Robert Seipp
(named in spring 1972)
Treasurer - Robert McLaughlin
Secretary - Councilman Betty Wilson

Mayor J. R. Blackmon
Honorable Gordon Clinton
Mayor Frank Curran
Mayor William Czuleger
Vice Mayor Frances Dias
Mayor James Hunter

William Mitchell
May Ross McDowell
Simon Russek
James Sands
Ruth Stevens
Mayor Norman Mineta
Rhoda Stewart
Howard Traver
Louis Wozar

James Sites named March 5, 1972 to fill
Rhoda Stewart's term

Paul Edwards named in June 1972 to fill
Simon Russek's term

This lively brochure details the sister city relationship between Dayton, Ohio and Augsburg, Germany. It also lists 1971 exchange delegates.

ANNUAL TOWN AFFILIATION CONFERENCE
AUGUST 16-19, SEATTLE, WASHINGTON
THEME: SISTER CITIES IN A CHANGING WORLD

1972

A conference is not all work and no play. Alan A. Reich enjoys a laugh with youth delegates.

The first Sister Cities International Youth Conference was held in conjunction with the Annual Conference in Seattle.

Alan A. Reich, deputy assistant secretary of state, Bureau of Educational & Cultural Affairs, U.S. Department of State, beams his approval to Mayor Tatsuo Miyazaki (right), Kobe, Japan, who is accepting an honorary membership in the Town Affiliation Association. F.W. Brittan, president (left) and Gordon Clinton, chairperson of the Seattle-Kobe Sister City Committee and former mayor of Seattle, also register their pleasure.

Chairman of the Board, F.W. Brittan, addresses the delegates about the importance of sister city partnerships.

Annual Awards 1972

Best Overall Program
Over 250,000: Portland, Oregon – sister city to Sapporo, Japan
75,000 – 250,000: Spokane, Washington – sister city to Nishinomiya, Japan
25,000 – 75,000: Monterey Park, California – sister city to Nachikatsuura, Japan
Under 25,000: Kent, Washington – sister city to Kiabara, Japan

Honorable Mention:
Glendale, California – sister city to Higashiosaka, Japan

Best Single Project
Over 250,000: Los Angeles, California – sister city to Lusaka, Zambia
75,000 – 250,000: Hialeah, Florida – sister city to Managua, Nicaragua
25,000 – 75,000: Kettering, Ohio – sister city to Steyr, Austria
Under 25,000: Santa Fe Springs, California – sister city to Mersin, Turkey

Honorable Mention:
Berkeley, California – sister city to Sakai City, Japan

Best U.S. International Sister City Award
Redondo Beach, California – sister city to La Paz and Ensenada, Mexico

Honorable Mention:
Seattle, Washington – sister city to Kobe, Japan

Tashkent (Uzbekistan) in the Union of Soviet Socialist Republics, signs a sister city agreement with Seattle, Washington. It is the first sister city linkage between Soviet and U.S. communities. Tashkent Mayor V. Kazimov wrote to Seattle, "We hope that establishing of permanent friendly contacts between our cities and citizens will serve the course of world peace, mutual understanding, and respect of nations."

Sponsored by the Reader's Digest Foundation
Source: Newsletter, Sister Cities International, September-October 1972

The State Represenative system (later known as state coordinators) is founded. Twenty-four state representatives are appointed in 20 states to help local sister cities programs.

The Charles T. Kettering Foundation presents a grant to develop an exhaustive study of the Town Affiliation program and to publish its findings.

George V. Allen National Youth Essay Contest - 1972
Second Annual Contest
Theme: "The Role of Youth in International Relations"

SENIOR DIVISION
First place – Joan D. Drexel, Omaha, Nebraska
Second place – Joan F. Kirby, Omaha, Nebraska
Third place – Robert A. Kraft, Leavenworth, Kansas

JUNIOR DIVISION
First place – Michael A. Parga, Santa Fe Springs, California
Second place – Rita Hasek, Rochester, New York
Third place – Margaret Holcombe, Detroit, Michigan
Honorable mention – Diane Watanabe, Whittier, California

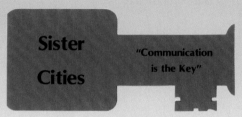

Sister Cities "Communication is the Key"

Joint Meetings: Help Communities Grow Their Sister City Programs

The Town Affiliation Association met jointly with the League of California Cities Committee on International Municipal Cooperation on October 15, 1972. Communication clinics covered: generating and sustaining interest in sister city programs, solving logistical problems in sister city relationships, and an "idea factory." Participants included: Tom Gittins, Thelma Press, Ethelda Singer, and Betty Wilson.

Sister City Leaders: Lou Wozar

Louis Wozar, a civic leader and industrialist from Dayton, Ohio, was elected third president of the association at the annual conference August 19, 1972, in Seattle, Washington. In taking over the reigns of leadership, Wozar stated, "Let us get on with the tasks of making the future of this organization an even greater adventure than the fifteen years we've just been through." Wozar became involved in international outreach in Dayton, Ohio in the 1960s. He became associated with the Dayton Council on World Affairs and then decided to initiate a program everyone in his community could participate in. He founded the Dayton sister city affiliation with Augsburg, then in West Germany, in 1964 and became its first chairperson. Wozar attended his first national sister cities conference shortly after that sister city relationship got off the ground. His commitment to the local program and his interest in the national program didn't go unnoticed. He was elected to the national board of directors during the annual conference in San Diego, California in 1970. He served as president from 1972 until 1978, when he became chairperson of the board. He traveled to more than 60 countries on behalf of the sister cities program at his own expense. "Lou Wozar is a living example of the true meaning of 'Volunteer.' He has devoted his personal talents and professional expertise to something in which he truly believes," said Jesse Philips, after a $100,000 endowment from the Philips Foundation was announced at the annual conference in 1981 honoring Wozar's many contributions to understanding between peoples of different nations.

Board of Directors 1972-1973

President - Louis Wozar
Chairman of the Board - Frederick Brittan
Vice President - Honorable Milton Graham
Vice President - Honorable James Hunter
Vice President - Honorable Frank Lamb
Vice President - Robert Seipp
Vice President - Ruth Stevens
Vice President - Mayor Betty Wilson

Treasurer - Robert E. McLaughlin
Secretary - William Mitchell
Frank Curran
Mayor William Czuleger
Mayor James McGee
Richard Neuheisel
James Sands
Ethelda Singer

Patrick Healy named in November/December 1972 to fill the term of Frank Curran.

Ambassador Joseph Palmer named in July/August 1973 to fill a vacancy.

Youth essay winner Vicki Winkler of Tempe, Arizona, smiles in appreciation to follow Arizonians (left) Milton Graham, Phoenix and Richard Neuheisel, Tempe. Both Graham and Neuheisel served on the Town Affiliation Association Board.

1973

Representatives of the U.S.S.R. Twin Towns Association and the Soviet Societies for Friendship and Cultural Relations with Foreign Countries met with Town Affiliation Association representatives to discuss guidelines for developing a sister city program between the two countries. This marked the dawn of a new era in sister city relationships, as communities across the U.S. and Soviet Union reached past cold war fears to forge friendship ties.

ANNUAL TOWN AFFILIATION CONFERENCE
SEPTEMBER 3-5, ATLANTA, GEORGIA

THIS IS THE LAST YEAR THAT "TOWN AFFILIATION CONFERENCE" WAS USED. STARTING IN 1974, ALL FUTURE CONFERENCES WERE CALLED THE "SISTER CITIES INTERNATIONAL CONFERENCE," ALTHOUGH THE ORGANIZATION WAS STILL KNOWN AS THE TOWN AFFILIATION ASSOCIATION.

Foreseeing a Bright Future
Landrum C. Bolling, Executive Vice President of the Lily Endowment, Inc. at the Friday luncheon: "I think the sister city concept is an exciting one and has tremendous potential for even more significant achievement in the years ahead. Not only in spreading its pattern, but also in extending the kinds of experiences that we can share together at the community level where we live and work."

A Program With Understanding and Meaning
The 1973 Annual Conference in Atlanta included remarks from the Honorable Jimmy Carter, then-governor of Georgia. He told delegates at the Opening General Session, "I don't believe there is a program with which I've become familiar since I've been in office that has a more understandable and penetrating meaning in these modern, confused, fast-changing, technological times than the sister city concept."

All ages were brought together during the Youth Session to talk about how to improve programs at the grassroots level.

George V. Allen National Youth Essay Contest - 1973
"How Youth Can Effectively Further International Relations Through the Sister City Program"

Group I – Grades 7-9
First place – Vicki Winkler, 8th grade, McKemy Junior High School, Tempe, Arizona
Second place – Michael Parga, 9th grade, Santa Fe High School, Santa Fe Springs, California
Third place –Kim Ellis, 9th grade, Marcos de Niza High School, Tempe, Arizona

Group II – Grades 10-12
First place – Joseph W. Giammona, 12th grade, Hillsdale High School, San Mateo, California
Second place – LeAnne Jewell, 11th grade, Redondo Union High School, Redondo Beach, California
Third place – Robert J. Tepper, 11th grade, Manzano High School, Albuquerque, New Mexico

L.A. Sister Cities On Display
Thanks to the efforts of TAA board member Ethelda Singer, five of Los Angeles, California's eleven (at the time) sister cities had exhibits at the International Sports, Vacation and Travel Show in 1973. Pictured, Los Angeles Mayor Tom Yorty (seated right) accepts a cup of coffee at the Tehran, Iran sister city booth. He also stopped at the booth for Bombay, India. Additional exhibits included handcrafts and slide shows highlighting Nagoya, Japan; Pusan, Korea; and Lusaka, Zamibia.

Rooted in Friendship: Torrance, California and Kashiwa, Japan
Mayor Ken Miller plants a tree at the Kashiwa City Shrine in 1973. On February 20, 1973, their sister city affiliation became official, with mayors Ken Miller of Torrance and Ryotaro Yamazawa of Kashiwa signing the agreement documents. This relationship is now more than 30 years old.

Sister Cities in Focus
Then-governor of California Ronald Reagan (far right) adds his approval to plans for the "Sister Cities in Focus" program. From left: California Museum Director William J. McCann, Whittier's Mayor Keith Miller representing President Nixon and Carol H. Tanaka, chairperson for the program for youth artists.

Annual Awards 1973

Best Overall Program
Over 250,000: Seattle, Washington – sister city to Kobe, Japan
75,000 – 250,000: Hialeah, Florida – sister city to Managua, Nicaragua
25,000 – 75,000: Coral Gables, Florida – sister city to Cartagena, Colombia
Under 25,000: Santa Fe Springs, California – sister city to Mersin, Turkey; Navojoa, Mexico; and Santa Fe, Argentina

Best Single Project
Over 250,000: Los Angeles, California – sister city to Bombay, India
75,000 – 250,000: Glendale, California – sister city to Higashiosaka, Japan
25,000 – 75,000: Palo Alto, California – sister city to Oaxaca, Mexico
Under 25,000: Palm Springs, California – sister city to Puerto Vallarta, Mexico

Outstanding Accomplishment Awards

Business/Professional Exchange:
Jacksonville, Florida

Cultural Exchange:
Portland, Oregon
Redondo Beach, California
Spokane, Washington
Los Angeles, California

Developing Local Awareness:
Jacksonville, Florida
San Jose, California
El Segundo, California

Educational Exchange:
Rochester, New York
Portland, Oregon
Redondo Beach, California
Spokane, Washington

Outstanding First Year Activity:
Glendale, Arizona

Overcoming Geographic Distance:
Jacksonville, Florida
Redford, Michigan
Tempe, Arizona

Providing Dramatic Help:
Tampa, Florida
Winchester, Virginia

Youth Programs:
Tucson, Arizona
Astoria, Oregon
Redondo Beach, California

Sponsored by the Reader's Digest Foundation
Source: Newsletter, Sister Cities International, September-October 1973

Elegantly dressed young ladies put on the southern belle charm to encourage delegates to attend the upcoming 1976 conference in Mobile, Alabama.

1974

ANNUAL SISTER CITIES INTERNATIONAL CONFERENCE
SEPTEMBER 18 – 21, PHOENIX, ARIZONA
THEME: COMMUNICATING FOR WORLD PEACE

Annual Awards Program winners share glowing smiles on either side of Kent Rhodes (center), from the Reader's Digest Foundation.

Robert G. Chollar (right), president and chairman of the Board of Trustees of the Charles F. Kettering Foundation, Dayton, Ohio receives the first "International Statesman" award from Sister Cities International President Lou Wozar. Chollar also delivered the keynote address for the conference, saying, "…time no longer gives us the luxury of not fully exercising the potential of organized private groups such as Sister Cities International to address critical issues in the international arena. The time has arrived to accept the responsibility commensurate with the opportunities your organization and its world-wide structure offers."

16 ANNUAL SISTER CITIES INTERNATIONAL CONFERENCE

U.S. SISTER CITY
taa
PROGRAM

SEPT. 18-24, 1974
PHOENIX ARIZON

Lou Wozar speaks to delegates, as well as a local television crew. Nearly 400 delegates from 100 U.S. cities representing 22 states, the District of Columbia and American Samoa attended the event. Ten additional nations were represented with delegates from Austria, Canada, France, Germany, Israel, Japan, Kenya, Mexico, Nicaragua and Nigeria.

This merry band from the Tucson Boys' Choir thrilled delegates.

A Grace Beyond Her Years...

Santa Cruz, California – Shingu , Japan
This little girl elegantly greets visitors from Santa Cruz, California, sister city to Shingu, Japan. Their sister city relationship began in 1974, and was initiated at the request of students at the Aikido School, a school for the martial arts. Shingu is a center for Aikido study and like Santa Cruz, is a small city on the coast between the sea and the mountains. The two communities have enjoyed many exchanges and in 1989, when an earthquake destroyed most of downtown Santa Cruz, Japanese schoolchildren collected funds to aid their Sister City.

"I am well aware of the fine efforts of the Sister City program in promoting closer ties of friendship and understanding with people throughout the world. It is both a pleasure and an honor for me to accept the Honorary Chairmanship of this fine organization."

-U.S. President Gerald R. Ford

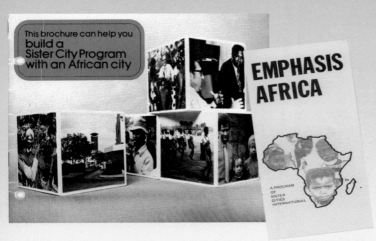

In 1974, Sister Cities International received funding for a new program, "Emphasis Africa" supported by the Lilly Endowment, Inc., Indianapolis, Indiana, to develop more links between U.S. communities and Africa.

George V. Allen National Youth Essay Contest - 1974
Contest Theme: How Our Community Can Celebrate America's Bicentennial Together with our Sister City"

Group I – Grades 7, 8, 9
First place – Merrill Johnson, Connolly Junior High School,
Tempe, Arizona – Skopje, Yugoslavia
Second place – Terry Sharrard, Cascade Junior High School,
Auburn, Washington – Kasuga-Cho, Japan
Third place – Jeanine Fahrlender, Lake Center,
Santa Fe Springs, California – Navojoa, Mexico; Mersin, Turkey; Santa Fe, Mexico

Group II – Grades 10, 11, 12
First place – Andrew T. Oram, Jamestown High School,
Jamestown, New York – Cantu, Italy; Jakobstad, Finland
Second place – Robert Tepper, Manzano High School,
Albuquerque, New Mexico – Chihuahua, Mexico; Sasebo, Japan
Third place – Paul Organ, Archbishop Rummel High School,
Omaha, Nebraska – Shizuoka, Japan

Group III – School newspapers
"Japanese, U.S. Cultures Meet in Sister Cities Programs'
by Marguerite Watt
The Troy In'voice
Auburn High School
Auburn, Washington – Kasugacho, Japan

Board of Directors 1973-74

President - Louis Wozar
Chairman of the Board - Frederick Brittan

Vice President - Milton Graham
Vice President - James Hunter
Vice President - Frank Lamb
Vice President - Robert Seipp
Vice President - Ruth Stevens
Vice President - Mayor Betty Wilson
Treasurer - Patrick Healy
Secretary - William Mitchell

Mayor William Czuleger
Philip Donohue
Vice Mayor David Lisk
Richard Neuheisel
Councilman Frank Ogawa
Mayor James McGee
Ambassador Joseph Palmer
James Sands
Ethelda Singer

In 1974, the Town Affiliation Association published a 138-page Sister City Handbook to help members enter the program and develop projects.

1974

In 1974, Dr. Oscar Rachetti, the "Intendente" of Montevideo, Uruguay met with Senator Hubert Humphrey as Rachetti began his study tour in the United States. Senator Humphrey praised the sister city program and called it, "certainly an ideal way to promote greater understanding." Rachetti's study tour was anchored by a long-term sister city relationship. Montevideo, Uruguay signed a sister city agreement with Montevideo, Minnesota in 1946. Dr. Rachetti praised the sister city program and looked forward to more links between the U.S. and Latin America. "Intendente" is a position roughly equivalent to a governor as well as a mayor of a city.

Annual Awards 1974

Best Overall Program
Over 250,000: *Jacksonville, Florida – sister city to Bahia Blanca, Argentina*
75,000 – 250,000: *Spokane, Washington – sister city to Nishinomiya, Japan*
25,000 – 75,000: *Portsmouth, Ohio – sister city to Orizaba, Mexico*
Under 25,000: *Oakwood, Ohio – sister city to Le Vesinet, France*

Best Single Project
Over 250,000: *Los Angeles, California – sister city to Bordeaux, France*
75,000 – 250,000: *Hialeah, Florida – sister city to Managua, Nicaragua*
25,000 – 75,000: *Glendale, Arizona – sister city to Delicias, Mexico*
Under 25,000: *Canisteo, New York – sister city to Wauchope, Australia*

Outstanding Achievement Awards

Business/Professional Exchange:
Coral Gables, Florida – sister city to Cartagena, Colombia
Portland, Oregon – sister city to Sapporo, Japan

Cultural Exchange:
Coral Gables, Florida – sister city to Cartagena, Colombia
Pueblo, Colorado – sister city to Puebla, Mexico
San Diego, California (3 awards) – sister city to Cavite City, Philippines; Leon, Mexico; and Yokohama, Japan

Developing Local Awareness:
Monterey Park, California – sister city to Nachikatsuura, Japan
Pueblo, Colorado – sister city to Puebla, Mexico
Redford, Michigan – sister city to St. Johann, Austria
Roanoke, Virginia – sister city to Wonju, Korea
Tempe, Arizona – sister city to Skopje, Yugoslavia

Educational Exchange:
Oakland, California – sister city to Fukuoka, Japan
Portland, Oregon – sister city to Sapporo, Japan

Outstanding First Year Activity:
Oceanside, California – sister city to Pago Pago, American Samoa
Pleasant Hill, California – sister city to Chilpancingo, Mexico

Overcoming Geographical Distance:
Santa Clara, California – sister city to Coimbra, Portugal

Providing Dramatic Help:
La Habra, California – sister city to Esteli, Nicaragua
Los Angeles, California – sister city to Bombay, India

Youth Programs:
Chula Vista, California – sister city to Irapuato, Mexico
San Jose, California (2 awards) – sister city to Okayama, Japan
Tempe, Arizona – sister city to San Jose, Costa Rica

Sponsored by the Reader's Digest Foundation
Source: Sister Cities International, Newsletter, September-October 1974

Board of Directors 1974-75

President - Louis Wozar
Chairman of the Board - Frederick Brittan
Vice President - Milton Graham
Vice President - David Lisk
Vice President - Frank Lamb
Vice President - Robert Seipp
Vice President - Mayor Betty Wilson
Treasurer - Patrick Healy
Secretary - William Mitchell
Philip Donohue
Mayor James McGee
Richard McGee
Richard Neuheisel
Councilman Frank Ogawa
Ambassador Joseph Palmer
Raymond Schultz
Don Shubert
Ethelda Singer
Mayor Charles Wheeler

Mayor John Belk, appointed March 1975
Victor Rockhill, appointed March 1975
Senator E. J. Garn, appointed March 1975

Did You Know?

An extensive year-long study of sister cities programs by the Charles F. Kettering Foundation in 1973-1974 showed that 25% of the sister city programs involved were organized and implementing programs to the extent that they could be classified as outstanding. Fifty percent were doing an adequate job in organizing and programming, although with increased service from the national associations, the researchers felt these programs could become outstanding. The remaining 25% significantly needed more help if they were to be expected to carry out any kind of international community-based programs.

Growing Friendship Ties
In 1975, Louis Wozar reported that 556 U.S. communities were affiliated with 705 communities abroad.

1975

To honor the 500th U.S. community joining Sister Cities International, U.S. President Gerald R. Ford praised the sister city program during a ceremony on May 25th at the White House Rose Garden with the executive officers of Sister Cities International. "I was very pleased to accept the Honorary Chairmanship of this program for which I have such high regard," said President Ford. "I have long been familiar with the Sister City Program, going back to my days in Congress, because of the many cities in Michigan involved," he continued. Louis Wozar, president of Sister Cities International presented the President with three volumes of American history and a Sister Cities International pin to mark this important milestone. Savannah, Georgia, affiliated with Patras, Greece, became the 500th U.S. community to join the growing sister city program.

500th U.S. Community Joining Sister Cities International Earns Accolades from President Ford

President Ford and Louis Wozar, right, president of Sister Cities International, share a lighter moment during the White House ceremony. President Ford is holding one of the books presented to him by Mr. Wozar. Standing behind President Ford are: (left) Sister Cities International vice president and Roanoke, Virginia vice mayor David K. Lisk and (right) Sister Cities International Board member and Dayton, Ohio mayor James McGee.

Participating in the Rose Garden ceremonies were (from left to right): John Richardson, Assistant secretary of state for educational and cultural affairs; Councilwoman Betty Wilson, Santa Fe Springs, California; Councilman Frank T. Lamb, Rochester, New York; Patrick Healy, former executive vice president, National League of Cities, Washington, D.C.; Senator Herman Talmadge, Georgia; Vice Mayor David K. Lisk, Roanoke, Virginia; President Ford; Mayor James McGee, Dayton, Ohio; F.W. Brittan, chairperson of the Board, Sister Cities International, Dover, Delaware; Thomas W. Gittins, executive vice president, Sister Cities International; Louis Wozar, president, Sister Cities International, Dayton, Ohio; Ambassador Joseph Palmer II, Bethesda, Maryland; and Mayor John P. Rousakis, Savannah, Georgia.

• The third National Youth Conference is held.
  The National Youth Committee is founded.
  A National Youth Chairperson and National Youth Board are elected.

Youth from Rehovot, Israel visited their sister city, Rochester, New York in 1975, and also stopped in Washington, D.C. to learn more about U.S. history and tour the capital city.

An educator talks to Baltimore, Maryland students about their community's sister city relationship with Gbarnga, Liberia.

This technical assistance program in Gbarnga, Liberia strengthened ties to Baltimore, Maryland.

The Gbarnga, Liberia Sister City Project

Gbarnga, Liberia and Baltimore, Maryland signed a sister city agreement in 1972. In 1981, Baltimore sent its sister city 3,000 desks, 1,500 desk chairs and 35,000 surplus textbooks. They have conducted cultural exchanges, provided technical assistance, established a pen pal program in the schools, hosted a teacher - ambassador exchange, and even administered a research tour in Liberia for nine educators under a Fulbright - Hays Groups Abroad grant. Two dozen schoolchildren joined embassy and government officials at the edge of Locust Point's Pier 3 to wave goodbye to the materials as they left on their journey across the ocean. The Firestone International Company provided free shipping for the materials, and the Chesapeake Operating Company donated crates and loading labor. These photos show a technical assistance project, as well as an educational exchange program. Historic ties between Maryland and Liberia date to the 19th century, when slaves repatriated to Africa founded the Republic of Liberia. Many of the repatriates were from Maryland and brought with them family and place names, such as Tubman and Maryland County.

Board of Directors 1975-76

President - Louis Wozar
Chairman of the Board - Frederick Brittan
Vice President - Frank Lamb
Vice President - David Lisk
Vice President - Richard McGee
Vice President - Richard Neuheisel
Vice President - Robert Seipp
Vice President - Honorable Betty Wilson
Secretary - William Mitchell
Treasurer - Patrick Healy
Gordon Clinton
Philip Donohue

Mayor James McGee
Elizabeth Moore
Councilman Frank Ogawa
Ambassador Joseph Palmer
Raymond Schultz
Donald Shubert
Ethelda Singer
Mayor Charles Wheeler

On March 13, 1975, a position for a Youth Representative on the Board of Directors is approved.

George V. Allen National Youth Essay Contest
1975

Category I: Grades 7-9
First Place – Michelle T. Mayer, Pleasant Hills, California
Second Place – Lucas Van't Hoog, Kettering, Ohio
Third Place – Daniel Papritz, Auburn, Washington

Category II: Grades 10-12
First Place – Gary Starr, Santa Fe Springs, California
Second Place – Gary Starr, Stephanie B. Prisch, Rochester, New York
Third Place – Celia Ann LaGreen, Omaha, Nebraska

Youth delegates share folk dances and forge new friendship ties during the conference. Youth organizers for the conference were Barbara Crutchfield of Manhattan Beach, California; LeAnne Jewell of Redondo Beach, California; and F. Robert Koch of Rochester, New York.

Kent Rhodes accepts an award for the Reader's Digest Foundation from Lou Wozar.

ANNUAL SISTER CITIES INTERNATIONAL CONFERENCE
AUGUST 6-9, ROCHESTER, NEW YORK
THEME: PLANNING FOR THE FUTURE

More than 75 young people attended the conference and began laying the groundwork for a national youth program. All sister city programs were encouraged to create a youth committee after the conference to nurture youth involvement.

Bahamas became the 74th country to join the growing sister city movement in special ceremonies marking an affiliation with Detroit, Michigan. Peter Drudge, Charge d' Affaires, Embassy of the Commonwealth of the Bahama Islands stands at the microphone and presents a flag to Laura Jackson, director of public information for the city of Detroit. Philip Donohue, board member for Sister Cities International from Hialeah, Florida holds the flag, while Mary Berrer, State Rep for Florida, looks on.

Annual Awards 1975

Best Overall Program
Over 300,000: San Jose, California – sister city to Okayama, Japan and San Jose, Costa Rica
100,000 – 300,000: Hialeah, Florida – sister city to Managua, Nicaragua
50,000 – 100,000: Redondo Beach, California – sister city to Ensenada, Mexico and La Paz, Mexico
Under 50,000: Coral Gables, Florida – sister city to Cartagena, Colombia

Best Single Project
Over 300,000: Jacksonville, Florida – sister city to Bahia Blanca, Argentina
100,000 – 300,000: Wichita, Kansas – sister city to Orleans, France
*50,000 – 100,000: Redford, Michigan – sister city to St. Johann, Austria
*50,000 – 100,000: Vallejo, California – sister city to Akashi, Japan
Under 50,000: Manhattan Beach, California – sister city to Culliacan, Mexico

** Note: two awards were given this year in the 50,000-100,000 Best Single Project category

Outstanding Accomplishment Awards

Business/Professional Exchange:
Santa Fe Springs, California – sister city to Navajoa, Mexico

Cultural Exchange:
Buffalo, New York – sister city to Kanazawa, Japan
Mobile, Alabama – sister city to Malaga, Spain; Puerto Barrios, Guatemala; Santo Tomas, Guatemala; and Pau, France
Glendale, California – sister city to Higashiosaka, Japan
Spokane, Washington – sister city to Nishinomiya, Japan

Developing Local Awareness:
Carson, California – sister city to Sinair, Philippines
Johnson City, Tennessee – sister city to Guaranda, Ecuador
La Habra, California – sister city to Esteli, Nicaragua and Tehuantepec, Mexico
Mobile, Alabama – sister city to Malaga, Spain; Pau, France; Puerto Barrios, Guatemala; and Santa Tomas, Guatemala
Pensacola, Florida – sister city to Chimbre, Peru and Miraflores, Peru
Pleasant Hill, California – sister city to Chilpancingo, Mexico

Outstanding First Year Activity:
Baltimore, Maryland – sister city to Gbarnga, Liberia
Concord, California – sister city to Kitakomi, Japan

Educational Exchange:
Charlotte, North Carolina – sister city to Arequipa, Peru
Los Angeles, California – sister city to Bordeaux, France
Pleasant Hill, California – sister city to Chilpancingo, Mexico

Overcoming Geographical Distance:
Darien, Connecticut – sister city to Mercara, India
Roanoke, Virginia – sister city to Wonju, Korea
Tempe, Arizona – sister city to Skopje, Yugoslavia

Providing Dramatic Help:
Hayward, California – sister city to San Felipe, Mexico

Youth Programs:
Anchorage, Alaska – sister city to Chitose, Japan
Azisa, California – sister city to Zacatecas, Mexico
Canoga Park, California – sister city to Taxco, Mexico
Lindsay, California – sister city to Ono City, Japan

Smile Award
May Ross McDowell – Johnson City, Tennessee

Sponsored by the Reader's Digest Foundation

CHIAVETTA'S CATERING **CHICKEN BAR·B·Q** WILL POULTRY CO.

Turkey SUB 69¢ ALL BEVERAGES 20¢

Turkey SUB 69¢

½CHICKEN BAR·B·Q

½ CHICKEN BAR·B·Q $199

½CHICKEN BAR-B-Q ROLL, SLICED TOMA. POTATO CHIPS, PICK. $199

39

TURKEY SUB 69¢

TURKE SUB 6

CHICK SANDWIC SLICED CHICKEN TOMATO SLICE LETTUCE SALAD DRESSING 3

AMERICA'S FAIR

In August 1976, more than 300 sister city visitors from Kanazawa, Japan, including these ladies in lovely kimonos, enjoyed an America's Fair and performed for their sister city in Buffalo, New York. Photo by Francis J. Passuite.

Growth and Expansion: The Third Decade

The "golden era" is the only way to summarize the third decade of the U.S. sister cities program. By this time, Sister Cities International had a solid reputation as an organization meeting the challenges of globalization and rapid change. Participating sister cities were demonstrating their capacity to deal successfully with new international contexts. In increasing numbers, sister city partnerships were closely connecting with the rest of the world.

1976

Annual Awards winners talk excitedly with Kent Rhodes from the Reader's Digest Foundation about their programs.

The 1976 conference in Mobile was an inclusive milestone – with more than 400 delegates in attendance representing nearly 100 U.S. communities from 35 states and 50 delegates from 22 nations.

"Youth has a distinct advantage. We are not afraid to reach out, to give of ourselves, to care. This attitude must not be lost. We must cultivate it and nurture it. We can do this by increasing our knowledge of our international partners," wrote Martha Dike, first-place finisher in the '76 George V. Allen National Youth Essay Contest. "Sister Cities News" noted that her thoughts accurately reflected those of the more than 60 youth delegates in Mobile.

Learning about outreach to new parts of the world was a key part of the conference.

INTERNATIONAL HORIZONS AND SISTER CITIES

20th ANNIVERSARY SISTER CITIES INTERNATIONAL CONFERENCE

AUGUST 25-28, 1976 MOBILE, ALABAMA

The conference agenda helped delegates navigate the 20th Anniversary conference in Mobile.

● National Youth Committee by-laws approved.
Youth State Rep System adopted.
Youth Board and officers elected.

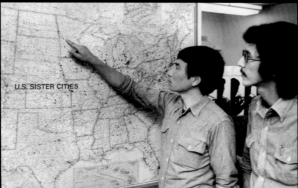

U.S. SISTER CITIES

Plotting A Journey of Friendship
Katsuyoshi Suzuki (left) and Hideaki Fujii (right) look at a map showing the locations of Japan's sister cities around the United States. They drove 25,000 miles for seven months to deliver bicentennial greetings of goodwill to all of Japan's sister cities.

Japan's Sister City Salute to America's Bicentennial

Katsuyoshi Suzuki and Hideaki Fujii, both young photojournalists from Tokyo, sum up the very special relationship that sister cities from all over the world had for their American counterparts during the 200th anniversary of the United States.

Suzuki and Fujii arrived in Washington, D.C. on June 14 after completing the first half of a "round the U.S. tour" in which they visited every U.S. city that has a Japanese sister city. They carried Bicentennial greetings from more than 100 cities in Japan and presented original Japanese paper carvings known as isekategami, a rare art form that dates back 1,200 years. The carvings were made especially for the trip by renowned artist Kikusui Takeushi.

Their journey actually began in 1974 when Fujii and Suzuki, then students in Japan, came up with the idea of being Bicentennial couriers to America in 1976. Their seven-month trip was officially recognized by the American Revolution Bicentennial Administration and the American Ambassador in Tokyo saw them off for their 25,000-mile road trip. Toyota Motor Sales, USA and Holiday Inns sponsored the event.

"The Buffalo"
The couriers named their car the "Buffalo" as a tribute to the American animal that represents the independent spirit of America celebrated during the Bicentennial. They also issued a "Buffalo Declaration" expressing their hopes for a peaceful world. Many sister cities from around the globe joined their U.S. counterparts for the Bicentennial celebration, marking a historic moment in history side-by-side.

An Impressive Gift Arrives at the White House
On the south lawn of the White House, Hideaki Fujii (left) and Katsuyoshi Suzuki (right) present a large traditional Japanese Carp to Milton Mitler, Deputy Special Assistant to the President for the Bicentennial. This and other gifts were presented to the White House as part of Japan's Sister City Salute to America's Bicentennial.

20th Anniversary

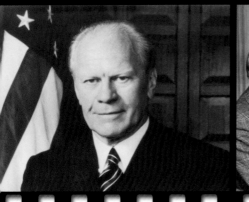

The U.S. Department of State was honored for its continuous support and encouragement of sister city activities during a luncheon in the United States capitol.

From left, Sister Cities International president Lou Wozar, presents John Richardson, assistant secretary of state for educational and cultural affairs, with a handsome plaque. To Wozar's right, Congressman Charles W. Whalen, Jr. of Ohio and Congressman Norman Y. Mineta of California participate in the ceremonies.

President Ford Praises Sister City Program

In a letter to Sister Cities International President Louis Wozar, President Gerald R. Ford praised the sister city program for its 20 years of accomplishments, saying, "When President Eisenhower proposed the establishment of a program of affiliation between American and foreign cities on September 11, 1956, no one could have anticipated how successful it would become in creating imaginative and valuable exchanges in the fields of education, culture, youth, business, local government and professional expertise. All who have given of their time and talent in this effort can take great satisfaction from their accomplishments."

Redondo Beach, California organized relief supplies for sister city La Paz, Mexico in 1976 after Hurricane Lisa wreaked havoc on the Mexican community.

Did you know?

Youth Program awards were presented for the first time this year.

Dues Structure

In 1977, the community dues structure for U.S. communities paying for membership in Sister Cities International was modified by the Board of Directors to become:

Over 500,000 in population	$650
300,001 – 500,000	$400
100,001 – 30,000	$325
50,001 – 100,000	$250
25,001 – 50,000	$200
10,001 – 25,000	$150
5,001 – 10,000	$100
Under 5,000	$50

Annual Awards 1976

Best Overall Program
100,000 – 300,000: Mobile, Alabama – sister city to Malaga, Spain; Pau, France; Puerto Barrios, Guatemala; and Worms, Germany
50,000 – 100,000: Palo Alto, California – sister city to Oaxaca, Mexico and Palo, Philippines
Under 50,000: Gardena, California – sister city to Huatabampo, Mexico; Ichikawa, Japan; Rosarita, Mexico

Honorable Mention:
Over 300,000: Denver, Colorado – Nairobi, Kenya
100,000 – 300,000: Hialeah, Florida – Managua, Nicaragua
50,000 – 100,000: Tempe, Arizona – Skopje, Yugoslavia
Under 50,000: Coral Gables, Florida – Cartagena, Columbia

Outstanding Accomplishment Awards
Business/Professional Exchange:
Cleveland, Ohio – sister city to Bangalore, India; Gdansk, Poland; Ibadan, Nigeria; Ljublijana, Yugoslavia; and Milano, Italy
Salt Lake City, Utah – sister city to Matsumoto, Japan

Cultural Exchange:
San Diego, California – sister city to Yokohama, Japan
St. Louis, Missouri – sister city to Stuttgart, Germany
Wichita, Kansas – sister city to Tlalnepantla, Mexico

Developing Local Awareness:
Monterey Park, California – sister city to Nachikatsuura, Japan
Pasadena, California – sister city to Mishima, Japan and Ludwigshafen, Germany
Redondo Beach, California – sister city to Ensenada, Mexico and La Paz, Mexico

Educational Exchange:
Los Angeles, California – sister city to Auckland, New Zealand

Overcoming Geographical Distance:
Arcadia, California – sister city to Newcastle, Australia
Jacksonville, Florida – sister city to Bahia Blanca, Argentina and Murmansk, USSR

Providing Dramatic Help:
Carson, California – sister city to Sinait, Ilocos Sur, Philippines
Sheboygan, Wisconsin – sister city to Rivas, Nicaragua

Providing Technical Assistance:
Redondo Beach, California – sister city to Ensenada, Mexico and La Paz, Mexico

Youth Programs:
Glendale, California – sister city to Higashiosaka, Japan
Orange, California – sister city to Queretaro, Mexico
Rochester, New York – sister city to Rehovot, Israel
Vallejo, California – sister city to Akashi, Japan

Smile Award
Terry Suzuki – Monterey Park, California

"Ike" Awards
(presented for the 20th anniversary of the sister city movement)
F.W. Brittan – St. Simon's Island, Georgia
Gordon S. Clinton – Seattle, Washington
Frank T. Lamb – Rochester, New York
May Ross McDowell – Johnson City, Tennessee
William R. Mitchell – Modesto, California
Ruth E. Stevens – Palm Beach, Florida
Betty Wilson – Santa Fe Springs, California
Patrick Healy – Washington, District of Columbia

Sponsored by the Reader's Digest Foundation

Edward Asner Named Goodwill Ambassador

Edward Asner, the popular motion picture, voice and television star, was named as a Goodwill Ambassador for Sister Cities International by Lou Wozar and Richard McGee in January 1976. Upon accepting his appointment, Asner said, "I am truly impressed with this program and I feel it is most meaningful in promoting world peace and understanding between people of different cultures. I look forward to assisting Sister Cities International in their efforts to accomplish the goals of international cooperation and understanding."

Edward Asner appeared in radio and television spots as part of the 20th anniversary of the sister city movement. Photo by Dana Gluckstein.

In presenting the awards, Mr. Kent Rhodes, president of the Reader's Digest Foundation said, "The Sister Cities Program is making tremendous strides in reducing international tensions. The 602 U.S. communities now affiliated with 781 sister cities in 75 other countries are reaching out in countless ways in order to diminish myths and understanding that so easily lead to hostility. The very essence of the Sister Cities program is its mutuality, its reciprocal, two way street of common concern for each other's well-being."

1976: A Busy Year for Sister City Activities

Many sister city groups organized celebratory events in honor of the bicentennial, including these pictured activities from Rochester, New York – Rennes, France and New Holland, Pennsylvania – Longvic, France. Mobile, Alabama hosted a delegation of 140 people from France to participate in the dedication of Fort Conde and assist with historical research and costuming for the event. The Sister City Committee in Carson, California worked with the Bicentennial Committee to hold a cultural fair honoring their three sister cities in Asia. Albuquerque, New Mexico planted cherry trees from Sasebo, Japan in the civic plaza as part of its activities. Poquosun, Virginia helped its French sister city find artifacts for a museum about Admiral de Grasse and his role in the defeat of Cornwallis at Yorktown.

Board of Directors 1976-1977

President – Louis Wozar
Chairman of the Board – Frederick Brittan
Vice President – Frank Lamb
Vice President – David Lisk
Vice President – Richard McGee
Vice President – Richard Neuheisel
Vice President – Raymond Schultz
Vice President – Mayor Betty Wilson
Secretary – William Mitchell
Treasurer – Patrick Healy

Youth Member to the Board – Richard Schultz

Mayor John Belk
Gordon Clinton
C. Dewey Crowder
George Henderson
Mayor James McGee
Elizabeth Moore
Frank Ogawa
Ambassador Joseph Palmer
Donald Shubert
Ethelda Singer
Barbara Watson
Mayor Charles Wheeler

On October 12, 1976, M.R. Vunda, mayor of Kitwa, Zimbabwe, shakes hands after signing a sister city agreement with Mayor C.A. Young of Detroit, Michigan.

In August 1976, more than 300 sister city visitors from Kanazawa, Japan visited their sister city, Buffalo, New York. Photo by Francis J. Passuite.

The delegation from Kanazawa, Japan performs in Buffalo, New York during a 1976 visit to their sister city. Photo by Francis J. Passuite.

These U.S. and Japanese Boy Scouts are sharing a common experience and learning from each other through the sister city program.

The George V. Allen Essay Contest was not held in 1977. It was retooled with new categories adding photography and poetry.

1977

Projects like this one helped communities in the developing world improve living standards and fostered mutual understanding.

Technical Assistance Program

The Technical Assistance Program (TAP) was established in 1977 to exchange technical expertise between communities in the United States and affiliated communities in developing countries. Supported in part with a grant from the U.S. Agency for International Development, TAP projects brought sister city partners from developing countries to the United States and helped communities work together to make life better. Hialeah, Florida, was the first U.S. city to receive a TAP grant to start a paramedics training program in its sister city, Managua, Nicaragua. Dozens more communities followed suit – developing projects in public safety, agriculture, health care, urban management of information systems, city planning, and vocational and special education. From 1987-1992, another grant was received from the U.S. Agency for International Development for the program. Funding cutbacks eventually closed this highly successful chapter in sister city history, but not before it laid the underpinnings of the Sister Cities Network for Sustainable Development.

Examples of TAP Projects in the 1970s:
- Burn Care & Reconstructive Surgery: Fort Lauderdale, Florida – Medellin, Colombia
- Burn Treatment Training: Austin, Texas – Maseru, Lesotho
- Eye Disease Control: Roanoke, Virginia – Kisumu, Kenya
- Farmers Credit Cooperative: Wilmington, Delaware – San Juan Sactegequez, Guatemala
- Management Training: Washington, D.C. – Dakar, Senegal
- Management Training & Urban Services: Miami-Dade, Florida – Kingston, Jamaica
- Market Reconstruction Project: Tuskegee, Alabama – Banjul, Gambia
- Medical Education: Los Angeles, California – Salvador, Brazil
- Municipal Water System Development: Scottsdale, Arizona – Alamos, Mexico
- Nurses Training & Public Health: Atlanta, Georgia – Montego Bay, Jamaica
- Potable Water Systems: Wichita, Kansas – Cancun, Mexico
- Reconstructive Surgery, Training & Teaching: Burbank, California – Gaborone, Botswana
- Sickle Cell Disease Screening: Charlotte, North Carolina – Port-au-Prince, Haiti
- Urban Sanitation Project: Dayton, Ohio – Monrovia, Liberia
- Urban Sanitation Project: Rochester, New York – Bamako, Mali
- Vocational Training: Denver, Colorado – Nairobi, Kenya
- Vocational Training for Disabled Youth: Oakland, California – Sekondi-Takoradi, Ghana

Improving lives and communities at the same time was a key part of the Technical Assistance Program.

Did You Know?
Riverside, California celebrated 20 years as a sister city to Sendai, Japan in 1977.

Volunteers in Chicago, Illinois staff an exhibit about sister city Warsaw, Poland. Displays like these educate thousands of people annually about sister city programs.

Technical expertise and funding for TAP projects also came from: Action Support Center for Ending Hunger, Avianca Airlines, Camp Virginia Jaycees for Retarded Citizens, Centre for Development and Population Activities, Children's Day School (Denver, Colorado), Clark College, the Coca-Cola Company, Denver University Graduate School of Social Work, the Ford Foundation, the Georgia Institute of Technology, the International Foundation, Interplast, Inc., Kaspers and Associates, Metro Dade Department of Youth & Family Development, Metro Dade Fire Department, National Association of Social Workers, Pan American Airlines, Ports of Call, Roanoke Association of Retarded Citizens, Rotary International Health, Hunger, and Humanity Program, Santa Clara Burn Treatment Center, Special Olympics, Stanford University, United Nations Fund for Population Activities, U.S. Agency for International Development Office of Foreign Disaster Assistance, U.S. Agency for International Development Office of Private and Voluntary Cooperation, U.S. Jaycees, University of Denver, University of West Virginia, and the Virginia Association for Retarded Citizens.

Board of Directors 1977-1978

President - Louis Wozar
Chairman of the Board - Frederick Brittan
Vice President - George Henderson
Vice President - Frank Lamb
Vice President - David Lisk
Vice President - Richard Neuheisel
Vice President - Raymond Schultz
Vice President - Mayor Betty Wilson
Secretary - William Mitchell
Treasurer - William Hanna

Youth Member to the Board - Richard Schultz

John B. Chandler
C. Dewey Crowder
Gordon N. Darling
Mayor James McGee
Richard J. Minkler
Frank Ogawa
Thelma Press
Ethelda Singer

The inspiring "Up-With-People" session opening the International Forum got things off to a rousing start. Delegates joined the singing and were invited by the performers to learn the international dances.

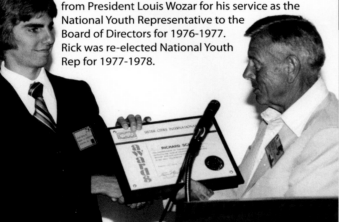

An Up & Coming Leader
Rick Schultz, National Youth Representative, Hialeah, Florida (left) accepts a "Certificate of Achievement" from President Louis Wozar for his service as the National Youth Representative to the Board of Directors for 1976-1977.
Rick was re-elected National Youth Rep for 1977-1978.

ANNUAL SISTER CITIES CONFERENCE
AUGUST 17-20, PALM SPRINGS, CALIFORNIA
THEME: INVOLVEMENT '77 AND SISTER CITIES

Delegates attend one of the many topical workshops, with discussions covering Africa, Asia, Europe, fundraising, Latin America, local organization and exchange, and technical assistance.

"Exchange of ideas and just getting to know each other on the level that the Sister City program provides plays an important role in maintaining good relationships between the U.S. and foreign relations. The Sister City program is based on a mutual situation – all countries experience urban problems – and from this common base we can move toward broader understanding to bring our diverse cultures closer together."

—U.S. President Jimmy Carter

Annual Awards 1977

Best Overall Program

*Over 300,000: San Diego, California – sister city to Cavite City, Philippines;
Leon, Mexico; Yokohama, Japan; and Tema, Ghana
100,000 – 300,000: Rochester, NY – sister city to Bamako, Mali; Caltanissetta, Italy;
Krakow, Poland; Rehovot, Israel; Rennes, France; and Wurzburg, Germany
50,000 – 100,000: Redondo Beach, California – sister city to Ensenada, Mexico and
La Paz, Mexico
Under 50,000: Johnson City, Tennessee – sister city to Guaranda, Ecuador*

Best Single Project

*Over 300,000: Oakland, California – sister city to Fukuoka, Japan
100,000 – 300,000: Hialeah, Florida – sister city to Managua, Nicaragua
50,000 – 100,000: Palo Alto, California – sister city to Oaxaca, Mexico
Under 50,000: Redford Township, Michigan – sister city to St. Johann, Austria*

Special Achievement Awards: International Involvement in America's Bicentennial

*Canoga Park, California – sister city to Taxco, Mexico
Cleveland, Ohio – sister city to Alexandria, Egypt; Bangalore, India; Brasov, Romania;
Gdansk, Poland; Heidenhein, Germany; Ibadan, Nigeria; Ljubijana, Yugoslavia;
Taipei, Republic of China; Milano, Italy
Dayton, Ohio – sister city to Augsburg, Germany; Monrovia, Liberia; and Oiso, Japan
Gardena, California – sister city to Huatabampo, Mexico; Ichikawa, Japan; and
Rosarito, Mexico
Hollywood, California – sister city to San Salvador, El Salvador
Littleton, Colorado – sister city to Bega, Australia
Los Angelos, California – sister city to Auckland, New Zealand; Bombay, India;
Bordeaux, France; Eilat, Israel; Lusaka, Zambia; Mexico City, Mexico; Nagoya, Japan;
Pusan, Korea; Salvador, Brazil; Tehran, Iran; and West Berlin, Germany
Mobile, Alabama – sister city to Ashod, Israel; Malaga, Spain; Pau, France;
Puerto Barrios, Guatemala; and Worms, Germany
Riverside, California – sister city to Cuautla, Mexico and Sendai, Japan
Roanoke, Virginia – sister city to Kisumu, Kenya and Wonju, Korea
St. Louis, Missouri – sister city to Accra, Ghana; Galway, Ireland; Lyon, France;
Stuttgart, Germany; and Suwa, Japan
Santa Monica, California – sister city to Fujinomiya, Japan; Hamm, Germany;
Mazatlan, Mexico
Seattle, Washington – sister city to Bergen, Norway; Dawson City, Canada;
Kobe, Japan; and Tashkent, U.S.S.R
Spokane, Washington – sister city to Nishinomiya, Japan
Tempe, Arizona – sister city to Regensberg, Germany and Skopje, Yugoslavia
York, Pennsylvania – sister city to Arles, France*

Sponsored by the Reader's Digest Foundation

Superpower Sister City Ties

By the end of 1977, there were five sister city linkages between the United States and the Soviet Union.

Deutschamerikaner Im Weissen Haus

Long time sister cities supporter Dave Rosenberg [at center with drums] shows President and Mrs. Carter some old fashioned cultural folk music in the Oval Office at the White House during Oktoberfest in 1977. President and Mrs. Carter stated that organizations like Sister Cities International, "help to bring together diverse cultures and ethnic groups to work together for better understanding and cooperation."

Did You Know?

There was a 70% increase in local sister city youth groups this year!

New Membership Categories

In 1977, the Board of Directors defined new membership categories for Sister Cities International for Individual Members ($15), Organizational Members ($50), and Corporate/Sustaining Members ($250).

Sister City Schools

Youth and Education – School Affiliation and "We Agree" Workshops in Global Education

In 1977, Sister Cities International established a school affiliation program to help bring students from around the globe together. Begun with a three-year grant from the Exxon Corporation, the program encouraged sister city partnerships to link elementary and secondary schools in the U.S. with their counterparts abroad. Organizers hoped to impact school curricula for the long-term, build knowledge among students about other cultures, and help students develop a global perspective. These school-to-school linkages included exchanging letters, ideas, pictures, films, tapes, and even people.

To expand the program, the Charles F. Kettering Foundation worked with Sister Cities International from 1977 to 1979 to sponsor "We Agree" Workshops in Global Education for community volunteers, parents, educators, and students. The workshops helped them establish global education goals, assess local resources, and make concrete plans to implement these goals.

With demand for the workshops continuing, the U.S. International Communications Agency provided additional funding to Sister Cities International to train leaders of the "We Agree" Workshop in Global Education. Forty-eight people from 27 U.S. cities, and 9 international participants were trained. In 1980, workshops were held in Tampa, Florida; Baltimore, Maryland; Kansas City, Missouri; Newark, New Jersey; and Rochester, New York.

School affiliation materials were available in English, French, German, Japanese, and Spanish. A 12-minute slide presentation was developed for the project and scripted in English and Japanese.

Sister Cities International: A Creative Force

"Sister Cities International serves as a creative force for international cooperation through community action. Its goal is to enhance world peace by promoting and serving sister city relationships between U.S. communities and their citizens and communities throughout the world."

— Honorable Tom Harkin
Congressman from Iowa, June 9, 1977
Congressional Record, Vol. 123

1978

Annual Awards 1978
Representatives from San Diego, California and sister city Tema, Ghana accept the award for best single project for a community over 300,000 in population.

President Carter Extols Sister City Program, Praises Wozar

U.S. President Jimmy Carter sent a message to President Lou Wozar at the conference, with warm regards to the delegates saying, "Sister Cities International has demonstrated how much ordinary people, visiting each other across national frontiers under a well-conceived program, can achieve in terms of international understanding. As you know, Mrs. Carter and I have been personally dedicated to this concept for many years. The strength of Sister Cities is its network of volunteers who devote their energy and imagination to improving cooperation between the people of the United States and citizens of other countries. The growth of this network in the past few years and the expansion of your program are impressive testimony to the interest of Americans in other cultures and to our abiding commitment to a more stable, compassionate world. Much of the recent success of the Sister Cities program can be attributed to the fine leadership of its outgoing President, Louis Wozar. He can be proud of his role in advancing the work of an organization which has been such a positive force in this interdependent world."

Who, me? Yes, You!
Dave Rosenberg, the U.S. Navy's director of intercultural programs, delivered an entertaining lecture on how to cross cultures for the opening youth conference session.

Cross-Cultural Communication
Delegates from Suwa, Japan; Zwedru, Liberia and Tel Aviv, Israel enjoy getting to know each other at the conference.

Betty Wilson of Santa Fe Springs, California

Learning Each Other's Traditions
Learning appreciation for other cultures helps young people develop tolerance and an appreciation for diversity. In a rapidly globalizing world, getting along with others is a necessity.

Sister City Leaders: Betty Wilson

Betty Wilson, mayor of Santa Fe Springs, California, was elected as the fourth president of Sister Cities International at the annual conference in St. Louis, Missouri on July 22, 1978. She became the first woman elected to this prestigious post. "A sister cities program," Wilson stated, "is a significant responsibility and we must continue to strive for excellence in our local programs and we must be prepared to meet new and difficult challenges in facilitating communications and cooperation among the citizens of our communities and citizens of towns and cities in other countries throughout the world." She served on the Board of Directors for many years and was long-remembered for her tireless efforts.

Betty Wilson holds a plaque honoring Sterling Wilson for his contributions to the sister city program, with Dick Neuheisel on her right and Ray Schultz on her left.

Board of Directors 1978-1979

President - Honorable Betty Wilson
Chairman of the Board - Louis Wozar
Vice President - George Henderson
Vice President - Frank Lamb
Vice President - David Lisk
Vice President - Richard Neuheisel
Vice President - Raymond Schultz
Vice President - Ethelda Singer
Secretary - William Mitchell
Treasurer - William Hanna

Youth Member to the Board - James Condrey

Charles Horn
Alice Pratt
Margaret Wells
John Belk
John Chandler
C. Dewey Crowder
Gordon Darling
James McGee
Richard Minkler
Frank Ogawa
Thelma Press
Charles Wheeler

GEORGE V. ALLEN NATIONAL TRI-MEDIA CONTEST 1978
THEME: "YOUTH VIEWS THE FUTURE: THE CHALLENGE OF SAVING OUR WORLD ENVIRONMENT"

GROUP 1 – GRADES 7-9
First Prize – Essay Cari Inoway, Salt Lake City, Utah
Second Prize – Essay Kimberly Leary, San Diego, California

First Prize – Poetry Jonthan Kranes, Salt Lake City, Utah
Second Prize – Poetry Kary Mauro, San Diego, California

First Prize – Photography Lincoln Fish, San Diego, California
Second Prize – Photography Russ Hollingsworth, Knoxville, Tennessee

GROUP 2 – GRADES 10-12
First Prize – Essay Sarah Love, Knoxville, Tennessee
Second Prize – Essay Todd Burgman, Omaha, Nebraska

First Prize – Poetry Sandra Huffman, Maroa, Illinois
Second Prize – Poetry Donald Crowther, Norwalk, California

First Prize – Photography John Peterson, Salt Lake City, Utah

This 1978 magazine produced by the Florida League of Cities promoted Florida's global affair with the world through the sister city program.

This 1978 magazine promoted the thriving sister city relationships nurtured by St. Louis, Missouri and their potential for stimulating economic growth.

Annual Awards 1978

Best Overall Program
100,000 – 300,000: Riverside, California – sister city to Cuautla, Mexico; Sendai, Japan; and Ensenada, Mexico
50,000 – 100,000: Redford Township, Michigan – sister city to St. Johann, Austria
Under 50,000: Coral Gables, Florida – sister city to Cartagena, Colombia and Quito, Ecuador

Best Single Project
Over 300,000: San Diego, California – sister city to Tema, Ghana
100,000 – 300,000: Torrance, California – sister city to Kashiwa, Japan
50,000 – 100,000: Canoga Park, California – sister city to Taxco, Mexico
Under 50,000: Gardena, California – sister city to Ichikawa, Japan

Outstanding Accomplishment Awards
Cultural Exchange:
Vandalia, Ohio – sister city to Lichtenfels, West Germany

Developing Local Awareness:
Vallejo, California – sister city to Asashi, Japan and Trondheim, Norway

Overcoming Geographic Distance:
Denver, Colorado – sister city to Nairobi, Kenya

Providing Technical Assistance:
Dayton, Ohio – sister city to Monrovia, Liberia
Hialeah, Florida – sister city to Managua, Nicaragua
Rochester, New York – sister city to Bamako, Mali

Youth and Educational Exchange:
Kettering, Ohio – sister city to Steyr, Austria
Sheboygan, Wisconsin – sister city to Esslingen, West Germany and Rivas, Nicaragua
Tempe, Arizona – sister city to Regensberg, West Germany and Skopje, Yugoslavia

Smile Award
Helen P. Cowell – Redondo Beach, California

Sponsored by the Reader's Digest Foundation

Your City Can Be A **VIP** [Very Important Program]

SISTER CITIES INTERNATIONAL

IN THE 1978 SISTER CITY AWARDS
Sponsored by THE READER'S DIGEST FOUNDATION

From the Great Rift Valley to the Mile High City: One Kenyan's Experience
Denver, Colorado – Nairobi, Kenya

It was the fall of 1978 and Jimmy Carter was president. The Broncos were up, the Nuggets down, and the brown smog was everywhere. This was Denver, Colorado. I had left my home in the beautiful open grasslands of Kenya's Great Rift Valley to travel to the Mile High City to be an exchange student sponsored by the Denver-Nairobi Sister Cities Committee. I was supposed to stay for one year; little did I know I would end up staying for seven.

I experienced a lot of culture shock when I arrived. What kind of people would take in a tall skinny stranger like me at the drop of a hat? The answer was a dear couple named Edna and John Mosley. I had an instant family that fed me well. I loved the sweet potato-pie and plum pudding. My first Thanksgiving and Christmas were amazing – the eggnog, the turkey and all the presents. I truly felt like a king!

However, my experience went beyond cuisine and gifts. Jim Reynolds, who then headed up the Colorado Civil Rights Commission, made sure I understood the value of the civil liberties and human rights many

Americans took for granted. I promised to one day take these to my home country.

The Denver-Nairobi Sister Cities Committee did their best to keep me on track studying and working a summer job. All these experiences taught me about the American work ethic. With lots of support, I graduated in 1979 and gained admission to the Graduate School of International Studies at the same university.

I am truly grateful for the kind hearts and helping hands extended to me during my time in Denver. They never failed to believe in me or teach me to appreciate the freedom I enjoyed in America. They also never doubted that I would take the knowledge and understanding I gained and give back generously to the place of my birth.

By John B. Gitari, who today works as a program officer for Human Rights and Social Justice for the Ford Foundation in West Africa.

1979

The Technical Assistance Program workshop drew rapt attention from attendees.

ANNUAL SISTER CITIES CONFERENCE
AUGUST 15-18, LOUISVILLE, KENTUCKY
THEME: VOLUNTEERS IN INTERNATIONAL PROGRAMS

These smiling youth delegates were never short of enthusiasm during a crowded conference session.

This happy group from Denver, Colorado received the "Best Overall Program" award for cities over 300,000 in population in 1979. At left, Kent Rhodes of the Reader's Digest Foundation talked to Genevieve N. Fiore, president of the Denver Sister Cities Committee.

Dr. Rose Lee Hayden
"Overall the response of the American educational and other systems to the challenge of preparing citizens for effective coping in an interconnected world is woefully inadequate," said Dr. Rose Lee Hayden, deputy director of the Peace Corps' Latin American and Caribbean regions at the conference luncheon on August 19, 1979. Dr. Hayden said that, "The role of sister cities has never been more important, the constraints never so real, and the rewards never so rich." She noted that, "This nation requires a cadre of experts about other peoples and cultures; professionals in business and government capable of successfully transacting transnational negotiations; scientists and technicians able to share and extend the frontiers of human knowledge on a global basis, and support tough leadership decisions and capable of participation in a democratic society...Persons such as yourselves are transnational carriers of global agreements – that governments ought to promote the general welfare of those they govern; that starvation is unacceptable; that the use of nuclear or biological weapons is unacceptable; and that cultural and ideological diversity should be tolerated. This is the seedling from which the new planetary awareness will sprout."

Louisville, Kentucky signed a sister city agreement with Tamale, Ghana during the conference. Pictured at a reception after the ceremonies are (from left to right): Ernest Tetteh, First Secretary, Embassy of Ghana; Betty Wilson, president of Sister Cities International; Mayor William B. Stansbury of Louisville; His Excellency Dr. Alex Quaison-Sackey, Ambassador of Ghana; Alhafi Rahjmu Gbadamosi, Headmaster of Tamale Secondary Schools, Ghana; and Louis Wozar, Chair of the Board of Directors for Sister Cities International.

West Coast Office
In 1979, Sister Cities International opened a West Coast Office in Los Angeles, California to help serve the growing number of affiliations on the West Coast.

St. Louis and San Francisco Form First Links with China

In fall 1979, St. Louis, Missouri and San Francisco, California become the first U.S. communities to link with communities in the People's Republic of China. The San Francisco "friendship city" accord with Shanghai was reached during a visit by Mayor Dianne Feinstein, who said, "We would like to see the great Pacific Ocean reduced to a river between our two countries." Peng Chong, chairperson of the Shanghai Municipal Revolutionary Committee responded, "And now, in the new historical context of normalized Sino-American relationship, our two cities will become friendly cities. We hail this happy event which, the first of its kind in the annals of Sino-American relationship, envisages broader prospects for the enhancement of friendship between our two countries in general and our two cities in particular." St. Louis formalized relations with Nanking in November.

Board of Directors 1979-1980
President - Honorable Betty Wilson
Chairman of the Board - Louis Wozar
Vice President - George Henderson
Vice President - Frank Lamb
Vice President - James Condrey
Vice President - Richard Neuheisel
Vice President - Raymond R. Schultz
Vice President - Ethelda Singer
Secretary - William Mitchell
Treasurer - William Hanna

Youth Member to the Board - James Condrey

C. Dewey Crowder
James McGee
Wylie Williams
Frank Ogawa
John Chandler
James Conway
Charles Horn
Michael Johnson
Richard Minkler
Alice Pratt
Thelma Press
Marge Wells
Dr. Charles Wheeler

SISTER CITIES 1979

Bringing The World Together

In 1979, Austin, Texas residents enjoyed a visit from Chief Masupha Seeiso (seventh from left) from sister city Maseru, Lesotho.

Annual Awards 1979

Best Overall Program
Over 300,000: Denver, Colorado – sister city to Brest, France; Karmiel, Israel; Nairobi, and Kenya; Takayama, Japan
100,000 – 300,000: San Bernardino, California – sister city to Mexicali, Mexico; Tachikawa, Japan; Tauranga, New Zealand; and Villa Hermosa, Mexico
50,000 – 100,000: Redondo Beach, California – sister city to Ensenada, Mexico and La Paz, Mexico

Best Single Project
Over 300,000: Los Angeles, California – sister city to Salvador, Brazil
100,000 – 300,000: Torrance, California – sister city to Kashiwa, Japan
50,000 – 100,000: Bakersfield, California – sister city to Wakayma, Japan
Under 50,000: Vandalia, Ohio – sister city to Lichtenfels, West Germany

Outstanding Youth Program
Pleasant Hill, California – sister city to Chilpancingo, Mexico and Cranbrook, Canada

Special Achievement Awards
Cultural Exchange:
Richmond, California – sister city to Shimada, Japan
Riverside, California – sister city to Cuautla, Mexico
Kettering Ohio – sister city to Steyr, Austria

Developing Local Awareness:
Delray Beach, Florida – sister city to Miyazu, Japan

Global Education Workshop:
Knoxville, Tennessee – sister city to Kaoshiung, Taiwan, China and Neuquen, Argentina

Houston, Texas – sister city to Baku, USSR; Chiba City, Japan; Heulva, Spain; Nice, France; Taipei, Taiwan, China

Program Revitalization:
Pensacola, Florida – sister city to Chimbote, Peru and Miraflores, Peru

Providing Technical Assistance:
Pensacola, Florida – sister city to Chimbote, Peru
Charlotte, North Carolina – sister city to Arequipa, Peru
Knoxville, Tennessee – sister city to Neuquen, Argentina
San Diego, California – sister city to Tema, Ghana

Youth Program Achievement:
St. Louis, Missouri – sister city to Accra, Ghana; Caracas, Venezuela; Galway, Ireland; Lyon, France; Kabul, Afghanistan; Stuttgart, West Germany; and Suwa, Japan
Sheboygan, Wisconsin – sister city to Esslingen, West Germany and Rivas, Nicaragua

Smile Award
Jacques C. Chicoineau – St. Louis, Missouri

Sponsored by the Reader's Digest Foundation

U.S.–Japan Education Program
In 1979 the Toyota 20th Anniversary Celebration fund awarded Sister Cities International a grant to establish a one-year U.S.–Japan Education Program with a focus on building sister school relationships. The project served as a clearinghouse for global education information, assisted post-secondary institutions with international affiliations, and built new exchange partnerships with other agencies. The project was extended through 1981 with funds from the Japan–U.S. Friendship Commission.

In the fall, San Francisco, California and St. Louis, Missouri became "friendship cities" with Shanghai and Nanking in the People's Republic of China. They are the first city-to-city affiliations between the United States and China

On December 26, 1979, students from Akashi, Japan stop for one last picture at City Hall before leaving their sister city, Vallejo, California.

Per Ketil, left, and Bente Riisem, students from Norway, are shown receiving a gift presented by Bill Chadbourne on behalf of students throughout Solano County. Chadbourne welcomed 11 students and three adults from Trondheim, Norway, Vallejo's sister city in 1979.

Vallejo, California welcomed a delegation of 11 students and three adults from sister city, Trondheim, Norway in 1979.

INDEPENDENCE, MISSOURI - HIGASHIMURAYAMA, JAPAN

Exploring History and Culture

The first Japanese delegation to visit Independence, Missouri from sister city Hiagashimurayama, Japan gets a taste of dress in the American West on January 27, 1978. The communities exchange delegations every five years and have exchanged more than 200 adults during their 25+ years as sister cities.

Giving Each Other a Lift

In October 1980, Mr. Koyama introduces his Festival Wagon Group to the delegation visiting Higashimurayama, Japan, from sister city Independence, Missouri. Delegates Bill and Joanne Shaw get a free ride!

1980

Barbara Schmitt receives the George V. Allen National Youth Award for 1980 from Sister Cities International President Betty Wilson. She also received a week-long trip to Washington, D.C. to observe foreign policy in action and to work at the Sister Cities International office. She was the president of Sheboygan Sister Cities Teen People in Wisconsin.

ANNUAL SISTER CITIES CONFERENCE
AUGUST 13-16, SAN DIEGO, CALIFORNIA
THEME: GOALS FOR THE 80'S

Sharing Culture: Sharing Smiles
Members of Kiriat Motzkin, Israel folk dance group, had delegates on their feet at the opening session. The dancers had just arrived from Tacoma, Washington, where their communities are linked.

Jon R. Kinghorn of the Charles F. Kettering Foundation addressed the delegates.

SISTER CITIES INTERNATIONAL

GOALS 80's ISSUES ACTION

23rd ANNUAL CONFERENCE AUGUST 13-16, 1980 SAN DIEGO, CALIFORNIA

This modern-looking logo encouraged members to get involved and attend the conference in San Diego.

Annual Awards 1980

Best Overall Program

Over 300,000: Wichita, Kansas – sister city to Cancun, Mexico; Orleans, France; and Tlalnepantla, Mexico

100,000 – 300,000: Stockton, California – sister city to Empalme, Mexico; Iloilo, Philippines; and Shimizu, Japan

50,000 – 100,000: Kettering, Ohio – sister city to Kettering, England and Steyr, Austria

Under 50,000: New Ulm, Minnesota – sister city to Ulm, West Germany and Neu Ulm, West Germany

Best Single Project

Over 300,000: San Antonio, Texas – sister city to Guadalajara, Mexico and Monterrey, Mexico

100,000 – 300,000: San Benardino, California – sister city to Mexicali, Mexico; Tachikawa, Japan; Touranga, New Zealand; and Villahermosa, Mexico

50,000 – 100,000: Richmond, California – sister city to Shimada, Japan

Under 50,000: Santa Fe Springs, California – sister city to Mersin, Turkey; Navojoa, Mexico; and Santa Fe, Argentina

Special Achievement Awards

Cultural Exchange:
Boston, Massachusetts – sister city to Kyoto, Japan
Gardena, California – sister city to Huatabampo, Mexico; Ichikawa, Japan; and Rosarito, Mexico
Minneapolis, Minnesota – sister city to Chunchon, Korea; Kuopio, Finland; and Santiago, Chile
Vandalia, Ohio – sister city to Lichtenfels, West Germany

Developing Local Awareness:
St. Louis, Missouri – sister city to Lyon, France; Nanjing, China; and Stuttgart, West Germany

Global Education Workshop:
Austin, Texas – sister city to Maseru, Lesotho and Saltillo, Mexico
San Jose, California – sister city to Okayama, Japan; San Jose, Costa Rica; Tainan, Taiwan, China; and Veracruz, Mexico
Torrance, California – sister city to Kashiwa, Japan

New Affiliation:
Salinas, California – sister city to Kushiniko, Japan

Providing Technical Assistance:
Minneapolis, Minnesota – sister city to Santiago, Chile

Sports Program:
Carson, California – sister city to Soka City, Japan

Technical Assistance Programs:
Baltimore, Maryland – sister city to Gbarnga, Liberia
Roanoke, Virginia – sister city to Kisumu, Kenya

Smile Award

Donna R. Harris – San Jose, California

Sponsored by the Reader's Digest Foundation

Caribbean/Central American Action Organization Formed

Lou Wozar, Chairman of the Board of Sister Cities International, was named to the Board of Trustees for Caribbean/Central American Action at its organizational meeting. The new organization was established to link people of the Caribbean and Central America with U.S. individuals and organizations. President Jimmy Carter said, "This action group represents a coming together of two concerns: first, our shared concern about the vital importance of the entire Caribbean region – that concern and interest has been growing lately – and secondly, a recognition that the friendship on a people-to-people basis must be the foundation for any progress that we envision taking place. The Sister Cities Program is one that can be expanded rapidly to encompass the people who live in the Caribbean Region."

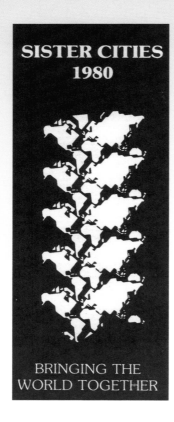

SISTER CITIES
1980

BRINGING THE
WORLD TOGETHER

Tri-Media Contest Ends

In 1980 the George V. Allen Tri-Media Contest, previously the George V. Allen Youth Essay Contest, was discontinued. It became the George V. Allen National Youth Award to honor an outstanding youth program.

25th Anniversary

1981

THE ORGANIZATION OFFICIALLY DROPS "TOWN AFFILIATION ASSOCIATION" AND ADOPTS "SISTER CITIES INTERNATIONAL" AS ITS NAME.

25th Anniversary Brings New Promotional Opportunities

The 25th Anniversary in 1981 brought new promotional opportunities for sister city programs. Many used this Community Action Toolkit and Public Relations Guide – which included sample press releases and advice on working with the press. A promotional magazine was also produced, and this fabulous photo of children and adults with a birthday cake helped promote participation.

Philip Morris, Inc. provided a grant for the 25th anniversary celebration in 1981. As part of that grant, the familiar logo of the world found on Sister Cities International publications was developed.

Did You Know?

In 1981, there were more than 740 U.S. cities, representing more than 85 million American people, affiliated with over 950 communities around the world in 77 other countries located on five continents.

Sister Cities Leaders: Richard Neuheisel

At the 25th anniversary conference, held in Kansas City, Missouri, August 19-22, 1981, Richard Neuheisel, of Tempe, Arizona, became the fifth president of Sister Cities International. Challenging the delegates, Neuheisel said, "Always do your best and the best will come back to you. If we all keep that view in mind as we proceed with our local programs the global impact of our work will do more for world peace than all the armorers and weaponry ever assembled. We owe it to ourselves, our children and future generations. It's what our founder, President Eisenhower, envisioned. It's his legacy to us. It's his challenge to us. It's our challenge." He served for 15 years as president, from 1981 to 1996.

I am proud to serve as Honorary Chairman of Sister Cities International and to be associated with a program whose human aspect reaches far beyond purely formal contacts between cities.

I well remember when President Eisenhower initiated this program in 1956 because of his deep personal convictions that it was incumbent upon all Americans to take responsibility for building world peace. Your record of accomplishment has proven this philosophy to be both sound and practical.

Twenty-five years have passed, and more than 700 cities linked with their counterparts on five continents have benefited from a wealth of invaluable experience and information. Moreover, Sister Cities International is just beginning to realize its full potential.

Because of your emphasis on the exchange of people and ideas, Sister Cities serves to promote better understanding and cooperation throughout the world. Out of this effort comes a spirit of friendship which, when multiplied by thousands of Sister Cities, results in improved economic, cultural, and social relationships between people everywhere.

My warmest congratulations to all Sister Cities as you celebrate this 25th anniversary of your founding and my best wishes for a most enjoyable and memorable celebration.

Sincerely,
Ronald Reagan

Annual Awards 1981

Best Overall Program

Over 300,000: San Diego, California – sister city to Cavite City, Philippines; Edinburgh, Scotland; Leon, Mexico; Tema, Ghana; and Yokohama, Japan
100,000 – 300,000: Rochester, New York – sister city to Bamako, Mali; Caltanissetta, Sicily, Italy; Cracow, Poland; Rehovot, Israel; Rennes, France; and urzburg, West Germany
50,000 – 100,000: Richmond, California – sister city to Shimada, Japan
Under 50,000: Coral Gables, Florida – sister city to Cartagena, Colombia and Quito, Ecuador

Best Single Project

Over 300,000: Los Angeles, California – sister city to Berlin, West Germany
100,000 – 300,000: Lakewood, Colorado – sister city to Sutherland Shire, Australia
50,000 – 100,000: Roanoke, Virginia – sister city to Kisumu, Kenya
Under 50,000: Vandalia, Ohio – sister city to Lichtenfels, West Germany

Special Achievement Awards

Cultural Exchange:
Norfolk, Virginia – sister city to Wilhelmshaven, West Germany
Pasadena, Texas – sister city to Hadano, Japan
Riverside, California – sister city to Cuautla, Mexico; Ensenada, Mexico; and Sendai, Japan
York, Pennsylvania – sister city to Arles, France

Technical Assistance:
Austin, Texas – sister city to Maseru, Lesotho
Charlotte, North Carolina – sister city to Port Au Prince, Haiti
Oakland, California – sister city to Sekondi Takoradi, Ghana
Wilmington, Delaware – sister city to San Juan Sacatepequez, Guatemala

Global Education and Youth Exchange:
Tampa, Florida – sister city to Barrangquilla, Colombia; Cordoba, Argentina; and Granada, Nicaragua

Global Education:
Baltimore, Maryland – sister city to Gbarnga, Liberia; Kawasaki, Japan; Niteroi, Brazil; and Odessa, USSR

Youth Exchange:
Bakersfield, California – sister city to Wakayama, Japan
Marietta, Georgia – sister city to Linz Am Rhein, West Germany

Youth Programs:
Baton Rouge, Louisiana – sister city to Ciudad Obregon, Mexico; Taichung, Taiwan, China; and Port Au Prince, Haiti
Houston, Texas – sister city to Baku, USSR; Chiba, Japan; Grampian Region, Scotland; Heulva, Spain; Nice, France; Stavenger, Norway; and Taipei, Taiwan, China
Kettering, Ohio – sister city to Kettering, England; Steyr, Austria
Mobile Alabama – sister city to Ashdod, Israel; Kagoshima, Japan; Malaga, Spain; Pau, France; Puerto Barrios, Guatemala; Worms, West Germany; Zakinthos, Greece
Pensacola, Florida – sister city to Chimbote, Peru; Escazu, Costa Rica; Kaohsiung, Taiwan, China; and Miraflores, Peru

Humanitarian:
Hialeah, Florida – sister city to Managua, Nicaragua
Salt Lake City, Utah – sister city to Matsumoto, Japan

Smile Award

Jessie Halverson – Riverside, California

Sponsored by the Reader's Digest Foundation

Remembered…As One Who Loved Every Day

"That the Sister City program has come to its present state is a great tribute to those who worked long and hard because of their strong faith in the Program. I would like to be remembered, if at all, as one who loved every day I was involved in the Sister City work, and hope that my faith in the good effect of communication between peoples around the globe played some small part in its present day greatness."

— F.W. Brittan, former president of the Board of Directors, in a letter dated May 13, 1981 to Richard Neuheisel in response to a request for memories for a 25th anniversary publication.

Richard Neuheisel addressed the conference delegates from the platform. As part of the 25th anniversary celebration, the board launched a major building fund project to help find a permanent home for the organization.

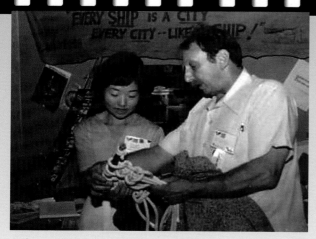

Delegates enjoyed sharing ideas. During the conference, the Jesse Philips Foundation announced a major grant to Sister Cities International to be known as the "Lou Wozar International Relations Endowment." The purpose of the endowment was to expand new affiliations and to assist more U.S. cities to enter the sister cities program.

Dwight David Eisenhower II Keynote
The keynote address for the 25th Anniversary Conference was delivered by Dwight Eisenhower II, grandson of President Eisenhower. He told delegates that the president's intentions in calling the White House conference on citizen diplomacy in 1956 was to "help build the road to enduring peace, to help people learn about each other so that people will say, 'how can we help each other?'"

This photo appeared in 1981 in the 25th Anniversary magazine produced about Sister Cities International. It shows youth intensely discussing international engagement.

The organization officially drops "Town Affiliation Association" and adopts "Sister Cities International" as its name

WHY SISTER CITIES?

A GUIDE FOR LOCAL PUBLIC OFFICIALS

This 1981 brochure helped involve more people in the sister city program.

Two Toledos Go to Washington

A twenty-nine member delegation from Toledo, Spain, accompanied by 16 hosts from sister city Toledo, Ohio, came to Washington, D.C., October 6, 1981. They were greeted the next day by then-Vice President George Bush who said, "the friendship between the two Toledos expresses better than any government official ever could the warm feeling that Americans have toward the Spanish people." Getting together for a picture after the ceremony were, from left: Charles Z. Wick, Director. U.S. International Communications Agency; Vice President George Bush; Mayor Juan deMesa, Toledo, Spain; and Carl Zerner, President, Toledo, Ohio Committee on Relations with Toledo, Spain. Later that day, the group was hosted at a luncheon by Congressman Ed Weber and attended a reception at the Embassy of Spain.

SUTHERLAND SHIRE, AUSTRALIA – LAKEWOOD, COLORADO

Teens from sister cities Sutherland Shire, Australia and Lakewood, Colorado become fast friends and make a peak of their own during a picnic in the Rocky Mountains in 1981.

Students for the 1985-1986 Lakewood, Colorado – Sutherland Shire, Australia student exchange are all smiles in this photo.

In 1981, Lakewood, Colorado students enthusiastically welcome the youth delegates from their sister city, Sutherland Shire in Australia. The emblem held on the right is the Australian high school's seal.

Fifty-three percent of member communities with over 300,000 in population reported in 1982 that business and trade relationships resulted from their sister city relationships.

New International Youth Initiative Unveiled

President Ronald Reagan announced on May 27, 1982 a new effort to expand international youth exchanges dramatically. He made the announcement to a group of 150 officers and international exchange organizers, saying that "Today we have a great opportunity to form new bonds through expanded exchanges among our youth, from all sections of our society. If we're to succeed, if we're to build human bridges across the seas and into the future as an investment for peace, we'll need more private support and cooperation than ever before." He continued, "And that, ladies and gentlemen, is why I invited you here today – to forge with me a new kind of cooperation between government and the private sector, between profit and nonprofit organizations, between families across our land and those abroad in an exciting exchange of our young people." Representing Sister Cities International at the full day of meetings were Jesse Phillips, a member of the International Executive Board for Sister Cities International and Thomas W. Gittins, executive vice president of Sister Cities International. A $90,000 grant was later given to Sister Cities International through the initiative.

U.S. – Soviet Relations Continue to Thaw

In 1982, Sister Cities International President Richard Neuheisel led a delegation to Moscow in the Soviet Union to meet with the Union of Soviet Societies for Friendship and Cultural Relations with Foreign Countries and to discuss twinning relationships. He signed a joint statement with V.S. Pestov pledging to improve the five existing U.S. – Soviet relationships, which included: Seattle, Washington – Tashkent; Jacksonville, Florida and Murmansk; Baltimore, Maryland and Odessa; Oakland, California and Nakhodka, and Houston, Texas and Baku. They announced a sixth sister city relationship between the two superpowers – Detroit, Michigan and Minsk.

Mayor Margaret Hance of Phoenix, Arizona and Paul Webb check out *Sister Cities News* at the Sister Cities International display during the 1982 National League of Cities convention.

Annual Honors
Kent Rhodes, chairman of the Reader's Digest Foundation, second from left, has a joyous smile for a big delegation from Waterloo, Illinois, which includes delegates from their sister city, Port Westfalica, West Germany.

ANNUAL SISTER CITIES
INTERNATIONAL CONFERENCE
AUGUST 18-21, TAMPA, FLORIDA
THEME: PEACE THROUGH PEOPLE

A Bundle of Youthful Energy...and Cash
These merry conference delegates have plenty to grin about. Sister Cities International received a $90,000 planning grant from the U.S. Information Agency to provide program support services for youth exchanges to U.S. communities with sister cities in Canada, Germany, Japan, Italy and the United Kingdom. The grant was part of President Reagan's Initiative on International Youth Exchange.

Warm Welcome
These brightly-costumed volunteers helped delegates register and served as interpreters.

Sister Cities International
International Executive Board – Appointed Members

William Anders
John Belk
Mayor Tom Bradley
Lucien Crosland
T. A. Dukes
Dwight Eisenhower II
Senator E.J. Garn
Bryant Gumbel
Ulrich Haynes
Bronson LaFollette

Paul McMullan
J.W. McSwiney
Norman Mineta
Patricia Neighbors
Jesse Philips
Joseph Palmer
Kent Rhodes
Charles Rhyne
Ambassador Claude Ross
G. Mennen Williams

Volunteers Show Longevity
A 1982 survey found that 48% of sister city committee members at the local level remained active for more than 3 years, 28% were active 3 years, 18% for 2 years, and 6% for 1 year.

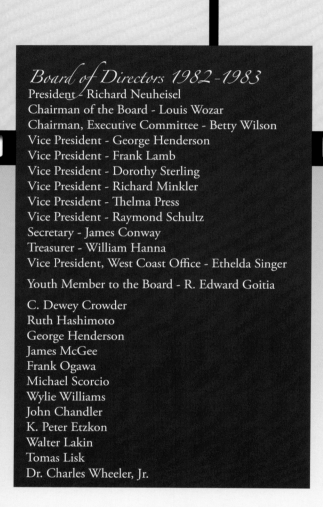

Annual Awards 1982

Best Overall Program
Over 300,000: Toledo, Ohio – sister city to Toledo, Spain
100,000 – 300,000: Wichita, Kansas – sister city to Cancun, Mexico; Orleans, France; Tlalnepantla, Mexico
50,000 – 100,000: Kettering, Ohio – sister city to Kettering, England; Steyr, Australia
Under 50,000: Vandalia, Ohio – sister city to Lichtenfels, West Germany

Best Single Project
Over 300,000: Denver, Colorado – sister city to Takayama, Japan
100,000 – 300,000: Louisville, Kentucky – sister city to Dublin, Ireland; Mainz, West Germany; Montpellier, France; Quito, Ecuador; and Tamale, Ghana
50,000 – 100,000: Pico Rivera, California – sister city to San Luis Potosi, Mexico
Under 50,000: Waterloo, Illinois – sister city to Porta Westfalica, West Germany

Best Overall Youth Program
Over 300,000: Baton Rouge, Louisiana – sister city to Port-au-Prince, Haiti; Ciudad Obregon, Mexico; and Taichung, Taiwan, China
100,000 – 300,000: Lakewood, Colorado – sister city to Sutherland Shire, Australia
50,000 – 100,000: Pensacola, Florida – sister city to Chimbote, Peru
Under 50,000: Vandalia, Ohio – sister city to Litchenfels, West Germany

Best Single Youth Project
Over 300,000: Tampa, Florida – sister city to Cordoba, Argentina; Barranquilla, Colombia
100,000 – 300,000: Chattanooga, Tennessee – sister city to Hamm, West Germany
50,000 – 100,000: Kettering, Ohio – sister city to Steyr, Austria
Under 50,000: Fredericksburg, Virginia – sister city to Frejus, France

Special Achievement Awards
New Affiliation:
Farmers Branch, Texas – sister city to Bassetlaw District, England
Fredericksburg, Virginia – sister city to Frejus, France

Professional Exchange:
Alexandria, Virgina – sister city to Dundee, Scotland
Spokane, Washington – sister city to Nishinomiya, Japan

Program Revitalization:
San Jose, California – sister city to San Jose, Costa Rica

Technical Assistance:
Coral Gables, Florida – sister city to Quito, Ecuador
Los Angeles, California – sister city to Lusaka Zambia and Salvador, Brazil
Miami, Florida – sister city to Bogota, Colombia
Roanoke, Virginia – sister city to Kisumu, Kenya

Youth Education:
Des Moines, Iowa – sister city to Kofu, Japan
Houston, Texas – sister city to Chiba, Japan
St. Louis, Missouri – sister city to Lyon, France; Nanjing, People's Republic of China; Stuttgart, West Germany; and Suwa, Japan

Youth Exchange:
La Vergne, Tennessee – sister city to Lavergne, France
Norfolk, Virginia – sister city to Wilhelmshaven, West Germany and Kitakyushu, Japan

Smile Award
John Yager – Toledo, Ohio

Sponsored by the Reader's Digest Foundation

1983

Two delegates from Sister Cities International represented the United States at the Fourth Congress of European Twinnings in Brighton, England, September 15-17, 1983.

The Sister City Relationship That Never Was

The Consulate of the United States in Trieste sent a letter to Sister Cities International in 1983 requesting help in establishing a sister city relationship between Key West, Florida and Lignano Sabbiadoro. Ironically – the linkage between the two communities sprang from the affection of one of the world's most renowned writers, Ernest Hemingway. Hemingway called Lignano "the Florida of Italy" and recounted his experiences there in his novel *Across the River and into the Trees*. The citizens of Lignano named a public park after the famous author. Alas, even with a letter of support from the Mayor of Lignano, the sister city effort linking Hemingway's favorite communities never got off the ground.

Ernest Hemingway enjoyed spending time in Lignano, Italy. A proposed linkage between Key West and Lignano unfortunately never took off.

Politics Don't Hamper Sister Cities
On March 9, 1983, all official, cultural and sports exchanges with China were severed by the United States. However, these policies did not affect sister city programs, and nine U.S. communities continued fostering their sister city relationships. When asked by *Sister Cities News,* Tom Eastham, press secretary to then-mayor Dianne Feinstein of San Francisco (sister city to Shanghai), said there was no let-up in activity, and added, "We have very substantial relationships in terms of exhibitions and other exchanges."

These merry conference delegates enjoyed networking in Phoenix.

Ruth Hashimoto proudly receives the Smile Award.

Rotary International Partners With Sister City Program

In 1983, the Rotary International Health, Hunger and Humanity program awarded $166,700 to the Roanoke/Kisumu project. The grant built on four years of technical assistance projects in environmental engineering and public health. The grant paid for equipment and material improvements for the Kisumu Rotary Youth Training Centre and for training additional Rotarians from other East African countries in vocational education programming.

Board of Directors 1983-1984

President - Richard Neuheisel
Chairman of the Board - Louis Wozar
Chairman, Executive Committee - Betty Wilson
Vice President - George Henderson
Vice President - Frank Lamb
Vice President - C. Dewey Crowder
Vice President - Richard Minkler
Vice President - Thelma Press
Vice President - Raymond R. Schultz
Secretary - James Conway
Treasurer - William Hanna
Vice President, West Coast Office - Ethelda Singer

Youth Member to the Board - R. Edward Goitia

William Chapman
Charles Wheeler
K. Peter Etzkorn
Ruth Hashimoto
Walter Lakin
Thomas Lisk
James McGee
Frank Ogawa
Michael Scorcio
Wylie Williams

Appointed – 1 year term - Annette Finesilver
Appointed – 2 year term - Lucien Crosland
Appointed – 3 year term - Spencer Bernard

Annual Awards 1983

Best Overall Program

Over 300,000: Houston, Texas – sister city to Baku, USSR; Chiba, Japan; Grampian Region, Scotland; Huelva, Spain; Nice, France; Perth, Australia; Stavanger, Norway; Taipei, Taiwan, China
100,000 – 300,000: Torrance, California – sister city to Kashiwa, Japan
50,000 – 100,000: Richmond, California – sister city to Shimada, Japan
Under 50,000: Arcadia, California – sister city to Newcastle, Australia and Tripolis, Greece

Best Single Project

Over 300,000: Toledo, Ohio – sister city to Toledo, Spain
100,000 – 300,000: Norfolk, Virginia – sister city toKitakyushu, Japan and Wilhelmshaven, Germany
50,000 – 100,000: Kettering, Ohio – sister city to Kettering, England and Steyr, Austria
Under 50,000: Steward, Alaska – sister city to Obihiro, Japan

Best Overall Youth Program

Over 300,000: Portland, Oregon – sister city to Sapporo, Japan
100,000 – 300,000: Lakewood, Colorado – sister city to Sutherland Shire, Australia
50,000 – 100,000: Orange, California – sister city to Orange, Australia and Queretaro, Mexico
Under 50,000: Pleasant Hill, California – sister city to Chilpancingo, Mexico

Best Single Youth Project

Over 300,000: St. Louis, Missouri – sister city to Lyon, France
100,000 – 300,000: Tampa, Florida
50,000 – 100,000: Carson, California – sister city to Soka, Japan
Under 50,000: Lindsay, California – sister city to Ono, Japan

Special Achievement Awards

Youth/Education Programs:
Centerville, Ohio – sister city to Waterloo, Canada
Oakland, California – sister city to Fukuoka, Japan and Nakhodka, USSR
San Bernardino, California
Santa Fe Springs, California
Wichita, Kansas – sister city to Cancun, Mexico

Technical Assistance:
Atlanta, Georgia – sister city to Montego Bay, Jamaica
Charlotte, North Carolina – sister city to Port Au Prince, Haiti
Dade County, Florida – sister city to Kingston, Jamaica
Denver, Colorado – sister city to Nairobi, Kenya
Miami, Florida – sister city to Bogota, Colombia
Naples, Florida – sister city to Espinal, Colombia
Roanoke, Virginia – sister city to Kisumu, Kenya
Wilmington, Delaware – sister city to San Juan Sacatepequez, Guatemala

Program Revitalization:
Baltimore, Maryland

Smile Award

Ruth Hashimoto – Albuquerque, New Mexico

Sponsored by the Reader's Digest Foundation

We Need a Second Language

The people of the world "need a second language – a language of understanding," said President Reagan when he convened members of his Council for International Youth Exchange at the White House in 1983. Jesse Phillips and Richard Neuheisel represented Sister Cities International and served on the Council.

We Meet Again: 491 Years Later

Four hundred and ninety one years to the day after the historic charter was signed supporting Christopher Columbus' voyage across the ocean in 1492, Santa Fe, Granada, Spain and Santa Fe, New Mexico formalized a sister city agreement. U.S. Ambassador to Spain Terence A. Todman called the linking, "a colorful and significant celebration that will take place to mark an event of enormous historical proportions."

Grant Awards

In 1983, the Reader's Digest Foundation awarded a grant to Sister Cities International to help new cities to enter the program. Benihana of Tokyo gave a grant to further youth exchanges and the U.S. Information Agency granted funds to Sister Cities International to offer "challenge grants" for youth exchange.

1984

Misako and Laurie (left) smile with other runners after their successful Olympic Torch Relay.

Olympic Torch Relay Brings Together 100 Japanese and U.S. Sister City Runners

In 1984, 100 runners from sister cities in California twinned with communities in Japan, carried the Olympic torch on a message of peace as it journeyed to Los Angeles, California. Fifty Japanese students traveled to the United States to take part in the project and home-stayed with 50 U.S. runners chosen to participate. The project was supported by businessman Shoji Kanazawa and his firm Maruko. Its impact on the young people participating in the project was profound, as demonstrated by these reflections from Misako Yamamoto. She wrote:

Running Partners Laurie Kempen from Bakersfield, California and Misako Yamamoto from Hyogo Prefecture, Japan.

18th July 1984. Perhaps that was for me the most important day of my life…My time in America was very short, but I experienced many things. But amongst these, the Olympic Torch Relay was undoubtedly the most important. I could only say "very great." The memories will glitter like diamonds in my heart as long as I live. Before I started to run I was very tense, however when I started running I could hear Laurie (my partner) calling out "Misako" in a very loud voice to encourage me…We were only together five days but I feel as if Laurie and I had been close friends since childhood. Although I am not very good at English I was able to make many friends. Perhaps that's because Americans treat everybody equally and openly. This was one fabulous week. My first flight in an aircraft, my first overseas trip, and meeting such wonderful people. I love Japan. I love the U.S.A.

Her running partner Laurie Kempson said:

There was great symbolism in our sharing the Olympic Torch Relay as well as sharing friendship. During the Relay, I lit Misako's torch, as our friendship and love had lit each other's hearts. After our run, we drove over to the beach. But because we had to be at a reception that evening, we could only stay a few minutes. But her eyes twinkled with excitement, and she said, "Oh, I am very happy! I have not been to the California coast before." We ran along the beach in our uniforms, feeling the combined ecstasy from the Torch Relay and newfound friendship. I learned that the Japanese have a lot of ceremonies, one of the saddest being the goodbye-line. On our last day together, as I came to Misako in the goodbye-line during the reception in Culver City, both of our eyes started filling with tears. We hugged each other and our eyes overflowed. …We will both always remember the great experience we shared and occasionally rekindle our flame through correspondence. With the purpose of the Olympics being world peace and friendship, it was very appropriate for sister city exchanges to be involved in the Sacred Torch Relay. I now feel an even closer kinship to Japan. It is a great country which I'll always love.

Continued Expansion and Support Are Critical

"In order to make sure that the chances of improved mutual understanding, which in the long run is the only answer to a stable and peaceful world, the sister cities program must continue to expand and receive support,"

— Ambassador Malcolm Toon, 1984

Glen Simoes (right), vice president of Benihana, Inc., Miami, receives a recognition plaque from President of the Board of Directors Richard Neuheisel for Benihana's sponsorship and funding of scholarships for students from 20 U.S. cities to visit their sister cities in Japan for 3-4 weeks to live with host families and carry out educational research projects.

ANNUAL SISTER CITIES INTERNATIONAL CONFERENCE
JULY 18-21, DENVER, COLORADO
THEME: A WORLD OF PEACE – HOPE FOR THE FUTURE

Youth delegates were an important part of the conference in 1984. A new round of Challenge grants was announced during the conference for 1984-85 and 11 countries added to the youth exchange initiative.

Growing Diversity
Nearly 600 delegates attended the conference. They represented 128 communities, 32 U.S. states and the District of Columbia, and 14 countries.

Standing 40 feet high and weighing 88 tons, this beautiful China Gate has graced the entrance to Philadelphia's Chinatown district since 1984. It was built through a cooperative venture between Philadelphia and sister city Tianjin, China. The Chinese lettering says, "Philadelphia-Chinatown-Tianjin."

Cities United: Portland, Maine and Shinagawa, Japan

Portland, Maine Mayor David Bernerman and Eitara Taga, mayor of Shinagawa, Japan congratulate each other after signing a proclamation officially designating their communities "sister cities." The City Hall ceremony was followed by an exhibition featuring music and dancers from both countries. Shinagawa sent a 26-member delegation to the event. Photo taken October 13, 1984 by Steve Nichols, photographer with the *Portland Evening Express*.

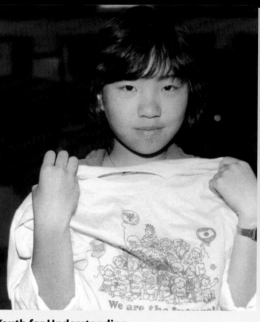

Youth for Understanding
Youth are the future! As demonstrated by an exchange student from Portland's sister city, Shinagawa, Japan. Photo taken August 3, 1985 by Steve Nichols, photographer with the *Portland Evening Express*.

Dancing to Celebrate and Share
Japanese dancers demonstrate Bon Odori folk dancing in Portland after the signing of Shinagawa's sister city agreement with Portland, Maine. Photo taken October 14, 1984 by Steve Nichols, photographer with the Portland Evening Express.

Cultural Exchange

Annual Awards 1984

Best Overall Program
*Over 300,000: Denver, Colorado – sister city to Brest, France; Cuernavaca, Mexico; Karmiel, Israel; Madras, India; Nairobi, Kenya; Potenza, Italy; and Takayama, Japan
100,000 – 300,000: Norfolk, Virginia – sister city to Kitakyushu, Japan and Wilhelmshaven, Germany
50,000 – 100,000: Tyler, Texas – sister city to Metz, France
Under 50,000: Waterloo, Illinois – sister city to Porta Westfalica, Germany*

Best Single Project
*Over 300,000: San Diego, California – sister city to Yokohama, Japan
100,000 – 300,000: Salt Lake City, Utah – sister city to Matsumoto, Japan
50,000 – 100,000: Schaumburg, Illinois – sister city to Schaumburg, Germany
Under 50,000: Arcadia, California – sister city to Newcastle, Autralia*

Best Overall Youth Program
*100,000 – 300,000: Mobile, Alabama
50,000 – 100,000: Wilmington, Delaware – sister city to Kalmar, Sweden
Under 50,000: Santa Fe Springs, California*

Best Single Youth Project
*Over 300,000: Austin, Texas
100,000 – 300,000: Lakewood, Colorado
50,000 – 100,000: Tyler, Texas – sister city to Metz, France
Under 50,000: Arcadia, California – sister city to Newcastle, Australia*

Special Achievement Awards
Technical Assistance:
*Austin, Texas – sister city to Maseru, Lesotho
Dade County, Florida – sister city to Kingston, Jamaica
Los Angeles, California – sister city to Salvador, Brazil
Roanoke, Virginia – sister city to Kisumu, Kenya
Washington, D.C. – sister city to Dakar, Senegal*

Education and Cultural Arts Program:
Baltimore, Maryland – sister city to Gbarnga, Liberia

Program Revitalization:
San Jose, California – sister city to San Jose, Costa Rica

Art Mobile Project:
Birmingham, Alabama – sister city to Hitachi, Japan

Musical Exchange Program:
Chattanooga, Tennessee – sister city to Hamm, Germany

Cultural Festival and Student Exchange Handbook:
Inependence, Missouri – sister city to Higashimurayama, Japan

Parks Project:
Lakewood, Colorado – sister city to Chester, England; Portsmouth, England; and Sutherlandshire, Australia

German-American Tricentennial Celebration:
Marietta, Georgia – sister city to Linz Am Rhein, Germany

10th Anniversary Celebration:
Pleasant Hill, California – sister city to Chilpancingo, Mexico

Chinese Art Exhibition:
San Francisco, California – sister city to Shanghai, China

10th Anniversary Celebration with Teacher Exchange:
Torrance, California – sister city to Kashiwa, Japan

Best First Year Program
*San Marino, California – sister city to San Marino, Republic of San Marino
Schaumburg, Illinois – sister city to Schaumburg, Germany
Tyler, Texas – sister city to Metz, France*

Sponsored by the Reader's Digest Foundation

In 1984, Mascara, Algeria officials look on while Elkader, Iowa Mayor Ed Olson signs a proclamation for twinning the two cities. Mohamed Khaldi, Mayor of Mascara, is shown at right.

Algerians in native costumes greet Elkader, Iowa city officials outside the city hall in Mascara in preparation for talks to twin the two cities in January 1984. The two cities represent the only sister city relationship between a U.S. city and an Algerian community. Both share the name Abd Elkader, known as the "George Washington" of Algeria, who was born in Mascara. Elkader, Iowa is the only city in the world that bears his name.

Continued Expansion and Support Are Critical

"In order to make sure that the chances of improved mutual understanding, which in the long run, is the only answer to a stable and peaceful world, the sister cities program must continue to expand and receive support,"

— Ambassador Malcolm Toon, 1984

1985

Networking was an important part of the conference. Ethelda Singer (far right) and Dick Neuheisel enjoy talking with delegates.

ANNUAL SISTER CITIES INTERNATIONAL CONFERENCE
JULY 10-14, BALTIMORE, MARYLAND
THEME: OUR WORLD – A FAMILY OF SISTER CITIES

"Our World – A Family of Sister Cities" was the conference theme.

Board member Ray Schultz presents a plaque to contributors from Madras, India for their support for the Building Fund for Sister Cities International.

Delegates enjoyed learning about history from this young man in costume while working as a guide on a ship deck in Baltimore's famous harbor.

Celebrating culture was an important part of the Baltimore conference.

A Leaping Gazelle Arrives in Detroit
Sculptor Marshall Fredericks (left) joins Detroit Chief Executive Assistant Fred Martin and Toyota, Japan Mayor Takashi Nishiyama to dedicate the "Leaping Gazelle" statue at Detroit's Belle Isle Park in 1985. Toyota, Japan is one of Detroit's five sister cities.

An Airplane Adventure
Denver, Colorado – Nairobi, Kenya Youth Exchange

The sister city program has seen many young people embark on grand adventures, but surely no one who was part of the first U.S. sister city exchange with a sub-Saharan African city in 1985, will ever forget their experience. Long delays at Kennedy Airport in New York kept the sixteen exchange students waiting, but they bided their time observing the many international travelers. Their learning adventures continued in Senegal when a French speaking crew boarded the plane. An emergency landing in Guinea because of a bomb scare added more adventure to the trip and caused them to miss their connection in Côte d'Ivoire for Nairobi. Only two days behind schedule, they finally arrived in Nairobi on Christmas Day. They busied themselves meeting host families and taking part in cultural activities. The Denver students and their Nairobi peers celebrated, shared and enjoyed each other's company immensely. The project was recognized with an Annual Award in 1987 as the Most Outstanding Youth Program that year – it was truly an adventure in discovery for many.

BALTIMORE, MARYLAND – GBARNGA, LIBERIA

Baltimore, Maryland and Gbarnga, Liberia conducted the Bong County Vocational Education Project in Liberia in 1985.

Annual Awards 1985

Best Overall Program

Over 300,000*: Albuquerque, New Mexico – sister city to Chihuahua, Mexico; Helmstedt, Germany; Hualien, Taiwan, China; and Sasebo, Japan; Baltimore, Maryland – sister city to Gbarnga, Liberia; Kawasaki, Japan; Luxor, Egypt; and Piraeus, Greece
100,000 – 300,000: Rochester, New York – sister city to Bamako, Mali; Caltanissetta, Italy; Krakow, Poland; Rehovot, Israel; Rennes, France; Waterford, Ireland; and Wurzburg, Germany
50,000 – 100,000: Richmond, California – sister city to Shimada, Japan
Under 50,000: Elkader, Iowa – sister city to Mascara, Algeria

* Albuquerque and Baltimore both received the "Best Overall Pprogram Award" in the over 300,000 population category which includes the "Best Single Project Award"

Best Single Project

100,000 – 300,000: Wichita, Kansas – sister city to Orleans, France
50,000 – 100,000: Palto Alto, California
Under 50,000: Reston, Virginia – sister city to Nyeri, Kenya

Best Overall Youth Program

100,000 – 300,000: Mobile, Alabama
Under 50,000: Pleasant Hill, California

Best Single Youth Project

100,000-300,000: Independence, Missouri
Under 50,000: Marietta, Georgia – sister city to Linz am Rhein, Germany

Special Achievement Awards

Anniversary Celebration:
Torrance, California – sister city to Kashiwa, Japan

Cultural Exchange:
Des Moines, Iowa – sister city to Kofu, Japan

Cultural/Heritage Development:
New Ulm, Minnesota – sister city to Neu Ulm, Germany and Ulm, Germany

Education Curriculum Development:
Tampa, Florida – sister city to Cucuta, Colombia

Foreign Language Development:
Tyler, Texas – sister city to Metz, France

Fund Raising:
Denver, Colorado

Technical Assistance Projects:
Dayton, Ohio – sister city to Monrovia, Liberia
Gainesville, Florida – sister city to Tegucigalpa, Honduras
Independence, Missouri – sister city to Blantyre, Malawi
San Diego, California – sister city to Tema, Ghana

Youth Exchange:
Chattanooga, Tennessee
Norfolk, Virginia – sister city to Wilhelmshaven, Germany

Best First Year Program

Elkader, Iowa – sister city to Mascara, Algeria

Best First Year Award with a City in a Developing Nation

Reston, Virginia – sister city to Nyeri, Kenya

Sponsored by the Reader's Digest Foundation

Source: Sister City News, Vol. 24, Number 3, August 1985

114

Japanese Garden Dedicated
Mr. Kinoshita, chief of Japanese Gardeners, performs a traditional ceremony of Blessing of the Friendship Garden on December 1, 1985 in Independence, Missouri for the garden from sister city Higashimurayama, Japan.

Words Spoken with Heartfelt Feeling
Greenville, South Carolina – Bergamo, Italy

Mayor Giorgio Zaccarelli was nervous – he wanted to make a good impression on his American hosts. So he studied English and prepared his remarks for the signing ceremony between Greenville, South Carolina and Bergamo, Italy in 1985. In his speech, the butterflies were not apparent. Zaccarelli recalled that the first time he met an American was in April 1945 during World War II. Forty years later he was pleased to establish an ongoing sister city relationship with the U.S. citizens, "who had sacrificed lives for my freedom, our common freedom." He also said, "We must cooperate so that Greenville and Bergamo can become good loving sisters. There are many fields in which we can work together." His remarks were truly inspiring for all.

Ambassador Program Initiated
In 1985, the Board of Directors approved the study of a proposal to create a Sister Cities International Young Ambassador Program to promote the active participation of young people ages 23-30.

Did You Know?

More than 100 youth delegates participated in the 1985 Annual Conference in Baltimore, Maryland.

U.S. Senator John McCain accepts an award from Richard Neuheisel in 1985 honoring his support of the sister city program.

PHOTO CONTEST ENTRY: YANGZHOU, CHINA – KENT, WASHINGTON, 1995

THE CHANGING WORLD: THE FOURTH DECADE

By the start of the fourth decade, cities, counties, states and other government jurisdictions had learned that if this is going to be a better world, if there is going to be a better standard of living, if there is to be some relief from human suffering, expanded opportunities for the young, security for the aged, increased health care for the sick, better education for children - it will be primarily because the citizens and their local governments across the world have insisted upon it and have mobilized the physical and human resources available to assure a better life.

Changing circumstances stimulated local governments to enter the international arena. Growing foreign investment and trade, overseas expansion by U.S. companies, and reduced federal support for economic development programs accelerated the emerging tradition of local government as an "economic activist." Local and state governments had to come to grips with the economic and social consequences of these shifts. The arrival of new immigrants expanded bilateral international relations, forged new trade and investment connections. Sometimes it also brought new urgency to human rights and health issues having international consequences for the localities where they settled.

Finally, this would be the decade when many nations made the slow, and often painful journey toward a democratic form of government. It was a time when barriers came down and global relations altered dramatically. What had originally started out as a program of goodwill and trying to win friends now emerged as a leader in fields never imagined by its founders.

Students of the Urban Gateway School view the Amezaiku craft exhibit at a museum in 1986 and learn about Chicago's sister city, Osaka, Japan.

1986

Sister Cities – We Are One

John Denver, the popular singer and writer, recorded "Sister Cities: We are One" in 1986 and the song was introduced at the 30th anniversary conference in Los Angeles. Performed by co-author and writing partner Dik Darnell and accompanied by "Kids of the Century" (who appeared on the popular television show "Fame"), the song was greeted enthusiastically by conference delegates who rose to their feet to sing the chorus. Unfortunately, Denver was not able to attend but he shared his hope for a world built around understanding, explaining "Music is indeed the universal language. It does bring people together and can give us a very real experience of being like someone else."

Exploring Culture Through Drama: Boston, Massachusetts and Melbourne, Australia, 1986.

SISTER CITIES
— WE ARE ONE —

MUSIC & LYRICS BY
JOHN DENVER AND DIK DARNELL
CHERRY MOUNTAIN MUSIC & VARIENA
© 1986

Sister Cities
(We Are One)

Sister Cities
We Are One
Music and lyrics by John Denver and Dik Darnell

Verse 1
The many flags behold
The four winds gently blow and seven seas break
on the shore of every land.
The spirit that we share, the love that's everywhere breaks
in our hearts and leads us all to understand.
Gone, gone are the days of separation,
long gone the threat of you or me.
The future of the world lies in the dreams of each and everyone.
So we will join together you and me.
Hand in hand we choose to be.

Chorus
We're all one dream, one voice of hope, hope for tomorrow,
we're all one life, one gift of love, one song forever.
Sister Cities, Brother Nations, hand-in-hand celebration.
Sister Cities, Brother Countries; one peaceful world,
one human nation. Yes, we are one.

Verse 2
For every mother's child,
For every father's joy and each and everyone
belongs to us all.
The life upon this earth, is dancing with the sons and
every silent voice awakes to join the call.
Gone, gone are the days of separation.
Long gone the threat of you or me.
The future of the world lies in the dreams
Of each and everyone.
So we join together you and me
Hand-in-hand we'll always be.

SISTER CITIES INTERNATIONAL

30TH ANNIVERSARY CONFERENCE

More than 1,100 people attended the Los Angeles conference, with delegates coming from 200 U.S. communities and 25 nations abroad. More than 200 youth delegates attended.

30TH ANNIVERSARY SISTER CITIES INTERNATIONAL CONFERENCE
JULY 16 – 19, LOS ANGELES, CALIFORNIA
THEME: SISTER CITIES: THE INTERNATIONAL KEY

Dick Neuheisel shakes hands with Los Angeles Mayor Tom Bradley. At the opening session, Bradley told delegates, "Sister Cities International has given us a unique opportunity to reach beyond our own borders and learn from people around the world. Los Angeles has the largest sister cities program in the nation. And without a doubt, that program has helped to expand the educational, commercial, cultural, and social links that make Los Angeles a leader in the global community."

Representatives of Slidell, Louisiana, smile as they receive the awards for the Best Overall Youth Program for a community with under 50,000 in population from Dick Neuheisel (right).

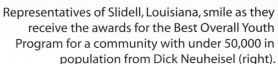

Dick Neuheisel presents a plaque to long-time sister city activists Doris and Bill Mitchell of Modesto, California, for their support and leadership as patrons for the Building Fund.

Washington D.C.'s Howard University Jazz Ensemble visits Beijing, China in October 1986.

Board of Directors 1986-87

President - Richard Neuheisel
Chairman of the Board - Louis Wozar
Chairman, Executive Committee -
Betty Wilson
Vice President - George Henderson*
Vice President - Frank Lamb
Vice President - C. Dewey Crowder
Vice President - Richard Minkler
Vice President - Thelma Press
Vice President - Raymond Schultz

Secretary - James Conway
Treasurer - William Hanna
Vice President, West Coast Office - Ethelda Singer
Youth Member to the Board - Abby Young
James Turner
Dr. Charles Wheeler
K. Peter Etzkorn * replaces George Henderson as
Vice President in early 1987
Annette Finesilver
Ruth Hashimoto

Walter Lakin
James McGee
Frank Ogawa
Joan Polivka
Michael Scorcio
Wylie Williams
Lucien Crosland
Spencer Bernard

Annual Awards 1986

Best Overall Program
Over 300,000: Denver, Colorado – sister city to Brest, France; Cuernavaca, Mexico; Karmiel, Israel; Kunming, China; Madras, India; Nairobi, Kenya; Potenza, Italy; and Takayama, Japan
100,000 – 300,000: Norfolk, Virginia – sister city to Kitakyushu, Japan and Wilhelmshaven, Germany
50,000 – 100,000: Des Plaines, Illinois – sister city to Cremona, Italy
Under 50,000: Temple City, California – sister city to Hawkesbury Shire, Australia and Magdalena, Mexico

Best Single Project
Over 300,000: New York City, New York – sister city to Tokyo, Japan
100,000 – 300,000: Tacoma, Washington – sister city to Kiryat, Motzkin, Israel; Kitakyushu, Japan; and Kunsan, Korea
50,000 – 100,000: Palo Alto, California – sister city to Oaxaca, Mexico
Under 50,000: Reston, Virginia – sister city to Nyeri, Kenya

Best Overall Youth Program
100,000 – 300,000: Mobile, Alabama
50,000 – 100,000: Orange, California
Under 50,000: Slidell, Louisiana

Best Single Youth Project
Over 300,000: Denver, Colorado – sister city to Brest, France; Cuernavaca, Mexico; Karmiel, Israel; Madras, India; Nairobi, Kenya; Potenza, Italy; and Takayama, Japan
100,000 – 300,000: Norfolk, Virginia – sister city to Kitakyushu, Japan and Wilhelmshaven, Germany
50,000 – 100,000: Schaumburg, Illinois – sister city to Schaumburg, Germany
Under 50,000: Santa Cruz, California – sister city to Sestri Levante, Italy

Special Achievement Awards

Anniversary Celebration:
St. Louis, Missouri – sister city to Lyon, France; Nanjing, China; and Stuttgart, Germany

Community/Cultural Awareness:
Arcadia, California – sister city to Newcastle, Australia and Tripolis, Greece
Brentwood, Tennessee – sister city to Brentwood, England
Seattle, Washington – sister city to Chongqing, China

Cultural Exchange:
Lakewood, Colorado – sister city to Chester, England; Portsmouth, England; Stade, Germany; and Sutherland Shire, Australia
Redford Township, Michigan – sister city to St. Johann, Austria

Professional Assistance:
East Providence, Rhode Island – sister city to Ribeira Grande, Azores, Portugal

Technical Assistance:
Baltimore, Maryland – sister city to Gbarnga, Liberia and Luxor, Egypt
Charlotte, North Carolina – sister city to Port au Prince, Haiti
Dade County, Florida – sister city to Kingston, Jamaica
Los Angeles, California – sister city to Lusaka, Zambia
Roanoke, Virginia – sister city to Kisumu, Kenya
Rochester, New York – sister city to Bamako, Mali
Washington, D.C. – sister city to Dakar, Senegal

Best First Year Program
Baltimore, Maryland – sister city to Rotterdam, The Netherlands
Fort Worth, Texas – sister city to Reggio Emilia, Italy

Sponsored by the Reader's Digest Foundation

"Blow, Silver Wind," a story of Norwegian immigration to the United States by Erik Bye, is performed in Houston, Texas, sister city to Stavanger, Norway. Stavanger is one of Houston's 16 sister city relationships.

Listening: To the Sounds of Peace

New York City Mayor Ed Koch listens intently to one of the cast members from the Beijing, China youth dancers. The fifty-six Beijing dancers, all around the age of 10, represented at the time the largest group of Chinese children ever involved in a cultural exchange between the U.S. and China. They joined children ages 8-14 from the National Dance Institute's public school programs in Manhattan, Brooklyn, Long Island, Jersey City, Westchester, California, Massachusetts and Maine in a production of over 1,500 children. The "China Dig" production was created by famed principal dancer Jacques d'Ambiose and also included Cloris Leachman, Mary Tyler Moore, Anne Ranking, the New York City Dancing Policemen, the Boys Choir of Harlem, Judy Collins and dancer Viktor Korjhan. The project was part of the Royal Pacific Cultural Exchange program funded by United Airlines. Photo by Joan Vitale.

This group from San Francisco, California is excited about the United Airlines Royal Pacific Cultural Exchange. Eleven U.S. cities and their 13 counterparts in Asia exchanged performing artists to help celebrate their links through performances and cultural exchange.

Kuumba Theater "The Heart of the Blues." The group performs the show in Osaka, Japan representing Chicago in the United Airlines Royal Pacific Cultural Exchange.

WHITE HOUSE STATEMENT ON THE 30TH ANNIVERSARY OF SISTER CITIES INTERNATIONAL

March 19, 1986

The President (Ronald Reagan) met today with the leadership of Sister Cities International to mark their 30th anniversary and receive their award for his contribution to international understanding. The President is the Honorary Chairman of Sister Cities International.

Over the years many ideas have been tried in the field of private international exchanges. For 30 years the Sister Cities programs have been among the most successful and effective. Sister Cities programs began after 1945 but became a full-scale national effort in 1956 when President Eisenhower initiated the People-to-People Program at the White House. Since then, Sister City relationships have been established between more than 745 U.S. cities, representing more than 90 million Americans and over 1,100 communities in 86 nations.

Sister Cities programs have worked to eliminate barriers of culture and language and have enhanced the opportunities for mutual understanding. Because of Sister Cities programs, thousands of young people have the opportunity each year to expand their horizons, American know-how is made available to help people in dozens of developing countries, and thousands of people around the world can see the American volunteer spirit at work.

Sister Cities International is also an important part of our effort to expand and broaden contacts and communications between the people of the United States and the Soviet Union. The President and General Secretary Gorbachev agreed in Geneva on the utility of broadening exchanges and contacts and finding new ways to increase cooperation. People-to-people programs can help build better understanding and genuine constituencies for peace.

The Sister Cities programs are an outstanding example of citizen and private sector participation at their best in the field of international exchange, understanding, and cooperation. We wish them well on their anniversary.

In 1986, Shoji Kanazawa, president of Maruko Group, Inc. and the first non-U.S. member of the International Executive Board for Sister Cities International, talks with Dwight David Eisenhower II about the new headquarters for Sister Cities International.

Metro-Dade Mayor Stephen P. Clark congratulates Miami-Dade County exchange students for their successful exchange program during July in Dade's sister city of Asti, Italy. From left: Glen Tibaldeo, Ricardo Nogueira, Lili Betancourt, Stacey Phillips, Mayor Clark, Lauren Ilvento, Humberto Rodriguez, and Michelle Ashby.

Metro-Dade Mayor Stephen P. Clark receives a gift from Italian exchange student Glauco Zitelli. Miami-Dade is a sister city to Asti, Italy.

Metro-Dade Mayor Stephen P. Clark welcomes Asti, Italy exchange students at the Government Center. From left: Stefano Spino, Francesco Bovio, Filippo Gaj, Corrado Elia, Valeria Ferrero, Mayor Clark, Silvia Marzo, Laura Toso, Laura Buffa, and Glauco Zitelli.

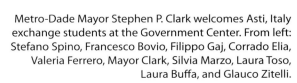

1987

The house in Alexandria had to be renovated. John Bebbling checks out the plans with Dick and Jane Neuheisel in what would become the conference room.

School groups and visitors from sister cities abroad were frequent guests at the headquarters at 120 South Payne Street in Alexandria, Virginia. This group of 9-10 year old boys from Washington, D.C. traveled to Beijing, China to play soccer and stopped by Sister Cities International for some advice on what to expect in 1988. The building was sold in the 1990s and the offices moved to downtown Washington, D.C.

The Kashiwa, Japan delegation stopped at 120 South Payne Street for a visit while touring Washington, D.C. Kashiwa is a sister city to Torrance, California. They also proudly admired the plaque showing the contributions of the Kashiwa Sister City Committee to the Building Fund.

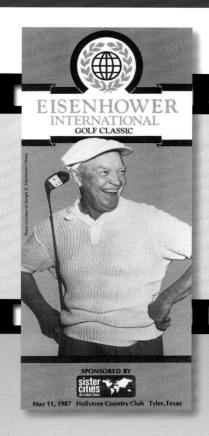

EISENHOWER INTERNATIONAL GOLF CLASSIC

SPONSORED BY
sister cities INTERNATIONAL

May 11, 1987   Hollytree Country Club   Tyler, Texas

The Eisenhower International Golf Classic

From 1987 through 1999, the University of Texas at Tyler and Sister Cities International joined together to sponsor the Eisenhower International Golf Classic. Half of the proceeds from the event supported Sister Cities International, including the Eisenhower International Scholarship Fund. Top PGA, LPGA and Senior PGA players and amateur golfers participated in the tournament, which raised money for the Eisenhower Scholarship Fund. The Golf Classic attracted star golfers and celebrities like Troy Aikman and Bill Bates of the Dallas Cowboys. As many as 10,000 people turned out for the annual three-day event, which also included the Young Artists Program and a 10K run.

This happy group has a good time while raising funds at the Eisenhower Golf Classic.

Spencer Christian of ABC's "Good Morning America" attended the Eisenhower International Golf Classic in 1987.

Mayor Tom Bradley presents "Ambassador Proclamations" to the 32nd Street Brass Quintet (photo with boys) and the Angelic Girls Glee Club in 1987. They were two of four musical groups traveling to the Auckland Fiesta to represent Los Angeles. The project was part of the United Airlines Royal Pacific Cultural Exchange.

Steve Loza, director of "UCLAtino" receives an "Ambassador Proclamation" from Mayor Tom Bradley in 1987. The group traveled to sister city Auckland, New Zealand to represent Los Angeles, California in Auckland Fiesta. The project was part of the United Airlines Royal Pacific Cultural Exchange.

125

Delegates enjoy networking time during the Annual Conference in Fort Worth.

Some of the young people attending the conference enjoyed meeting this group of KISS impersonators.

Annual Sister Cities International Conference
July 15-18, Fort Worth, Texas
Theme: Friendship Without Boundaries

"Friendship Without Boundaries" was the theme of the 1987 Annual Conference in Fort Worth, Texas. A July 15th editorial in the *Fort Worth Star-Telegram* wrote that the conference theme, "is especially appropriate because it not only reminds us of what might be accomplished worldwide through friendship and understanding, but, in a special sense, it also summarizes the big, friendly, Texas-size welcome Fort Worth is extending to our visitors."

Meeting people from other cultures and backgrounds has always been an important part of Annual Conference.

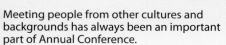

Dave Rosenberg and his cultural group entertained Dr. Michael Rehs from Stuttgart, Germany, as well as a local television crew.

Happiness: Finding a Sister Community
While on a visit to Tashkent, Uzbekistan (then in the Union of Soviet Socialist Republics) in 1987, Sculptor Yakov Shapiro presented to the sister city delegation his gift – "Happiness" – for the city of Seattle. It wasn't the first time the two communities used public spaces to salute their friendship - in 1974 Seattle inaugurated Tashkent Park.

Lunching for Peace
Mayors from sister cities Seattle, Washington and Tashkent, Uzbekistan get ready to enjoy lunch in a cafe. Pictured is: Royce Morrison, Roy Farrell, Vladimir Serjantov, Rosanne Royer, and Allan Doan. Seattle signed the first sister city agreement with a community in the former Soviet Union in 1973. Ironically, the relationship stemmed from a promotional tour organized by Alaska Airlines in 1971, when mayors from Tashkent, Irkutsk and Sochi visited Seattle and really hit it off with Seattle-ites.

Did You Know?

By the close of 1986, 756 U.S. communities were linked with 1,100 counterparts in 86 countries.

Annual Awards 1987

Best Overall Program
Over 300,000: Baltimore, Maryland – sister city to Cadiz, Spain; Gbarnga, Liberia; Genoa, Italy; Kawasaki, Japan; Luxor, Egypt; Odessa, USSR; Piraeus, Greece; Rotterdam, Netherlands; and Xiamen, China
100,000-300,000: Tempe, Arizona – sister city to Lower Hutt, New Zealand; Regensburg, Germany; and Skopje, Yugoslavia
50,000-100,000: Schaumburg, Illinois – sister city to Schaumburg, Germany
Under 50,000: New Brunswick, New Jersey – sister city to Fukui/Tsuruoka, Japan

Best Single Project Award
Over 300,000: Denver, Colorado – sister city to Brest, France; Cuernavaca, Mexico; Karmiel, Israel; Kunming, China; Madras, India; Nairobi, Kenya; Potenza, Italy; and Takayama, Japan
100,000-300,000: Pasadena, California – sister city to Jarvenpaa, Finland; Ludwigshafen am Rhein, Germany; and Mishima, Japan
50,000-100,000: Richmond, California – sister city to Shimada, Japan
Under 50,000: Decatur, Georgia – sister city to Ouahigouya/Bousse, Burkina Faso

Best Overall Youth Program Award
Over 300,000: Denver, Colorado – sister city to Brest, France; Cuernavaca, Mexico; Madras, India; Potenza, Italy; Takayama, Japan; Karmiel, Israel; and Nairobi, Kenya
100,000-300,000: Lakewood, Colorado – sister city to Chester, England and Sutherland, Australia
50,000-100,000: No winner selected
Under 50,000: Slidell, Louisiana – sister city to Panama City, Panama

Best Single Youth Project Award
Over 300,000: Houston, Texas – sister city to Stavanger, Norway
100,000-300,000: Orange, California – sister city to Orange, Australia and Queretaro, Mexico
50,000-100,000: Kettering, Ohio – sister city to Kettering, England and Steyr, Australia
Under 50,000: Santa Cruz, California – sister city to Sestri Levante, Italy and Shinju, Japan

Special Achievement Awards

Technical Assistance:
Reston, Virginia – sister city to Nyeri, Kenya
Palo Alto, California – sister city to Palo, Philippines
Austin, Texas – sister city to Maseru, Lesotho
Atlanta, Georgia – sister city to Montego Bay, Jamaica

Special Event
Dade County, Florida – sister city to Kingston, Jamaica

Humanitarian Assistance:
Prescott, Arizona – sister city to Caborca, Mexico

Educational Exchange:
Norfolk, Virginia – sister city to Kitakyushu, Japan; Norfolk County, England; and Wilhemshaven, Germany

Cultural Exchange:
Waterloo, IL – sister city to Porta Westfalica, Germany
El Cajon, California – sister city to Municipio de Comondu, Mexico

Cultural Art Exchange
St. Louis, Missouri – sister city to Lyon, France; Stuttgart, Germany; and Suwa, Japan

Best First Year Program
Salem, Oregon – sister city to Kawagoe, Japan and Simferopol, USSR
Flint, Michigan – sister city to Changchun, China
Decatur, Georgia – sister city to Ouahigouya/Bousse, Burkina Faso

Sponsored by the Reader's Digest Foundation

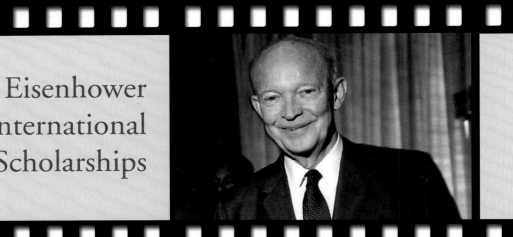

Eisenhower International Scholarships

EISENHOWER INTERNATIONAL

SCHOLARSHIP FUND

SPONSORED BY

sister cities INTERNATIONAL

The Eisenhower International Scholarship program began in 1987. It provided more than $100,000 in scholarship funds to over 100 international college students from 30 countries twinned with 47 U.S. sister cities. Funds to support the program were raised through the Eisenhower International Golf Classic. The program ended in 2000 due to limited funding.

"I'm very lucky to be an Eisenhower International Scholar because this has made it possible for me to attend college here. I'm very thankful and I'm trying hard to achieve my goal in life."
- Ricardo Espinosa of Panama, sister city to Pearl City, Louisiana, 1990

"The hospitality of sister cities members reminds me of home because people always want me to join them for dinner, skiing or other activities. I only hope I have been a good ambassador. I'm grateful for this opportunity, and if I named people to thank the list would be long."
- Madani Dia, Mali, sister city to Rochester, New York, 1990

"The things I am learning here will help me develop our community to its fullest potential."
- Welmer Delgado, Costa Rica, sister city to Anderson Valley, California, 1990

1990
Ricardo Espinosa – Panama/Pearl River, Louisiana
Madani Dia – Mali/Rochester, New York
Welmer Delgado – Costa Rica/Anderson Valley, California
Magdeline Seloane – Mamelodi, South Africa/Reston, Virginia
Gilda De Regil Lopez – Cancun, Mexico/Wichita, Kansas
Mirfotih Agzamov – Tashkent, Union of Soviet Socialist Republics/Seattle, Washington
Murad Alimov – Tashkent, Union of Soviet Socialist Republics/Seattle, Washington
David Griffiths – Ireland/Lexington, Kentucky
Jacksonville, Florida
Des Plaines, Illinois
Salt Lake City, Utah
Scottsdale, Arizona
Washington, D.C.
Louisville, Kentucky
Tyler, Texas
Miami-Dade County, Florida
Dayton, Ohio

1991
Edward Etale – Nambute, Kenya/Amesbury, Massachusetts
Sergei Dyakin – Petrozavodsk, Union of Soviet Socialist Republics/Duluth, Minnesota
Juan Carlos – Esquivel, Costa Rica/Anderson Valley, California
Lizi Xiao Ying – Xiamen, China/Baltimore, Maryland
Manasa Nabeta – Fiji/Des Plaines, Illinois

Claudia Barba – Bahia Blanca, Argentina/Jacksonville, Florida
David Griffiths – Ireland/Lexington, Kentucky
Catalina Alvarez – Ecuador/Louisville, Kentucky
Katherine Lauer – Germany/Louisville, Kentucky
Helen Bertaux – France/Louisville, Kentucky
Anna Fyodorova – Union of Soviet Socialist Republics/Modesto, California
Ricardo Espinoza – Panama/Pearl River, Louisiana
F.M. Sipamla – Kenya/Reston, Virginia
Ibrat Ismanou – Union of Soviet Socialist Republics/Seattle, Washington
Raushanbeck Dakimou – Union of Soviet Socialist Republics/Seattle, Washington
Ndiouga Pieng – Dakar, Senegal/Washington, D.C.
Charles Menclas – Ecuador/Winchester, Kentucky

1994
Deauville, France – Lexington, Kentucky
Morogoro, Tanzania – Fresno, California
Sibiu, Romania – Columbia, Missouri
Strasbourg, France – Boston, Massachusetts

1997
Alexey Vladimirovich Dotsenko – Murmansk, Russia/Jacksonville, Florida
Maria Fernanda de la Torre – Quito, Ecuador/Louisville, Kentucky
Lasha Janashia – Poti, Georgia/LaGrange, Georgia
Assem Arstanova Marmyrbaeva – Almaty, Kazakhstan/Tucson, Arizona
Gaiane G. Melkumova – Dubna, Russia/La Crosse, Wisconsin

Dmitry Mescheryakov – Kharkiv, Ukraine/Cincinnati, Ohio
Inna Ivanova Moroz – Cherkassy, Ukraine/Santa Rosa, California
Anna Nickolaeva – Petrozavodsk, Russia/Duluth, Minnesota
Leyla Rzulakieva – Baku, Azerbaijan/Houston, Texas
Isabella Sarkisyan – Yerevan, Armenia/Cambridge, Massachusetts

1999
Andrei Lozovik – Chelyabinsk, Russia/Columbia, South Carolina
Tendai Manyau – Harare, Zimbabwe/Cincinnati, Ohio
Agnes B. Amasa – Esabalu, Kenya/Amesbury, Massachusetts
Anna Nikolaeva – Petrozavodsk, Russia/Duluth, Minnesota
Katerina A. Shaustyuk – Uzhgorod, Ukraine/Corvallis, Oregon
Vita Kusleikiene – Siauliai, Lithuania/Omaha, Nebraska
Viktoriya N. Prudska – Smila, Ukraine/Newton, Iowa
Elzbieta Ksiezyk – Ziebice, Poland/Brighton, Colorado

2000
Robin Joska – Olomouc, Czech Republic/Owensboro, Kentucky
Anna Nikolaeva – Petrozavodsk, Russia/Duluth, Minnesota
Julie Berthelot – Strasbourg, France/Boston, Massachusetts
Anne Pannier – Strasbourg, France/Boston, Massachusetts

1988

EISENHOWER INTERNATIONAL
GOLF CLASSIC

HOLLYTREE COUNTRY CLUB • TYLER, TEXAS

MAY 16, 1988

sister
cities
INTERNATIONAL

Larry Gatlin (center) and brothers Steve (left) and Rudy (right) were featured performers at the barbecue at the Eisenhower International Golf Classic in Tyler, Texas, May 15-16, 1988. They also played as amateur golfers in the tournament. "With the Gatlins, Mickey Mantle, David Eisenhower, David Graham, and some of the world's greatest PGA golfers, the Eisenhower Classic is developing as one of the most prestigious – and fun – tournaments in the world – for golfers and non-golfers alike," said George F. Hamm, Tournament Chairman. The 1988 event drew 14,000 spectators.

Golfer Chi Chi Rodriquez participated in the Eisenhower International Golf Classic.

Golfer Fred Couples participated in the Eisenhower International Golf Classic.

Board of Directors 1987-88

President - Richard Neuheisel
Chairman of the Board - Louis Wozar
Chairman, Executive Committee
Betty Wilson
Vice President - K. Peter Etzkorn
Vice President - Wylie Williams
Vice President - C. Dewey Crowder
Vice President - Richard Minkler
Vice President - Thelma Press
Vice President - Raymond Schultz
Secretary - James Conway
Treasurer - William Hanna
Vice President, West Coast Office
Ethelda Singer

Youth Member to the Board - Mike Griffith
Richard Donohue
Annette Finesilver
Launa Kowalski

Amanda Wash
Ruth Hashimoto
James McGee
Frank Ogawa
Michael Scorcio
James Turner
Dr. Charles Wheeler

Appointed - Clark Johnson
Appointed - Ambassador
Charles Nelson
Appointed - Maureen Yandle Sanchez
Honorable Betty Wilson

During the March 1988 meeting, the Board of Directors voted to make the President of the Ambassador's Association a full voting member of the board for a one-year term. They also voted to allow six appointed positions.

In August 1988, the Festival of Friends features bands from Stratford-Upon-Avon, England, United Kingdom, Stratford, Connecticut, USA; and Stratford, Canada.

Nearly 100 youth delegates attended the conference. They brought their own enthusiasm and ideas to the table.

ANNUAL SISTER CITIES INTERNATIONAL CONFERENCE
JULY 20 – 24, LEXINGTON, KENTUCKY
THEME: EXPLORING NEW HORIZONS

J. Edward Hall, President of the Reader's Digest Foundation, addresses the delegates. It was the 26th year Reader's Digest had sponsored the awards program.

How Do You Move a Six-Ton Hyperbaric Chamber?

Santa Barbara, California – Puerto Vallarta, Mexico
How do you get a six-ton hyperbaric chamber from Santa Barbara, California to Puerto Vallarta, Mexico? By borrowing a C-130 plane from the Air National Guard! That's how Evie Treen and her sister city colleagues delivered the donated 18-foot-long chamber, valued at a half million dollars, to Puerto Vallarta in 1988, where the Mexican Navy now maintains it. The chamber has been used to treat divers suffering from the bends, as well as diabetes, smoke inhalation, and other injuries and illnesses.

In 2002, Mexican Navy officers meet with Jaime Velasquez, former president of Puerto Vallarta/Santa Barbara Sister Cities and Evie Treen at the Navy base to review the decompression chamber and its operation.

In 1988, the Board of Directors and state representatives met at the Wingspread Conference Center in Wisconsin to take up the challenge of defining "Sister Cities: Leadership and Direction into the 90's."

Annual Awards 1988

Best Overall Program
Over 300,000: Denver, Colorado – sister city to Brest, France; Cuernavaca, Mexico; Karmiel, Israel; Kunming, China; Madras, India; Nairobi, Kenya; Potenza, Italy; and Takayama, Japan
100,000 – 300,000: Raleigh, North Carolina – sister city to Kingston-Upon-Hull, England and Shinyanga, Tanzania
50,000 – 100,000: Kettering, Ohio – sister city to Kettering, England and Steyr, Australia
Under 50,000: Santa Cruz, California – sister city to Alushta, USSR; Puerto la Curz, Venezuela; Santa Curz de Tenerife, Spain; Sestri Levante, Italy; and Shingu, Japan

Best Single Project
Over 300,000: Charlotte, North Carolina – sister city to Arequipa, Peru
100,000 – 300,000: Tempe, Arizona
50,000 – 100,000: Schaumburg, Illinois – sister city to Schaumburg, Germany
Under 50,000: Sonoma, California – sister city to Chambolle Musigny, France; Greve, Italy; and Kanev, USSR

Best Overall Youth Program
Over 300,000: Baltimore, Maryland – sister city to Cadiz, Spain; Genoa, Italy; Kawasaki, Japan; Luxor, Egypt; Odessa, USSR; Rotterdam, Netherlands; and Xiamen, China
100,000 – 300,000: Lakewood, Colorado – sister city to Chester, England; Portsmouth, England; and Sutherland Shire, Australia
50,000 – 100,000: Stratford, Connecticut – sister city to Stratford, Canada
Under 50,000: Slidell, Louisiana

Best Single Youth Project
Over 300,000: Houston, Texas – sister city to Taipei, Taiwan, China
100,000 – 300,000: Norfolk, Virginia – sister city to Kitakyushu, Japan and Wilhelmshaven, Germany
50,000 – 100,000: Salinas, California – sister city to Kushikino, Japan
Under 50,000: Elkader, Iowa – sister city to Mascara, Algeria

Special Achievement Awards

Community Awareness:
Tyler, Texas – sister city to Metz, France

New Haven, Connecticut – sister city to Avignon, France
Youth and Educational Exchange:
Dade County, Florida – sister city to Santo Domingo, Dominican Republic; Kingston, Jamaica; Cayman Islands, British Best Indies; and Asti Province, Italy

Anniversary Celebration:
Palo Alto, California – sister city to Palo, Philippines; Hagerstown, MD; and Wesel, Germany

Community Outreach:
Wichita, Kansas

Culinary Exchange:
Chattanooga, Tennessee – sister city to Wuxi, China

Diversity of Exchange:
Seattle, Washington – sister city to Tashkent, USSR
Portland, Oregon – sister city to Sapporo, Japan

Program Revitalization:
Ogden, Utah – sister city to Hof, Germany

Technical Assistance:
Amesbury, Massachusetts – sister city to Esabalu, Kenya
Baltimore, Maryland – sister city to Luxor, Egypt
Palo Alto, California – sister city to Palo, Philippines

Best First Year Program
Wilmington, North Carolina – sister city to Dandong, China
Sebastopol, California – sister city to Yamauchi, Japan

Sponsored by the Reader's Digest Foundation

Board of Directors 1988-89

President - Richard Neuheisel
Chairman of the Board - Louis Wozar
Chairman, Executive Committee
Betty Wilson
Vice President - K. Peter Etzkorn
Vice President - Wylie Williams
Vice President - Rick Donohue
Vice President - Richard Minkler
Vice President - Thelma Press
Vice President - Raymond Schultz
Secretary - James Conway
Treasurer - William Hanna
Youth Member to the Board - Miki Edelman

President of the Ambassador's Association
Kathy Hogan

Donna Harris
Ruth Hashimoto
James McGee
Frank Ogawa
John Raeside
Jane Tublin
Linda Whitton
Annette Finesilver
Ann Galloway
Launa Kowalski

Ambasssador Charles Nelson
Maureen Sanchez
Ethelda Singer
Dr. Robert Swart
James Turner
Amanda Wash
Dr. Charles Wheeler

Appointed - James Amato
Appointed - Clark Johnson
Appointed - John Kearns
Appointed - Mayor Sue Myrick

These dancers from sister city Beijing, China display beauty and grace.

The delegation representing Dakar, Senegal rode on a colorful float in the parade.

Washington D.C. Proclaims "International Sister Cities Days"

Mayor Marion Barry, Jr. was joined by the ambassadors from the District of Columbia's sister cities in a parade and ceremony at Freedom Plaza on October 8, 1988. The event honored the bond of friendship Washington shares with its sister cities Beijing, China; Dakar, Senegal; and Bangkok, Thailand. Also hosting the event was special guest and Tony Award winner Jennifer Holliday. The D.C. Department of Recreation and the International Capital Cities Friendship Council sponsored the festivities, which began with a parade on historic Pennsylvania Avenue. The mayor issued a proclamation stating: "Whereas, the District of Columbia has forged bonds of unwavering friendship with the preeminent cities of Bangkok, Thailand; Dakar, Senegal; and Beijing, China; and Whereas, the partnership between the District of Columbia and its cherished Sister Cities has resulted in numerous cultural, educational and technical exchanges; and Whereas, to celebrate and confirm the happiness brought about by Bangkok, Dakar and Beijing's close affiliation with Washington, D.C., a two-day celebration will take place October 7-8, 1988: Now, Therefore, I, The Mayor of the District of Columbia, do hereby proclaim October 7-8, 1988, as 'International Sister Cities Days' in Washington, D.C. and invite all citizenry to observe and commend this vibrant celebration."

A young visitor to the celebration checks out the beautiful bell presented to Washington, D.C. by Bangkok, Thailand in honor of their sister city relationship. Signed on July 4, 1963, the agreement between Washington and Bangkok represents the capital city's oldest sister city relationship.

Thousands of Washingtonians turned out for the festivities and enjoyed traditional dancing and learning about the District's sister cities.

Peace Through People
Jacksonville, Florida has very
active sister city programs.

МУРМАНСК
ГОРОД·ГЕРОЙ

Jacksonville
Welcomes
Murmansk City Council Youth Committee
And "Sputnik Club" Delegation

October 16-23, 1988

A Warm Welcome: In Many Languages
This multilingual 1988 brochure welcomed the
Murmansk City Council's Youth Committee and the
"Sputnik Club" for a visit to Jacksonville, Florida.

PEACE
THROUGH
PEOPLE

JACKSONVILLE
SISTER CITIES
PROGRAM

Bahia Blanca, Argentina
Murmansk, U.S.S.R.
Masan, Korea
Nantes, France
Yingkou, China

"Our Sister's Children"

This photo entered in the 40th Anniversary Photo Contest was taken five
years earlier in Murmansk in what was then the Soviet Union by Ann
Fontane of Jacksonville, Florida. A documentary focusing on everyday
life in Murmansk was filmed in 1990 and producer David Gold told the
Florida Times-Union newspaper that, "It was literally the most moving
experience I've ever had. To be in such a different place and yet find such
kindred spirits was overwhelming."

Children in a
classroom in
Murmansk in
the Soviet Union.
Jacksonville had
one of the first
sister city
partnerships
with the
Soviet Union.

Third Eisenhower International Golf Classic
May 6-8, Tyler, Texas

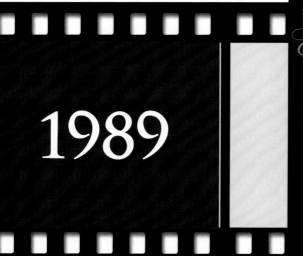

"I am honored and proud to lend my name to an organization that has encouraged better international understanding in the fields of education, culture, economic, and social relationships. Thank you for extending me the privilege of being associated with the United States Sister Cities Program."

-U.S. President George Bush, Honorary Chairman of Sister Cities International

Horticulturalist David Driver from Lower Hutt, New Zealand, works in Tempe Arizona's City Hall Gardens in 1989. He visited Tempe through a sister city exchange program.

**Warm Hospitality: Kumamoto City, Japan
San Antonio, Texas**

The 1987 sister city agreement between San Antonio, Texas and Kumamoto City in Japan stressed long-term reciprocity and linked two communities with a long history of hospitality. To date, over 250 programs have resulted from their partnership, including the debut of the Kumamoto Castle before 150,000 guests in the 1989 Kumamoto City Fair. And that's not the only example of how their arts and culture programs have contributed to understanding. Kumamoto sent living national treasures to construct an authentic Japanese garden – the Kumamoto En – at the San Antonio Botanical Center. In exchange, San Antonio sent an authentic 19th century prairie cabin to Kumamoto's Botanical Center.

Youth delegates led attendees into the Opening General Session. The opening session included 1,100 delegates from 200 U.S. communities and 24 countries.

Young Artists Program Winners 1989

1st - Bakary Quattaro and Tiemoko Dico – Bamako, Mali (sister city to Rochester, New York)
2nd - Merrill Ann White – Charlotte, North Carolina
3rd - Tsubasa Nakano – Kameoka, Japan (sister city to Stillwater, Oklahoma)
4th - Denise Funderburg – La Mirada, California
5th - Karla Sylling – Mankato, Minnesota
6th - Soe Murayma – Narashino, Japan (sister city to Tuscaloosa, Alabama)
7th - Carmen M. Trochez – New Brunswick, New Jersey
8th - Armando Avita – Pico Rivera, California
9th - Kim Cammack – Tempe, Arizona
10th - Constaniti Siouretri – Tripolis, Greece (sister city to Arcadia, California)
11th - Derrick Nevels – Tuscaloosa, Alabama
12th - Darryl Eschmann – Waterloo, Illinois

ANNUAL SISTER CITIES INTERNATIONAL CONFERENCE
JULY 18-23, PORTLAND, OREGON
THEME: BUILDING HARMONY AMONG NATIONS

Sister Cities Leaders: Thelma Press
Thelma Press certainly doesn't look like a sister city veteran in this 1989 photograph during the Portland conference – but she already was! She became involved with the sister city program 30 years earlier when Tachikawa, Japan linked with San Bernadino, California. She served on the Board of Directors for 20 years from 1978 through 1998. She served as co-chair of the First Sino-U.S. Sister Cities Conference in Beijing in 1995.

U.S. Information Agency Director Bruce Gelb told delegates, "Your efforts have helped millions of people around the world to better understand America. Many whose lives you have touched, also now think of America as a caring friend."

The dance group from Ashekelon, Israel, sister city to Portland, Oregon was a big hit. A special U.S. – Israel Sister Cities Conference was held July 18-19 and drew more than 100 participants.

The conference logo, which featured flags of the U.S. and U.S.S.R. "shaking hands" with each other, is visible in this photo.

FIRST U.S. – U.S.S.R. SISTER CITIES CONFERENCE
MAY 29-31, TASHKENT, UZBEKISTAN, UNION OF SOVIET SOCIALIST REPUBLICS
THEME: TASHKENT '89

Nearly 500 delegates from more than 40 U.S. cities and their counterparts in the Soviet Union traveled to Tashkent in the Uzbek republic within the Union of Soviet Socialist Republics to attend the first U.S. – U.S.S.R. Sister Cities Conference. "As hosts, the Uzbeks are second to none," wrote Hib Sabin of Santa Fe, New Mexico in the *Sister City News*. Sabin noted how important language is to an individual's sense of identity and reflected that "I must tackle the Uzbek language if I am to truly know my Uzbek brother." Delegates attended workshops on communications, program development and affiliation possibilities. After the three-day conference concluded, the U.S. delegates journeyed with their Soviet counterparts home for a visit to their sister city. At the time of the conference, Sister Cities International recorded 36 affiliations between communities in the U.S. and U.S.S.R., with an additional 40 communities investigating the possibility of signing a sister city agreement.

Sister Cities International President Richard Neuheisel, would later reflect that this conference was one of the most historic events in the history of the sister city movement.

Arriving delegates are greeted with traditional food by their Uzbek hosts.

More than 500 delegates from the U.S. and U.S.S.R. attended the event to discuss how sister city relationships could be formed and strengthened.

This merry group of young dancers performs for delegates visiting Tashkent for the conference.

Ambassador Association Forms

The Sister Cities International Ambassador Association, for 23-35 year olds, was formally announced during the Los Angeles conference in July 1986 and Eddie Goitia, of Phoenix, Arizona, was elected its first president.

Annual Awards 1989

Best Overall Program
Over 300,000: Baltimore, Maryland – sister city to Cadiz, Spain; Gbarnga, Liberia; Genoa, Italy; Kawasaki, Japan; Luxor, Egypt; Odessa, USSR; Piraeus, Greece; Xiamen, China
100,000 – 300,000: Lexington, Kentucky – sister city to County Kildaire, Ireland; Deauville, France; and Shizunai, Japan
50,000 – 100,000: Palo Alto, California – sister city to Enschede, Netherlands; Linkoping, Sweden; Oaxaca, Mexico; and Palo, Philippines
Under 50,000: New Ulm, Minnesota – sister city to Neu Ulm, Germany and Ulm, Germany

Best Single Project
Over 300,000: Phoenix, Arizona – sister city to Himeji, Japan
100,000 – 300,000: Torrance, California – sister city to Kashiwa, Japan
50,000 – 100,000: Stratford, California – sister city to Stratford, England and Stratford, Canada
Under 50,000: Saratoga, California – sister city to Muko-Shi, Japan

Best Overall Youth Program
Norfolk, Virginia – sister city to Kitakyushu, Japan; Norfolk County, England; and Wilhelmshaven, Germany
50,000 – 100,000: Ogden, Utah – sister city to Hof, Germany
Under 50,000: Slidell, Louisiana – sister city to Panama City, Panama

Best Single Youth Project
Over 300,000: Tampa Florida
100,000 – 300,000: Tempe, Arizona – sister city to Regensburg, Germany
50,000 – 100,000: Battle Creek, Michigan – sister city to Takasaki, Japan
Under 50,000: Pearl River, Lousiana – sister city to Anton, Panama

Special Achievement Awards

Anniversary Celebration:
Independence, Missouri – sister city to Higashimurayama, Japan
Pasadena, California – sister city to Ludwigshafen am Rhein, Germany
Wyandotte, Michigan – sister city to Komaki, Japan

Cultural Exchange:
Arcadia, California – sister city to Newcastle, Australia and Tripolis, Greece
Duluth, Minnesota – sister city to Petrosavodsk, USSR; Thunder Bay, Canada; and Vaxjo, Sweden
Jacksonville, Florida – sister city to Bahia Blanca, Argentina; Holon, Israel; Masan, Korea; Murmansk, USSR; Nantes, France

Orange, California – sister city to Orange, Australia and Orange, France
Sonoma, California – sister city to Kanev, USSR
Waterloo, California – sister city to Porta Westfalica, Germany

Community Involvement:
Fort Worth Texas – sister city to Nagaoka, Japan; Reggio Emilia, Italy; Siena Provincia, Italy; and Trier, Germany

Diversity of Exchange:
Dade County, Florida – sister city to Lima, Peru; Sao Paulo, Brazil; Santo Domingo, Dominican Republic; Kingston, Jamaica; Cayman Islands, British West Indies; and Asti Province, Italy
Santa Cruz, Calfironia – sister city to Alushta, USSR; Puerto La Cruz, Venezuela; Santa Curz de Tenerife, Spain; Sestre Levante, Italy; and Shingu, Japan

Educational Exchange:
Salem, Oregon – sister city to Kawagoe, Japan
Stillwater, Oklahoma – sister city to Kameoka, Japan

Performing Arts:
Temple City, California – sister city to Hawkesbury, Australia

Programming Revitalization:
Seattle, Washington – sister city to Limbe, Cameroon

Technical/Professional Exchange:
Dayton, Ohio – sister city to Monrovia, Liberia
Riverside, California – sister city to Ensenada, Mexico

Unique Exchange:
Denver, Colorado – sister city to Brest, France

Best First Year Program
Spokane, Washington – sister city to Makhachkala, USSR
South San Francisco, California – sister city to Atotonilco El Alto, Mexico
Corning, New York – sister city to L'vov, USSR

Sponsored by the Reader's Digest Foundation

1990

These folklore dancers from LeZion, Israel received rave reviews from conference delegates.

From left: U.S. Ambassador to Mexico John D. Negroponte, Dick Neuheisel and Mexican Ambassador to the United States Gustavo Petricioli, share a hearty handshake for the future of U.S./Mexico sister city exchanges prior to the opening of the conference.

Conference attendees included these students from Bukhara, Uzbekistan in the Soviet Union. They attended the conference as part of an exchange visit with sister city Santa Fe, New Mexico.

Traditional Mexican dancers and entertainers celebrated the many historic sister city linkages between Mexico and the U.S.

Youth delegates enjoyed interactive workshops. Miki Edelman wrote in the newsletter that, "If there is anything to be said about this conference it is that it was a great forum for learning…We were forced in many ways to re-assess who we are and where we are going."

A Historic Conference in Argentina
Sister Cities International President Dick Neuheisel, left, presents a gift to Argentina President Carlos Saul Menem during the first conference sponsored by the Sister Cities Foundation of Buenos Aires. The September 13-17 conference drew more than 250 delegates from six nations and marked an historic milestone in efforts to foster sister city ties. At right is Buenos Aires Mayor Carlos Grosso.

Let's Hear It For Sister Schools!
Ten students from Fremont's Mission San Jose High School visited Fukaya, Japan in 1990 to start a sister school relationship with Fukaya High School of Commerce. Students from Fukaya visited their peers in California the following year.

Did You Know?

In 1990, Sister Cities International developed a three-year program for youth exchange and training between U.S. cities and their Mexican counterparts through a grant from the W.K. Kellogg Foundation.

Board of Directors 1990-91

Board of Directors 1990-1991
President - Richard Neuheisel
Chairman of the Board - Louis Wozar
Chairman, Executive Committee
Betty Wilson
Vice President - James Amato
Vice President - Wylie Williams
Vice President - Ann Galloway
Vice President - Richard Minkler
Vice President - Thelma Press
Vice President - Raymond Schultz
Secretary - K. Peter Etzkorn
Treasurer - Rick Donohue

Youth Member to the Board - Miki Edelman
President of the Ambassador's Association
Len Olender
Johnel Bracey
Donna Harris
Ruth Hashimoto
Clark Johnson
John Kearns
Launa Kowalski
James McGee
Mayor Sue Myrick
Ambassador Charles Nelson
Frank Ogawa

Carlton Parker
John Raeside
Ethelda Singer
Dr. Robert Swart
Jane Tublin
James Turner
Dr. Charles Wheeler
Linda Whitton
Ex Officio - Dr. George Hamm

Mayor Rodger Randle was elected by a special vote of the Board in early 1991. His term ran through 1993.

This photo was taken in 1990 at the Sister Cities exhibit in Sacramento, California's Children's Festival.

Delegates from Matsuyama, Japan pause in 1991 for a photo during the festivities for Sacramento, California's Camellia Festival. When this photo was taken, a delegation from Matsuyama had participated in the event annually for a decade.

Dr. Silvia Chetrari (left) and Pat Buchanan (both in white) talk with Moldovan women lawmakers about strengthening the laws to protect abused women.

Dr. Silvia Chetrari and a young woman at the first woman's crisis center in Moldova.

Domestic Violence Prevention (DVP) Program
Lakeland, Florida - Balti, Moldova

This look inside one of the programs receiving funding from a grant for domestic violence prevention programs through Sister Cities International demonstrates the powerful impact a sister city program can have on lives and communities.

When Moldova gained its independence in 1991, the former Russian republic lost nearly all its revenue sources. Manufacturing companies, medical facilities, equipment producers and other markets all disappeared. The country found itself with a highly educated generation of professionals - due to the free education provided by the old Soviet Union - but there was no money to pay them.

With nothing left but people and fertile land, making vodka and wine became this small country's primary source of income, as well as their national pride. But because there still was no money - the average salary was $30 a month and many were paid in liquor - alcohol abuse subsequently became a huge problem. And with it came a huge rise in domestic violence.

Determined to solve this crisis, Dr. Silvia Chetrari stepped forward. As a proponent for women's rights in Moldova, she opened the first woman's crisis shelter in the country in 1999 and later opened two more centers. She also wrote a book about the problem of female trafficking in Moldova and other surrounding countries.

Dr. Chetrari visited Lakeland to learn about a Florida Domestic Violence Prevention Program, which she used as the model for a customized program for Balti. Back home, she enlisted university legal students who after a short training period could serve as advocates for abused Moldovan women, who often feared police and wouldn't confront their abusive partners. These trained volunteers provide support for the women before the police appear on the scene, which has led to more women being willing to file complaints.

Although no one expects to change a system and culture overnight, Lakeland and Balti have made an auspicious start toward a better future for the women of Moldova, by working together.

Advocates at the clinic wear special badges and prepare to advocate for families in crisis. The favorite saying in Moldova at the time was "A woman that hasn't been beaten is like a rug that hasn't been swept." These women were trying to change that.

United in Friendship
Springfield Illinois Mayor Ossie Langfelder and Ashikaga, Japan Mayor Yukihisa Machida sign a sister city agreement on October 10, 1990. Robert Church, executive director of the Office of the Mayor, looks on from above.

Mayor W. Wilson Goode, city of Philadelphia, Pennsylvania greets Jean Yango, executive director for city planning in sister city Douala, Cameroon.

Young Artists Program Winners 1990 *

1st – Quyen Le - La Mirada, California
2nd - Higashimurayama, Japan
3rd - Tempe, Arizona
4th - Narashino, Japan
5th - Des Plaines, Illinois
6th - Tuscaloosa, Alabama
7th - Virginia, Minnesota

8th - Tyler, Texas
9th - Ensechede, Netherlands
10th - Prince George's County, Maryland
11th - Toledo, Ohio
12th - Nagasaki, Japan

* Names of all youth winners are not available

1990 Annual Award Winners – presented in Albuquerque, New Mexico
July 25-28, 1990
Sponsored by the Reader's Digest Foundation

Best Overall Program
Over 300,000: Fort Worth, Texas – sister city to Nagaoka, Japan; Reggio Emilia, Italy; and Trier, West Germany
100,000 – 300,000: Eugene, Oregon – sister city to Chinju, Korea; Irkutsk, USSR; Kakegawa, Japan; and Kathmandu, Nepal
50,000 – 100,000: Stratford, California – sister city to Stratford, Canada and Stratford-Upon-Avon, England
Under 50,000: Richmond, Indiana – sister city to Serpukhov, USSR

Best Single Project
Over 300,000: Prince George's County, Maryland – sister city to Ziguinchor Region, Senegal
100,000 – 300,000: Wichita, Kansas – sister city to Orleans, France
50,000 – 100,000: Greenville, South Carolina – sister city to Bergamo, Italy
Under 50,000: Anderson Valley, California – sister city to Guayabo, Costa Rica and La Fortuna, Costa Rica

Best Overall Youth Program Award:
Over 300,000: Not Awarded
100,000-300,000: Norfolk, Virginia – sister city to Kitakyushu, Japan; Norfolk County, England; Wilhelmshaven, West Germany; and Toulon, France
50,000-100,000: Not Awarded
Under 50,000: Sonoma, California – sister city to Chambolle Musignov, France; Greve, Italy; and Kanev, USSR

Best Single Youth Project Award
Over 300,000: Jacksonville, Florida
100,000-300,000: Fort Wayne, Indiana – sister city to Takaoka, Japan
50,000-100,000: Santa Fe, New Mexico – sister city to Bukhara, USSR
Under 50,000: Montgomery, Ohio – sister city to Neuilly-Plaisance, France

Special Achievement Awards

Anniversary Celebration:
Omaha, Nebraska – sister city to Shizuoka, Japan

Community Awareness:
Kettering, Ohio – sister city to Kettering, England and Steyr, Australia
Louisville, Kentucky – sister city to Montpellier, France

Community Outreach:
Charlotte, North Carolina – sister city to Krefeld, West Germany
Corning, New York – sister city to Lvov, USSR
Greater Portland, Maine – sister city to Arkhangelsk, USSR
St. Mary's, Ohio – sister city to Hokudan, Japan

Cultural Exchange:
Binghamton, New York – sister city to Borotvitchi, USSR

Diversity of Exchange:
Quincy, Illinois – sister city to Herford, West Germany

Development Exchange:
Des Plaines, Illinois – sister city to Nailuva, Fiji

Economic Development:
Cincinnati, Ohio – sister city to Karkov, USSR
San Francisco, California – sister city to Shanghai, China

Educational Exchange:
Rice Lake, Wisconsin – sister city to Miharu-Machi, Japan

Environmental Exchange:
Cambridge, Massachusetts – sister city to Yerevan, USSR

Technical Assistance:
Houston, Texas – sister city to Guayaquil, Ecuador

Youth Exchange:
Orange, California – sister city to Orange, Australia and Queretaro, Mexico

Best First Year Program
Glens Falls, New York – sister city to Saga City, Japan

Special Recognition for New Horizons
State of Maryland

Sponsored by the Reader's Digest Foundation

1991

EISENHOWER INTERNATIONAL GOLF CLASSIC
WILLOW BROOK COUNTRY CLUB
TYLER, TEXAS
MAY 6

Young Artists Program Winners 1991
Theme: Expressions of Harmony

1st - Izumi Ariyoshi – Kameoka, Japan
2nd - Kevin Clayton – Stillwater, Oklahoma
3rd - Llja Dukov – Serpukhov, USSR
4th - Brendan Higgings – County Kildare, Ireland
5th - Carrie Horwitz – Des Plaines, Illinois
6th - Yoo Kyung Lee – Charlotte, North Carolina
7th - Lai-Ping Look – Seattle, Washington
8th - Sid Mohede – La Mirada, California
9th - Eric Norman – Kettering, Ohio
10th - Eri Okuno – Kakegawa, Japan
11th - Wu Rong – Beihai, China
12th - Wendy Winanen – Virginia, Minnesota

Sid Mohede, La Mirada,
California

Brendan Higgins, County
Kildare, Ireland, sister city to
Lexington, Kentucky

Reflections at 35
By Dwight David Eisenhower II

I was just a small boy when my grandfather announced his People-to-People program at the White House in 1956. I well remember his enthusiasm for the idea and his deep belief in the importance of international citizen involvement. He said of the concept, "The assumption is that all people want peace. The problem is for all people to get together – to leap governments if necessary, to evade governments – to work out not one method but thousands of methods by which people can gradually learn a little more of each other."

Thirty-five years later I traveled to Denison, Texas, the birthplace of my grandfather, to participate in the Centennial of his birth. While there, I learned of the great enthusiasm for a newly forming sister city link between Denison and Cognac, France, and I thought how pleased he would have been. The people of Denison are already planning for dozens of exchanges with Cognac to learn a little more about each other.

This was his vision, and sister city activists are bringing his words to life every day.

When this program started, some cynics scoffed at the idea that a city could be organized to carry out exchanges with a partner many thousands of miles away across national boundaries and cultures. You have demonstrated that it can be done and hundreds of America's cities, along with their counterparts in every world area, are celebrating their 10th and 15th, and some their 30th or more, anniversaries. The level of exchange has deepened as the years flowed by. Today, cities are not only involved in tens of thousands of people exchanges, but are deeply committed to finding the answers to many of the critical issues that affect all humanity.

Your emphasis on the exchange of ideas and long-term cooperation, gives continuity to improving human relations between people. Out of this effort these sister cities are helping to build the road that can lead to peace. You are weaving together the fabric of civilization, person-to-person, family-to-family, city-to-city, nation-to-nation. This is your agenda and your goal. It must continue and it must grow as we approach the 21st century if we want a world for our children, and their children, to grow up in where we can truly work for the common good of all.

The conference sessions inspired many delegates to take their sister city programs to new heights of achievement.

35TH ANNIVERSARY SISTER CITIES INTERNATIONAL CONFERENCE
JULY 15-20, CHICAGO, ILLINOIS
THEME: CELEBRATE SISTER CITIES

This ad encouraged sister city members to attend the conference in Chicago. And boy did they ever! More than 1,200 delegates attended representing 34 countries. Ambassador Henry E. Catto, director of the U.S. Information Agency told attendees, "Citizen diplomacy can be hard work. You know it. I know it. It can be fascinating, various, eye-opening and enormously satisfying, but it does not happen just by wishing and hoping."

Scene from the 1991 conference in Chicago.

Maori dancers from the Waiuheta Cultural Group of Lower Hutt, New Zealand delighted conference delegates with their enthusiasm and energy.

143

Tenth Anniversary Sister State Celebration State of Maryland and Kanagawa Prefecture, Japan
Governor William Donald Schaefer and Governor Kazuji Nagasu lead the 150-member Kanagawa delegation past applauding Marylanders into the Governor's Mansion for the official welcome ceremony on October 15, 1991.

Sister Cities International: Praised by Senator McCain
"Sister Cities International is a valuable way to promote the exchange of ideas at the grassroots level. America's role as a model for developing nations owes a debt to the tireless work of those at Sister Cities International.
- *Senator John McCain, Arizona, 1991*

Annual Awards 1991

Best Overall Program
Over 350,000: San Francisco, California – sister city to Abidjan, Cote D'Ivoire; Cork, Ireland; Haifa, Israel; Osaka, Japan; Manila, Philippines; Seoul, Korea; Shanghai, China; Sydney, Australia; Taipei, Taiwan, China; and Thessaloniki, Greece

100,000 – 350,000: Rochester, New York – sister city to Bamako, Mali; Caltanissetta, Italy; Krakow, Poland; Novgorod, USSR; Rehovot, Israel; Rennes, France; Waterford, Ireland; and Wurzburg, Germany

50,000 – 100,000: Kettering, Ohio – sister city to Kettering, England and Steyr, Autralia
Under 50,000: Dixon, Illinois – sister city to Dickson, USSR

Best Single Project
Over 350,000: Jacksonville, Florida – sister city to Murmansk, USSR
100,000 – 350,000: Louisville, Kentucky – sister city to Quito, Ecuador
50,000 – 100,000: Palo Alto, California – sister city to Oaxaca, Mexico
Under 50,000: Amesbury, Massachusetts – sister city to Esabalu, Kenya

Best Overall Youth Program
Over 350,000: Fort Worth, Texas – sister city to Bandung, Indonesia; Budapest, Hungary; Nagaoka, Japan; Reggio Emilia, Italy; and Trier, Germany

100,000 – 350,000: Raleigh, North Carolina – sister city to Compiegne, France; Kingston-Upon-Hull, U.K; and Shinyanga, Tanzania

Under 50,000: Stillwater, Oklahoma – sister city to Kameoka, Japan

Best Single Youth Project
Over 350,000: Houston-Galveston, Texas – sister city to Stavanger, Norway

100,000 – 350,000: Greece, New York – sister city to Vitre, France

Under 50,000: Rice Lake, Wisconsin – sister city to Miharu-Machi, Japan

Special Achievement Awards

Community Awareness and Outreach:
Montgomery, Ohio – sister city to Neuilly-Plaisance, France
Pocatello, Idaho – sister city to Iwamizawa, Japan

San Jose, California – sister city to Dublin, Ireland; Okayama, Japan; Tainan, Taiwan, China; and Veracruz, Mexico
Sonoma, California – sister city to Chambolle-Musigne, France; Greve-In-Chianti, Italy; and Kanev, USSR
Toledo, Ohio – sister city to Poznan, Poland; Qinhuangdao, China; Szeged, Hungary; and Toledo, Spain

Cultural Awareness:
Cincinnati, Ohio – sister city to Kharkov, USSR
Charlotte, North Carolina – sister city to Arequipa, Peru; Baoding, China; Krefeld, Germany; and Port-au-Prince, Haiti
Lexington, Kentucky – sister city to County Kildare, Ireland; Deauville, France; and Shizunai, Japan
Phoenix, Arizona – sister city to Taipei, Taiwan, China
Waterloo, Iowa – sister city to Porta Westfalica, Germany

Economic Development:
Greenville, South Carolina – sister city to Kortrijk, Belgium

Educational Development:
Redondo Beach, California – sister city to Ensenada, Mexico

Expanding Horizons:
Prince George's County, Maryland – sister city to Nantou County, Taiwan, China; Rishon LeZion, Israel; and Ziguichor County, Senegal

State of Maryland – sister city to Anhui Province, China; Kanagawa Prefecture, Japan; Lodz Region, Poland; Nord-Pas de Calais, France; Rio de Janeiro, Brazil; and Walloon Region, Belgium

Humanitarian Assistance:
Waukesha, Wisconsin – sister city to Kokchetov, USSR

Technical Assistance:
Reston, Virginia – sister city to Nyeri, Kenya

Best First Year Program
Council Bluffs, Iowa – sister city to Tobolsk, USSR
Greece, New York – sister city to Vitre, France

OKLAHOMA STATE UNIVERSITY-KYOTO

In May 1990, Mayor Yoshihisa Taniguchi welcomes the first class to attend Oklahoma State University's branch campus in Kameoka, Japan. The students studied for two years in Japan and then traveled to Stillwater, Oklahoma for two additional years of instruction. During their twenty-year sister city relationship, the two communities have nurtured active sister school affiliations and have had several winners in the Young Artists Competition.

Board of Directors 1991-92

President - Richard Neuheisel
Chairman of the Board - Louis Wozar
Chairman, Executive Committee
Betty Wilson
Vice President - James Amato
Vice President - Wylie Williams
Vice President - Ann Galloway
Vice President - Richard Minkler
Vice President - Thelma Press
Vice President - Raymond Schultz
Secretary - K. Peter Etzkorn
Treasurer - Rick Donohue

Youth Member to the Board - John Bowman
President of the Ambassador's Association
Catherine Ross

Henry Cole
Mary Cort
Donna Harris
Luther Jordan
John Raeside
Jane Tublin
Linda Whitton
John Kearns
Launa Kowalski
Mayor Sue Myrick
Ambassador Charles Nelson
Mayor Rodger Randle
Ethelda Singer
Dr. Robert Swart
James Turner
Dr. Charles Wheeler
Ex Officio - Dr. George Hamm

The Board of Directors adds a state coordinator liaison position in 1992

Cincinnati-Kharkiv project founder, Bud Haupt (center) stands ready to greet the Kharkiv delegation while a woman nearby readies a traditional Slavic welcome of bread and salt. In writing about the conference on September 13, the *Cincinnati Post* editorialized, "Through Cincinnati's own two year relationship with the city of Kharkiv in the Ukraine, we have learned just how invaluable these exchanges are. Nothing can break down the barriers of culture and language, or destroy false stereotypes more effectively than one-to-one interaction."

SECOND U.S. – U.S.S.R. SISTER CITIES CONFERENCE
SEPTEMBER 12-14, CINCINNATI, OHIO
THEME: TOGETHER FOR THE FUTURE

Arriving at the airport, a delegate from Dubna, Russia, embraces sister city counterpart Chuck Hanson, chair of the La Crosse – Dubna sister city project. In a letter to conference delegates, President George Bush said, "It is my hope that the bonds of friendship that are formed by Sister Cities and other programs will help to foster not only democratization throughout the Soviet Union but also greater mutual understanding between our two peoples."

U.S. delegates hold their sister city signs high as they eagerly look to see who will be the first Soviet arrivals off the Aeroflot charter to Cincinnati. Sister Cities International President Dick Neuheisel (center right) leads the welcome. The conference brought together 240 U.S. delegates with 210 counterparts from 65 communities and 11 republics within the Soviet Union.

1992

Youth delegate Lance Welch talks to delegates about the promise youth hold for the future.

A delegate smiles with a performer in Native American dress.

Delegates enjoy the opening session at the conference in Tulsa, Oklahoma.

Space Bridge: San Diego – Vladivostok Forge New Citizen Linkages

On January 25, 1992, 3,000 Russians and 400 Americans laughed at the antics of cross-cultural mimes, cheered the dancing of young Americans and Russian sailors, and ogled each other. The vast distances across the Pacific Ocean and the barriers of the Cold War evaporated into irrelevance for San Diego, California and sister city Vladivostok, Russian Federation, thanks to the Space Bridge. A technological triumph, the Space Bridge allowed live interaction between Russian and American audiences and marked the end of Vladivostok's isolation in Soviet Asia. For the one-month-old San Diego-Vladivostok Sister City Society, raising the $38,000 needed for the project in only six weeks seemed an insurmountable task – but hard work, publicity in the community, and an 11th hour grant from Alaska Airlines made the Space Bridge possible.

Bringing Kansas City to the World: Expo '92 Seville, Spain

Because of its twenty-five-year sister city relationship with Seville, Kansas City was the only city to participate in the largest universal exposition of the 20th century – Expo 92 in Spain. The exhibit marketed Kansas City to the world and showcased the diversity of the U.S. heartland. Approximately 1.7 million visitors streamed through the exhibit in 176 days, and the 32 project staffers on both sides of the Atlantic worked around the clock.

Kansas City Exhibit Draws Royal Interest
King Juan Carlos and Queen Sophia of Spain enjoy their conversation with Mrs. Fred Bush, wife of Ambassador Fred Bush, at Expo '92.

Young Artists Program Winners 1992

1st - Andrew Kleindolph – Muscatine, Iowa
2nd - Tatiana Stefanco – Philadelphia, Pennsylvania
3rd - Errick Braggs – Tulsa, Oklahoma
4th - Yao Ke – Changsha, China
5th - Jason Forbes – Seattle, Washington
6th - John Schnittker – Sacramento, California

7th - Ann Christensen – St. Paul, Minnesota
8th - Natasha Kartashova – Magadan, Russia
9th - Amber Simpson – Lakeland, Florida
10th - April Fourt – Tuiscaloosa, Alabama
11th - Heidi Wolfe – Toledo, Ohio
12th - Kanae Takamuki – Kameoka, Japan

1992 – FIRST U.S.-AFRICA SISTER CITIES CONFERENCE
MARCH 6-7, WASHINGTON, DC.
THEME: IMPROVING COMMUNICATION AND AWARENESS AMONG U.S. AFRICAN SISTER CITIES

THE FOURTH DECADE 1986-1995

Grandmas The World Over Want Peace
This photo was taken in 1992 for the Sister Cities International photography competition and submitted by the Archangelsk (Russia) Committee from Portland, Maine.

On December 4, 1992, Philadelphia's mayor Edward G. Rendell (left) presents a replica of the Liberty Bell to Mayor Shlomo Lahat of Tel Aviv, Israel.

Annual Awards 1992

Best Overall Program
Over 350,000: Forth Worth, Texas – sister city to Bandung, Indonesia; Budapest, Hungary; Nagaoka, Japan; Reggio Emilia, Italy; and Trier, Germany
100,000 – 350,000: Bryan/College Station, Texas – sister city to Kazan, Russia
Under 50,000: Sonoma, California – sister city to Chambolle-Musigny,France; Greve, Italy; and Kaniv, Ukraine

Best Single Project
Over 350,000: Cincinnati, Ohio – sister city to Kharkiv, Ukraine
100,000 – 350,000: Durham, North Carolina – sister city to Arusha, Tanzania; Durham City, England; Kostroma, Russia; and Toyama, Japan
50,000 – 100,000: Palo Alto, California – sister city to Oaxaca, Mexico
Under 50,000: Ephrata, Pennsylvania – sister city to Eberbach am Neckar, Germany

Special Achievement Awards

Anniversary Celebration:
Saline, Michigan – sister city to Brecon, Wales

Communications Project:
San Diego, California – sister city to Vladivostok, Russia

Economic Development:
State of Maryland – sister city to Anhui Province, China; Kanagawa Prefecture, Japan; Kyongsangnam-Do, Korea; Lodz Region, Poland; and Walloon Region, Belgium

Education and Training:
Cambridge, Massachusetts – sister city to Yerevan, Armenia

Medical Assistance:
Jacksonville, Florida – sister city to Murmansk, Russia

Sports Exchange:
Burlington, Vermont – sister city to Yaroslavi, Russia

Youth Community Service Exchange:
Wichita, Kansas – sister city to Cancun, Mexico

Youth Music Project:
St. Paul, Minnesota – sister city to Changsha, China; Culiacan, Mexico; Modena, Italy; Nagasaki, Japan; and Novosibirsk, Russia

Best First Year Program
Winchester, Massachusetts – sister city to St. Germain-en-Laye, France

Let the First Strike Be a Knock on the Door
Council Bluffs, Iowa- Tobolsk, Russian Federation

In 1988 the national organization Ground Zero paired a Council Bluffs peace group with Tobolsk in Siberia. The theme of the project was "Let the First Strike Be a Knock on the Door." A box filled with letters was mailed to Tobolsk and opened the door for a sister city partnership. Educators, business people, city officials, medical personnel, farmers, lawyers, consultants, engineers and students traveled on exchanges between the two communities.

They established a satellite link in Tobolsk and published a cookbook featuring Russian and American cuisine alongside personal stories about their cross-cultural friendships. "I never dreamed that an old Joe like me would ever play music for Americans in Tobolsk," said an elderly accordion player.

During a farewell dinner in August 1992, Nick Benzing rose and said, "President Eisenhower once said that peace will come only when ordinary citizens rise up and demand it from their leaders. I think that's what Sister City it all about, ordinary citizens making peace and friendship between our great countries."

The Mayor of Tobolsk, Sergei Belken rose next. "I have been thinking very hard about this all week. On your first day here, I met Ridge [Hein-Snyder]. We discovered that we not only are the same age, but served in our military service at the same time - I in Moscow, Ridge in Vietnam. I thank God that we never had to clash on the field of battle."

That evening they raised their glasses in the sincere hope that in some way their friendship and alliance would assure lasting peace and prosperity for both countries.

Did You Know?

Sister Cities International was asked to develop a municipal education and training initiative with the Commonwealth of Independent States (formerly known as the Soviet Union) by the U.S. Information Agency, and the Reader's Digest Foundation funded a two-year global youth volunteerism program.

1993

U.S. – N.I.S. Municipal Education & Training Program 1992-1993

This one-year grant provided training opportunities to local government officials from the Newly Independent States (N.I.S.) of the former Soviet Union. The program was funded by the U.S. Information Agency.

During a 1993 visit, Prince George's County, Maryland executive Wayne Curry presents a key to Meir Nitzon, mayor of Rishon LeZion, Israel.

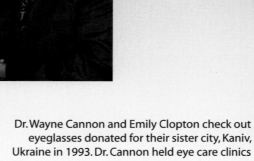

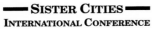

Dr. Wayne Cannon and Emily Clopton check out eyeglasses donated for their sister city, Kaniv, Ukraine in 1993. Dr. Cannon held eye care clinics in Kiev and Kaniv, and the "Lion in Sight" team saw more than 2,500 people in seven days.

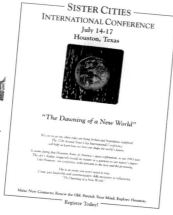

Young Artists Program Winners 1993

1st - Dimitry Belyayer – Ivanova, Russia (sister city to Plano, Texas)
2nd - Vivienne Byrne – County of Kildare, Ireland (sister city to Lexington, Kentucky)
3rd - Benjamin Graham – Seattle, Washington
4th - Ivo Hausle – Senshachtel, Eberbach, Germany (sister city to Ephrata, Pennsylvania)
5th - Andrew Kleindolph – Muscatine, Iowa
6th - Le Ouyen – Norwalk, California
7th - Jay Pengan III – Carson, California
8th - Zho Shjiring – Tianjlin, China
9th - Olga Sheravehova – Stavropol, Russia (sister city to Des Moines, Iowa)
10th - John S. Skinner – Tyler, Texas

President Bill Clinton Praises Sister Cities International

"The Sister Cities International program has been instrumental in breaking down barriers between cultures and in fostering better relations between peoples separated by oceans. I applaud your efforts to build lasting bridges between peoples separated by oceans. I applaud your efforts to build lasting bridges between people of different nations in a rapidly changing world. I am committed to working for a more peaceful planet and am impressed with your organization's ongoing work toward this goal. I am happy to offer my support as Honorary Chairman."

- President Bill Clinton

Community Service Learning Youth Exchange Program 1992-1994

Funded in part with a grant from the Reader's Digest Foundation, this program engaged youth in community service learning projects chosen by the young people and the sister city committees in both paired cities. Projects carried out included: caring for the elderly, building nature trails, preserving natural resources, working with inner city youth, assisting special education teachers, rehabilitating abandoned buildings, and initiating drug awareness campaigns.

Sister City Ties Overcome Political Barriers
Mobile, Alabama-Havana, Cuba

Society Mobile-Alabama, a non-profit, was formed in 1993 as a citizen's organization to support the sister city relationship between Mobile and Havana, Cuba. The society has sponsored numerous delegations of visitors both to and from Havana, promoting business and educational development, as well as cultural exchange. The society is focused on laying a foundation for the future, noting that, "The political environment will one day change to allow unfettered exchanges of all kinds typically enjoyed by sister cities, and the Society plans to be there, and be prepared, when that day comes."

In 1994, Sarah Marston, 15, wrote the following about her experiences in Cuba: "I am always intrigued by mysterious and exotic countries, and I want to find out about these places for myself. I don't have the baggage of Cold War. I want to make my own judgment about Cuba…Basic necessities like soap are missing in Cuba. Yet the people are very generous in every way. They don't give you the cold shoulder. They want to find out about the United States." She was most touched by the children, "They came up and asked for gum and money, but mostly they wanted to practice their English…I really feel for the Cuban children, they suffer so much. Many eat only two meals a day, breakfast and supper. I bought them lunch for three days, and that is why I didn't bring back any souvenirs."

Annual Awards 1993

Best Overall Program
Over 350,000: State of Maryland – sister city to Anhui Province, China; Kanagama Prefecture, Japan; Kyongsangnam-Do Province, Korea; Lodz Region, Poland; and Walloon Region, Belgium
100,000 – 350,000: Torrance, California – sister city to Kashiwa, Japan
50,000 – 100,000: Redford, Michigan – sister city to Gau-Algesheim, Germany; Georgina, Canada; and St. Johann, Austria
Under 50,000: Waterloo, Illinois – sister city to Porta Westfalica, Germany

Best Single Project
Over 350,000: Houston/Galveston, Texas – sister city to Stavanger, Norway
100,000 – 350,000: Tempe, Arizona – sister city to Lower Hutt, New Zealand; Regensberg, Germany; Skopje, Macedonia; Timbuktu, Mali; and Zhenjaing, China
50,000 – 100,000: Greenville, South Carolina – sister city to Kortrijk, Belgium and Bergamo, Italy
Under 50,000: Rice Lake, Wisconsin – sister city to Niharu, Japan

Special Achievement Awards

Anniversary Celebration:
Riverside, California – sister city to Senia, Japan
Bakersfield, California – sister city to Wakayma, Japan

Cultural Exchange:
Kansas City, Missouri – sister city to Seville, Spain
Merced California – sister city to Somoto, Nicaragua
Phoenix, Arizona – sister city to Hermosillo, Mexico
Tinley Park, Illinois – sister city to Budingen, Germany

Education and Training:
Cincinnati, Ohio – sister city to Kharkiv, Ukraine
Scottsdale, Arizona – sister city to Alamos, Mexico

Educational Development:
Binghamton, New York – sister city to Borovichi, Russia
Portsmouth, Ohio – sister city to Orizaba, Mexico

Humanitarian Assistance:
Rochester, New York – sister city to Novgorod, Russia
Boyertown, Pennsylvania – sister city to Bogodukhov, Ukraine
Jacksonville, Florida – Murmansk, Russia
Sonoma, California – Kaniv, Ukraine

Best First Year Program
Canon City, Colorado – sister city to Valdai, Russia
Hanover Park, Illinois – sister city to Cape Coast, Ghana

Sponsored by the Reader's Digest Foundation

1994

SISTER CITIES

INTERNATIONAL CONFERENCE
Louisville, Kentucky • July 26-30, 1994
Weaving A Patchwork Of Peace

Be there when Louisville welcomes the world.

From the graceful sounds of "ROARchestra" to the fast paced excitement of the first Sister Cities International Youth Soccer Cup. Enjoy the historic charm of Locust Grove and travel back in time on the Belle of Louisville riverboat. There will be festive entertainment, celebrities and surprises!

It's the Bluegrass State at its best in 1994.

Delegates to the 1994 conference helped "weave a patchwork of peace" by sending twelve-inch patches to Louisville that were sewn together to create 26 quilts.

Sister Cities World Cup:
Louisville, Kentucky Welcomes the World

In the summer of 1994, the world came to Louisville, Kentucky to attend the Sister Cities conference and the MasterCard International Sister Cities Cup. Just nine days after the finals of the World Cup was played, soccer teams from sister cities in Scotland, Australia, Ireland, Argentina, Germany, Russia, the Ukraine, Costa Rica, Ghana, and the U.S. converged on Louisville for the youth tournament. The Cup was sanctioned by FIFA and the U.S. Youth Soccer Association and was comprised of both boys' and girls' divisions, ages 8 through 18. Each team played a minimum of three games with a champion being crowned in each age division. Little did Louisville know that this soccer tournament would be the first of many to come and that it would give thousands of young people from around the world an opportunity to create friendships and memories that would last a lifetime.

Young Artists Program Winners 1994

1st - Kevin Austin Keller – Owensboro, Kentucky
2nd - Kathleen Murphy – Winchester, Massachusetts
3rd - Inbal Shem-Tov – Irvine, California
4th - Chantel Titus – New Port Richey, Florida
5th - Adam Hand – Scottsdale, Arizona
6th - Rika Kohchi – Yao City, Japan
7th - Madonna Nakamura – Lexington, Kentucky
8th - Jason Lail – Charlotte, North Carolina
9th - Thomas Kirchheim – Wandersleben, Germany
10th - Maxim Smolov – Ekaterinberg, Russian Federation

Louisville-area soccer players were on hand as John Douglas, a senior vice president of Mastercard International, presented Mayor Jerry Abramson with a check for $100,000 to sponsor the 1994 Mastercard International Sister Cities Cup. Louisville, Kentucky is the birthplace of MasterCard.

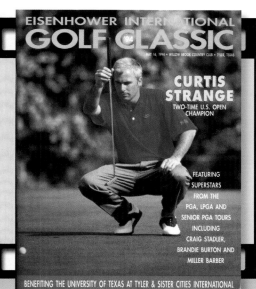

EISENHOWER INTERNATIONAL
GOLF CLASSIC
MAY 16, 1994 • WILLOW BROOK COUNTRY CLUB • TYLER, TEXAS

CURTIS STRANGE
TWO-TIME U.S. OPEN CHAMPION

FEATURING SUPERSTARS FROM THE PGA, LPGA AND SENIOR PGA TOURS INCLUDING CRAIG STADLER, BRANDIE BURTON AND MILLER BARBER

BENEFITING THE UNIVERSITY OF TEXAS AT TYLER & SISTER CITIES INTERNATIONAL

Golfer Cindy Rarick was one of many featured professional golfers at the Eisenhower International Golf Classic.

Board of Directors 1993-94

President - Richard Neuheisel
Chairman of the Board - Louis Wozar
Chairman, Executive Committee -
Betty Wilson
Vice President - James Amato
Vice President - Nancy Eidam
Vice President - Ann Galloway
Vice President - James Turner
Vice President - Thelma Press
Vice President - Raymond Schultz
Secretary - Henry Cole
Treasurer - Wylie Williams
Chairman International Executive Board
- Dr. George Hamm

Youth Member to the Board - Lance Welch
President of the Ambassador's
 Association - Melissa Anderson
State Coordinator Liaison - Priscilla Harris

Johnel Bracey
Toni Brown
Mary Cort
Geraldine Ferraro
Glenn Hughes
Launa Kowalski
Thomas Miner
Sue Myrick
Ambassador Charles Nelson
Carlton Parker
John Raeside
Honorable Rodger Randle
Shirley Rivens Smith
Patricia Sanders
Stephen Schwartz
Jane Tublin
Dr. Charles Wheeler
Linda Whitton
Shelley Zeiger

Theater Exchange Shares Cultures: Philadelphia, Pennsylvania – Torun, Poland
The Philadelphia/Torun Theater Exchange practices in Philadelphia's Walnut Street Theater in 1994. Today Philadelphia has sister city relationships with Abruzzo, Italy; Aix-en-Provence, France; Douala, Cameroon; Florence, Italy; Incheon, Republic of Korea; Kobe, Japan; Nizhni Novgorod, Russian Federation; Tel Aviv, Israel; Tianjin City, Taiwan, China; and Torun, Poland. Philadelphia also has a partner for peace relationship with Mosul, Iraq.

Annual Awards 1994

Best Overall Program
Over 350,000: Phoenix, Arizona – sister city to Chengdu, China; Ennis, Ireland; Grenoble, France; Hermosillo, Sonora, Mexico; Himeji, Japan; and Taipei, Taiwan, China
100,000 – 350,000: Sioux Falls, South Dakota – sister city to Pottsdam, Germany and Strabane, Northern Ireland
50,000 – 100,000: Tyler, Texas – sister city to Metz, France; Yachiyo, Japan; Jelenia Gora, Poland
Under 50,000: Sonoma, California – sister city to Chambol-Musigny, France; Greve, Italy; and Kaniv, Ukraine

Best Single Project
Over 350,000: Chicago, Illinois – sister city to Accra, Ghana; Casablanca, Morocco; Goteburg, Sweden; Kiev, Ukraine; Milan, Italy; Osaka, Japan; Prague, Czech Republic; Shenyang, China; Toronto, Canada; and Warsaw, Poland
100,000 – 350,000: Tacoma-Pierce County, Washington – sister city to Kitakyushu, Japan; Kunsan, Korea; Alesund, Norway; and Kiryat Motzkin, Israel
50,000 – 100,000: El Cajon, California – sister city to Ciudad Constitucion, Baja, California and Sur, Mexico
Under 50,000: Santa Cruz, California – sister city to Jinotepe, Nicaragua

Special Achievement Awards

Community Awareness:
Rochester, New York – sister city to Rehovot, Israel; Caltanissetta, Italy; Krakow, Poland; Novgorod, Russia; Bamako, Mali; Waterford, Ireland; Rennes, France; and Wurzburg, Germany
Centerville, Ohio – sister city to Bad Zwishenahn, Germany

Cultural Exchange:
Delray Beach, Florida – sister city to Miyazu, Japan
Rice Lake, Wisconsin – sister city to Miharu-Machi, Japan
Aspen, Colorado – sister city to Shimukappu, Japan

Educational Development:
Cincinnati, Ohio – sister city to Liuzhou, China
Stillwater, Oklahoma – sister city to Kameoka, Japan

Humanitarian Assistance:
Atlanta, Georgia – sister city to Tbilisi, Republic of Georgia
St. Louis, Missouri – sister city to Stuttgart, Germany; Nanjing, China; and Suwa, Japan
Waterloo, Illinois – sister city to Porta Westfalica, Germany

Medical Assistance:
Yonkers, New York – sister city to Ternopil, Ukraine
Canon City, Colorado – sister city to Valdai, Russia

Sports:
Round Rock, Texas – sister city to Lake MacQuarie, Speers Point, New South Wales, Australia

Youth Exchange:
Albuquerque, New Mexico – sister city to Guadalajara, Jalisco, Mexico
Portsmouth, Ohio – sister city to Orizaba, Veracruz, Mexico
San Bernardino, California – sister city to Mexicali, Vilahermosa, Mexico
Lexington, Kentucky – sister city to County Kildare, Ireland
San Diego, California – sister city to Edinburgh, Scotland

Best First Year Program
Orange, California – sister city to Novo Kosino, Russia
Las Cruces, New Mexico – sister city to Nienburg, Germany
Colombia, Illinois – sister city to Gedern, Germany

Sponsored by the Reader's Digest Foundation

Summit of the Americas
The 1994 Summit of the Americas in Miami, Florida featured U.S. President Bill Clinton. The summit involved 34 nations and established ground rules for hemispheric relationships. Sister city programs were involved in the report about the conference and highlighted for their work building understanding and appreciation of cultural heritage.

U.S. – Japan Volunteerism Internship Program, 1994-1997

In 1994, this innovative program involved six U.S. – Japan sister city pairs. Each community sent one intern to its sister city to study the concept and practice of volunteerism, including how services are provided in their sister city. Interns were encouraged to link similar organizations between the two communities. An additional six pairs were selected in 1996 and participating communities were asked to organize a follow-up exchange or project in 1997.

"Before leaving home, many of my friends were concerned because I tend to be independent. Many told me to behave. At no time did I experience chauvinism, however. Everyone treated me very well. My most uncomfortable time was when they insisted on paying for everything, including many of the souvenirs which I brought back. They were very generous with their time, resources and warmth. I was able to develop a warm relationship with my guide, who "mothered" me, even though she was younger than my youngest child. My trip is an experience that I shall never forget. I am happy I took the risk! Thank you very much for the opportunity."
-U.S. intern

"When full-time American workers join volunteer activities, how do they manage their daily lives? Isn't it hard for them to participate fully in their jobs?"
- Japan intern

"The purpose of the Women's Action Exchange is to promote acceptance of women in business and professions and to advance knowledge, community responsibility, and the business and professional interests of its members. The meeting was held from 6:45am to 8:15am. It was an unbelievable experience to me to join such a meeting held early in the morning. To my additional surprise, they have meetings twice a month. The topics were very interesting, but I could not help thinking about the breakfast table without wife or mother. I have never heard of having meetings so early in the morning in Japan. The members were very attractive, sophisticated and full of confidence, but I wonder what made them gather to the meeting. I was overwhelmed by their vitality."
- Japan intern

"One of the big surprises for me, was how much we are alike. Volunteers in my sister city are just like volunteers I know in the United States. Dedicated, caring, involved individuals…One volunteer told me, 'After age 45, return to society what you have received.' And she followed that advice."
- U.S. intern

"The expression "helping others to succeed is its own reward" is a shared sentiment among American and Japanese volunteers."
- U.S. intern

"I attended a sister city meeting in my sister city. I was amazed to see them talking pleasantly and freely after they had done their one day's job. In Japan we are used to having supper and tea before we have a meeting."
- Japan intern

1995

PEACEFUL COMMUNICATION

Young Artists Program Winners 1995

1st - Irene Lerner – Des Plaines, Illinois

2nd- Matt Mayer – Montgomery, Alabama

3rd - Gary Aubert – Tourrettes, France
(sister city to Fredericksburg, Virginia)

4th - John Anderson – Tuscaloosa, Alabama

5th - Chen Xiaolin – Chengdu, China
(sister city Phoenix, Arizona)

6th - Kevin Koller – Owensboro, Kentucky

7th - Han Haijian – Beihai, China
(sister city to Tulsa, Oklahoma)

8th - Siri Okamoto – Seattle, Washington

9th - Alicia Smith – Phoenix, Arizona

10th - Michael Wingard – Charlotte, North Carolina

World Peace Blanket Includes Santa Clara, California

In 1995, 50 years after the end of World War II, the World Peace Blanket project was initiated and people all over the world were invited to submit peace blanket contributions, along with a message of hope for world peace. With the project originating in the region of Japan where its sister city Izumo is located, Santa Clara, California was asked to participate. Working with a regional quilting organization, Betty Sampson, created "peaceful communication" showing stylized kites on a background of clouds in a light blue sky. More than 4,200 quilt patches and 800 messages from 45 countries were received and assembled into 288 smaller World Peace Blankets. These smaller sections were then combined into a larger blanket which was displayed during a World Peace Forum held in Matsue City, Japan. Parts of this larger blanket were sent to the Hiroshima Peace Memorial Hall and the United Nations. Their message of peace has been displayed all over the world.

United Nations Global Youth Forum Includes Sister City Delegation

Santa Clara, California sent a delegation of six middle school students to the Untied Nations Environmental Program Global Youth Forum in Shimane, Japan in 1995. Themed, "plea for the preservation of a green earth," the students gave presentations on Santa Clara's environmental projects, interacted with students from around the globe, and learned about Japanese culture while staying with host families. The delegates were also able to visit the region and talk with officials from Izumo, Santa Clara's sister city.

Board of Directors 1994-95

President - Richard Neuheisel
President-Elect - Rodger Randle
Chairman of the Board - Louis Wozar
Chairman, Executive Committee -
Betty Wilson
Vice President - Launa Kowalski
Vice President - Ambassador Charles Nelson
Vice President - Ann Galloway
Vice President - Mary Palko
Vice President - Thelma Press
Vice President - Pat Sanders
Secretary - Nancy Eidam
Treasurer - Shirley Rivens Smith
Chairman, International Executive Board
- Dr. George Hamm

Youth Member to the Board - Janet Downey
President of the Ambassador's Association
- Lawrence Roybal
State Coordinator Liaison - Paula West

Jerry E. Abramson
James Amato
Johnel Bracey
Toni Brown
Henry Cole
Zelda Faigen
Geraldine Ferraro
Glenn Hughes
David Lisk
Thomas Minder
David Perez-Ginart
Carlton Parker
John Raeside
Bonnie Talley
Jane Tublin
James Turner
Dr. Charles Wheeler
Shelley Zeiger

Indianapolis offered a warm welcome to Annual Conference delegates.

SISTER CITIES INTERNATIONAL ANNUAL CONFERENCE
JULY 25-29, INDIANAPOLIS, INDIANA
THEME: RACING TOWARD WORLD UNDERSTANDING

A Mexican delegate walks through the Pan-Am Plaza at the International Delegates Parade in Indianapolis. A pre-conference event, the "Western Hemispheric Forum," expanded upon issues discussed at the Summit of the Americas in 1994 and showcased sister city programs in the Americas.

Colorful costumes were highlights of the International Delegates Parade.

Sister Cities International Leads Mayors Delegation to South Africa

Sister Cities International, working in conjunction with the U.S. Information Agency, sponsored a mayors' mission to South Africa to promote economic development, municipal cooperation and free trade. Mayors from Albuquerque, Galveston, Oakland, Rochester, Newark, East Orange, Winston-Salem, Rockford, Toledo and North Little Rock invited business leaders to join them on the trip. They visited Cape Town, Durban, Johannesburg and Pretoria. President Richard Neuheisel praised the trip and said, "Sister Cities has once again demonstrated its ability to act as the international arm of city halls across America."

Congressman Norman Mineta talks with an exchange student visiting Washington, D.C. Congressman Mineta has a long history with the sister cities program. He served on the Board of Directors for Sister Cities International from 1970-1972, on the International Executive Board in 1982 and was very supportive of the sister city program in San Jose, California.

Sister Cities Leaders: Congressman Mineta Speaks Out in Favor of Sister Cities

The following is a speech given by Congressman Norman Mineta in 1995 urging House members to vote against the Gilman amendment. This piece of legislation, which passed in the House, cut funds for exchange programs.

Mr. Chairman, this amendment would further cut funding for one of the most successful programs our Nation operates – the Sister Cities Program, as well as other important cultural exchange programs.

As a former member of the board of directors of Sister Cities International, I have seen first hand the benefits the program brings.

My own city of San Jose, California, has built strong relationships with such cities as Okayama, Japan and Dublin, Ireland.

When the San Francisco Bay Area suffered the Loma Prieta earthquake in 1989, the citizens of San Jose, Costa Rica, another of our Sister Cities, generously sent supplies and aid for the relief centers.

The Sister Cities Program, Mr. Chairman, brings people of different nations together in friendship and understanding. It builds relationships that strengthen the bonds between the United States and the other nations of the world.

Mr. Chairman, as we seek to reduce the federal budget, we must do so responsibly. In cutting funding for cultural exchange programs like Sister Cities, this amendment goes far beyond what is reasonable, and will cripple programs that are of very great importance.

I urge my colleagues to oppose the Gilman amendment.

Student Twinning Mission With Scotland

Mount Dora (Florida) exchange students travel to Forres, Scotland for a month-long stay in mid-June and to attend Forres Academy until the summer break. The Forres students stay in Mount Dora for two weeks in October during the "Tattie holidays," a throwback to the days when youth were needed to harvest potatoes. In this photo, U.S. exchange students Lucas Koester and Daviann Ryder attend a sister city tree planting event in June 1995 at Applegrove Primary School in Forres, Scotland. The exchange program began in 1994.

Board of Directors 1995-1996

President - Richard Neuheisel
President-Elect - Rodger Randle
Chairman of the Board - Louis Wozar
Chairman, Executive Committee - Betty Wilson
Vice President - Launa Kowalski
Vice President - Ambassador Charles Nelson
Vice President - Ann Galloway
Vice President - Mary Palko
Vice President - Thelma Press
Vice President - Pat Sanders
Secretary - Nancy Eidam
Treasurer - Shirley Rivens Smith

Chairman, International Executive Board - Dr. George Hamm
Youth Member to the Board - Janet Downey
President of the Ambassador's Association - Lawrence Roybal
State Coordinator Liaison - Paula West
Jerry E. Abramson
James Amato
Johnel Bracey
Toni Brown
Henry Cole
Zelda Faigen

Geraldine Ferraro
Glenn Hughes
David Lisk
Thomas Minder
David Perez-Ginart
Carlton Parker
John Raeside
Bonnie Talley
Jane Tublin
James Turner
Dr. Charles Wheeler
Shelley Zeiger

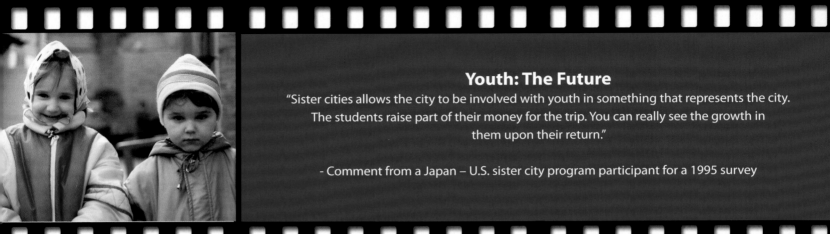

1995 International Camp

This 1995 International Camp brought together U.S. and Russian youth from the Greater Tri-Cities, Tennessee/Virginia and Rybinsk, Russian Federation.

This community service project planting and moving trees in 1995 with Girls Inc. brought together sister city youth and helped improve the community for the Greater Tri-Cities in Tennessee and Virginia. They have sister city relationships with Guaranda, Ecuador; Ronneby, Sweden; Rybinsk, Russian Federation; and Teterow, Germany.

The Great Wall of China

FIRST U.S. – SINO SISTER CITIES CONFERENCE
NOVEMBER 3-13, BEIJING, PEOPLE'S REPUBLIC OF CHINA

Conference attendees, including Mayor Rosemary Corbin of Redmond, California (wearing red jacket) enjoy a meal during the First Sino-U.S. Sister Cities Conference in Beijing.

President of the Board of Directors, Dick Neuheisel, and his wife Jane, visited the Great Wall of China during the First Sino-U.S. Sister Cities Conference in Beijing in 1995.

Changing Lives and Perspectives

"…the American students, before going to Japan, think that we are poor and that the Japanese are wealthy – then they see how small the houses are there, and how hard they have to work…They come back with a better appreciation and big hopes for the future. The first student that we sent has now opened a trade business. Others are in our Japanese sister city as teachers or artists."

- Comment from a Japan – U.S. sister city program participant

Annual Awards 1995

Best Overall Program
Muscatine, Iowa – sister city to Crespo, Argentina; Ichikawadaimon, Japan; Koslovodsk, Russia; Lomza, Poland; Parana, Argentina; and Paysandu, Uruguay
Durham, North Carolina – sister city to Arusha, Tanzania; KostOman, Russia; and Toyama, Japan
Kettering, Ohio – sister city to Kettering, England and Steyr, Australia
The State of Maryland – sister city to Anhui Province, China; Jalisco, Mexico; Kanagawa Prefecture, Japan; Kyongsangnam-Do, Korea; Leningrad Region, Russia; Lodz Region, Poland; Nord-Pas de Calais, France; and Walloon Region, Belgium

Best Single Project
Over 300,000: Fort, Worth – sister city to Budapest, Hungary
100,000 – 300,000: Fort Wayne, Indiana – sister city to Plock, Poland; Gera, Germany; and Takaoka, Japan
Under 50,000: Corvallis, Oregon – sister city to Uzhgorod, Ukraine

Special Achievement Awards

Trade and Tourism Devleopment:
Jacksonville, Florida – sister city to Bahia Blanca, Argentina; Nantes, France; Masan, Korea; Murmansk, Russia; Yingkou, China
Phoenix, Arizona – sister city to Chengdu, China
San Diego, California – sister city to Vladivostok, Russia

Youth:
Cincinnati, Ohio – sister city to Lizhou, China
Cambridge, Massachusetts – sister city to Yerevan, Armenia
Bloomington, Indiana – sister city to Posoltega, Nicaragua
Torrance, California – sister city to Kashiwa, Japan
Boyertown, Pennsylvania – sister city to Bobodukhiv, Ukraine

Arts and Culture:
Denver, Colorado – sister city to Takayama, Japan
Philadelphia, Pennsylvania – sister city to Florence, Italy

Commemorative:
Sacramento, California – sister city to Matsuyama, Japan
Tampa, Florida – sister city to LeHavre, France
Duluth, Minnesota – sister city to Ohara, Japan

Cultural Diversity:
Cincinnati, Ohio – sister city to Kharkiv, Ukraine

Environment:
Hazleton, Pennsylvania – sister city to Gorzow Wielkopolski, Poland

Best First Year Program
Oklahoma City, Oklahoma – sister city to Puebla, Mexico
Palo Alto, California – sister city to Albi, France

Volunteer of the Year
Barbara Seitz Martinez (Bloomington, Illinois)
Eleanor Kahle (Toledo, Ohio)
Jane Fleetwood (Jacksonville, Florida)

President's Award
Raymond R. Schultz

A 5,000 EGG OMELET MARKS 20 YEARS OF FRIENDSHIP

How do you cook a 5,000 egg omelet? With a year of organizing, a special plan, chevaliers (chefs) from France, and 5,000 onlookers. More than 157 people from France and across the United States were part of this remarkable 20th anniversary celebration in 2000 marking the twinning between Fredericksburg, Virginia and Frejus, France. The 157 guests were housed throughout Fredericksburg and their ten-day visit resulted in lasting friendships. The highlight of the event was of course the omelet! It contained 5,000 eggs, 52 pounds of butter, four gallons of chopped onions, a pound of pepper, and twenty pounds of Virginia ham. One hundred loaves of French bread were also served. The Confrerie tradition stipulates that the omelet is always provided for free to guests, and stems from a Napoleonic legend about villagers feeding the famous warrior's hungry army in a gesture of hospitality. The omelet later became a tradition for Christians, reminding them to feed the poor at Easter and is now a symbol of worldwide friendship.

LOOKING BACK AND LEAPING FORWARD: THE FIFTH DECADE

Growth, technology, and innovation best summarize the fifth decade of the U.S. sister cities program. Moving full force into the 21st century, Sister Cities International has responded to vast cultural expansion and emerging technologies with a variety of programs and partnerships.

Sister cities have sought out new linkages and partnerships to strengthen the efforts and brought us full swing into a modern era. New partnerships with the State Department, international organizations and local governments have helped us move forward, with a common purpose.

Rapid globalization and an emerging global perspective spurred Sister Cities International to respond by creating the Youth & Education Network and the Sister Cities Network for Sustainable Development.

This has been a time to leap forward into new beginnings, new partnerships and new networks, and also look back at the power and success of person-to-person diplomacy.

1996

Weaving Strands of Peace
A girl works at a loom in 1992 in Kargopol, Russian Federation, near Archangelsk. Photo by Mary K. Hall from Weymouth, Massachusetts. Submitted to Amateur, Category: Color Modern

SISTER CITIES INTERNATIONAL 40TH ANNIVERSARY PHOTO CONTEST

A photo contest was held in 1996 by Sister Cities International to celebrate the 40th anniversary of the sister city movement. These images celebrated the beauty and power of sister city friendships and programs.

A mother and baby greet a sister city visitor in January 1996 in Archangelsk, now in the Russian Federation and a sister city to Portland, Maine. Photo by Dennis Marrotte and submitted by the Greater Portland, Maine sister city program. Submitted to Amateur, Category: Color Modern.

FIRST PLACE, AMATEUR, ILLINOIS

"Welcome to Ghana"
Mayor's Residence, Cape Coast, Ghana. Photo by Hanover Park, Illinois - Cape Coast, Ghana Sister Cities Participant.

Max in America
This photo was taken in Kharkiv, Ukraine in spring 1995 during a sister city visit when Maxim Alexandrovich Livinov was four years old. Photo by Richard Jameson of Cincinnati, Ohio and chair of the Individual Liberties Committee for the Kharkiv Sister City Project. Submitted to Division: Amateur, Category: Color Modern

Street Vendor
Submitted to Division: Amateur, Category: Color Modern Photo by Mayene Miller from Kent, Washington with the Yangzhou Sister City Committee.

New Beginnings Head Start of Tioga
Submitted by the Philadel-phia-Douala, Cameroon Education Exchange. Photo by Ralph Graves, December 1995. Honorable Mention, Amateur.

Riders play "ulak Tartysh," a traditional horse game of the nomadic Kyrgyz culture at an Independent Day celebration in Bishkek. Bishkek is a sister city to Colorado Springs, Colorado. Photo taken by Hermine Dreyfuss.

10th Eisenhower Golf Classic benefiting
Sister Cities International and the University
of Texas at Tyler - May 13, Tyler, Texas

Cross-Cultural Ties:
Chinese Week in Phoenix, Arizona

Organized through a partnership between Phoenix Sister Cities and the Chinese Week Committee, this vibrant week-long cultural celebration wows Phoenix residents every year with performing artists, acrobatics, dances and traditional costumes. The highlight of the week is the Culture & Cuisine Festival featuring arts and crafts, dragon dances, martial arts demonstrations, and musical performances. The Children's Pavilion draws thousands and entire busloads of students roll in for the festivities. Phoenix has sister city relationships with Chengdu, China and Taipei, Taiwan, China.

MEMBER STORY

Omaha's Cross Travels to Lithuania's Hill of Crosses
Omaha, Nebraska – Siauliai, Lithuania

When Siauliai and Omaha officially became sister cities in May 1996 with a signing ceremony, the festivities included the dedication of a cross on the Hill of Crosses in Lithuania. Originating in 1847, the historic hill was filled with thousands of crosses – which oppression could never fully eliminate. Every time the hill was razed or burned, the people would again place crosses on it. Viktoras Aras-Arlauskas, an Omaha-based Lithuanian woodcarver crafted an ornate wooden cross. It was mounted onto a wooden chapel constructed by Omaha-based carpenter, Greg Peterson. A wooden plaque inscribed with "Omahos gyventojai" lets others know its origin. Pictured, Ieva Ripinskas with Omaha's cross on the Hill of Crosses.

Sister Signings: Irving, Texas and Leon, Mexico

Irving, Texas and Leon, Mexico have been sister cities since 1996. This copy of their signing agreement includes a signature from George W. Bush, then governor of Texas. Signing ceremony festivities included an International Celebration, which is held annually in Irving and honors the cultures of its many sister cities. Irving's other sister cities are: Merton, England (United Kingdom); Mario, Italy; Boulogne-Billancourt, France; and Espoo, Finland.

This ink drawing of the Sister Cities International headquarters building in Alexandria was used on the Annual Report issued for 1996-1997. Only a year later, the building was sold and the offices moved to downtown Washington, D.C.

"Interlocking Lives"
Lindsey Hook, Seattle, Washington
"I wanted to show that people are different everywhere. It doesn't matter what you look like or who you are, we are all people and we all have to live on this planet together."

"Celebrating 40 Years…"
Nayabei Vanwoekom Barroso, 14, Oaxaca, Mexico, sister city to Palo Alto, California
"The faces, though they are different faces, are able to be considered like equals. The hands signify strength and love at the same time, that's why in the painting they appear intertwined."

Young Artists Program Winners 1996

1st – Nayabei Vanwoerkom Barroso, Esuipulas Xoxo, Oaxaca, Mexico (sister city to Palo Alto, California)

2nd - Nick Freeman - Des Plaines, Illinois

3rd - Tamara N. Friedrich - Scottsdale, Arizona

4th - Lindsey Hook - Seattle, Washington

5th - Yan Jin - Chengdu, China (sister city to Phoenix, Arizona)

6th - Yenhin (Nikki) Saepharn - Sacramento, California

7th - Stefanie Schah - Schotndor, Germany (sister city to Tuscaloosa, Alabama)

8th - Kim Wu - Del Ray Beach, Florida

9th - Laura Zaze - Liepaja, Latvia (sister city to Bellevue, Washington)

"Pieces of Unity"
Nick Freeman, 17, Des Plaines, Illinois
"A mixed media representation of the people of the world adding their own individual piece to the puzzle."

1996-Magazine

The cover of the 1996 magazine is a fused glass art construction depicting a variety of cubistic and expressionist faces designed and executed by students in the Design and Materials art classes at Maine East High School in Park Ridge, Illinois. The piece was donated to the Des Plaines, Illinois Sister Cities organization in celebration of the "40 Years…Many Faces…One World" theme.

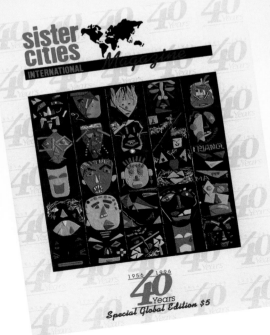

Reflecting on the Experience of a Lifetime
U.S. and Ukrainian students write in their journals about their experiences in Uzhgorod, Ukraine. Uzhgorod is paired with Corvallis, Oregon. Pictured from left to right: Heidi Gallagher, Anya Shamshura, Ina Ovchinnikova, and Abby Curtia.

Friendship Knows No Borders
Vanessa Rupp of Tooele City, Utah enjoys the friendship of several children of Kambarka, Russia. She is one of 16 Russian and United States students who have participated in Sister Cities International summer exchanges.

U.S. – N.I.S. Sister Schools Initiative

In 1996, Sister Cities International launched a pilot program to support school linkages between communities in the United States and the Newly Independent States. The 18-month project led to the exchange of more than 100 educators and students, collaborative global learning projects, and online resources. The project was funded by the N.I.S. Secondary School Initiative at the United States Information Agency's Bureau of Educational and Cultural Affairs.

Participating Partnerships
Santa Rosa, California – Cherkassy, Ukraine
Sebastopol, California – Chihirin, Ukraine
Cambridge, Massachusetts – Yerevan, Armenia
Corvallis, Oregon – Uzhgorod, Ukraine
Waukesha, Wisconsin – Kokshetau, Kazakhstan

Hidden Hunger Initiative

When announcing the Hidden Hunger Initiative in 1996, two billion people world-wide were affected by hidden hunger, a form of malnutrition that causes learning disabilities, mental retardation, poor health, low work capacity, blindness, and premature death. Many of the effects of hidden hunger are not readily apparent and not easily associated with nutritional deficiencies. It is caused by a lack of vitamins and minerals, such as Vitamin A, iodine, and iron.

Sister city programs were encouraged to fight hidden hunger among children by:
- Creating multicultural teaching kits for elementary schools.
- Sponsoring teacher exchanges to foster creativity in classrooms and communities.
- Developing "Super-Nutrient Sports Days" for youth and adults – with athletic events, music, art, and cooking competitions.
- Participating in international training programs for teachers, parents, and civic leaders.

They were also encouraged to hold town meetings and discuss with their sister city partners how this problem could be addressed. They were urged to start workplace nutrition programs, work with the food industry to increase the supply of vitamin-fortified food, foster scientific exchanges to assure high quality food manufacturing, support business-to-business exchange, and begin industry recognition programs. Through this initiative, many sister city partners worked together to fight hidden hunger – prolonging lives and making communities healthier places to live.

Board of Directors 1996-97

President - Rodger Randle
President-Elect - Jim Amato
Chairman of the Board - Richard Neuheisel
Vice President - Launa Kowalski
Vice President - Ambassador Charles Nelson
Vice President - Ann Galloway
Vice President - Mary Palko
Vice President - Thelma Press
Vice President - John Raeside
Secretary - Henry Cole
Treasurer - Charles Stokke
Chairman, International Executive Board -
  Dr. George Hamm

Youth Member to the Board - Josh Lader
President of the Ambassador's Association -
  Marcus Newton
State Coordinator Liaison - Priscilla Harris

Jerry Abramson
Don Brandes
John Clarke
Nancy Eidam
Dr. Stelle Feuers
Nancy Huppert
David Lisk
Sandra McCormick
Bob McConnell

Thomas Miner
Carlton Parker
Dr. David Perez-Ginart
Sharon Receveur
Shirley Rivens Smith
Bonnie Talley
Jane Tublin
James Turner
Paula West
Dr. Charles Wheeler
Joseph Wilkinson
Honorable Betty Wilson
Louis Wozar
Shelley Zeiger

Mary Palko and Jane Neuheisel. Palko chaired the 40th Anniversary Sister Cities International conference.

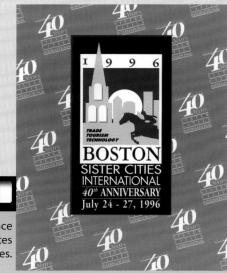

The 1996 40th Anniversary conference in Boston included 1,300 delegates from 49 states and 31 countries.

Conference attendees enjoyed performances by these dancers from Maui, Hawaii.

Youth participants at the conference had a great time and learned more about citizen diplomacy.

Annual Awards 1996

Best Overall Program
St. Mary's, Ohio
Louisville, Kentucky
Phoenix, Arizona

Best Single Project
Santa Barbara, California
Orange, California
Illinois State Chapter

Special Achievement Awards

Technology:
Tyler, Texas
Seattle, Washington

Trade:
New Brunswick, New Jersey
The State of Maryland

Tourism:
Lexington, Kentucky

Volunteers of the Year
Merv Lapin (Vail, Colorado)
Jean Cappellino (Rochester, New York)

Youth Leadership Development
Portsmouth, Ohio
Cincinnati, Ohio

Diverse Community
Gresham, Oregon
Springfield, Missouri
Charlotte, North Carolina and Tulsa, Oklahoma (Tie)

The Richard G. Neuheisel Award for
Outstanding Achievement
Tempe, Arizona

"The fundamental concept of Sister Cities International, as envisioned by President Dwight D. Eisenhower 40 years ago, continues to offer opportunities to people who are committed to work toward furthering world understanding."

- Vice President Ann Galloway,
40th Anniversary Magazine, Sister Cities International

The dancers from Nairobi are welcomed at the airport by a crowd of 500 people, with traditional dancers, drumming and merrymaking.

Nairobi dancers share their culture and focus on communicating through dance while visiting Denver.

One Spirit, Many Voices
Denver, Colorado – Nairobi, Kenya

In 1995 the Denver-Nairobi Sister Cities Committee, Cleo Parker Robinson Dance, the Metropolitan State College of Denver and the Denver Black Arts Festival, Inc. formed a partnership and won a grant from the United States Information Agency for a Creative Arts Exchange project.

In the fall, Cleo Parker-Robinson and Dr. Akbarali Thobhani traveled to Kenya to study the history of Kenyan Dance and select dancers for the exchange. They learned that there are 40 ethnic groups in Kenya, with just as many types of dance. They observed how Kenyan dancers use dance to express their culture and themselves.

In 1996, the project's first phase took Cleo Parker Robinson Dance Ensemble to Kenya for three exciting weeks to serve as resident artists in Nairobi. This became an incredible exchange of educational experiences and the dance company conducted workshops and learned dances from several fascinating Kenyan cultural traditions.

In July, Kenyan entertainers journeyed to the Mile High City where they were greeted with a grand reception of cheers, banners, dancing, drumming and singing by 500 citizens. They stayed for three weeks to conduct master classes, workshops and educational seminars.

During this extraordinary exchange of culture all participants focused on communicating "sound…through dance." Life-long relationships were built and the participants felt that they were able to unify race, class, culture and voices in one joyous spirit.

Connecting the World…..One Community at a Time
Youth Baseball Exchange

In 1988, two businessmen - one in Tacoma, Washington and the other in Kitakyushu, Japan – agreed to develop a baseball exchange for young men from their two cities. In 2003, this program celebrated its fifteenth exchange.

The purpose of this ongoing program is to promote cultural understanding among young people. It gives them an opportunity to learn about people from other parts of the world. What they often find is that they are more alike than they are different.

Playing baseball has been a vehicle to expose these youngsters to people from other cultures, and to help mold their thoughts globally and culturally.

"The games we've won and lost are probably even, but the final score of the game is not what's important," said Tony Anderson, chairman of the project. "The interaction between our young people, the opportunity to learn more about a different culture and way of life is the key and the focus."

Since the beginning of this exchange, more than 600 youngsters from both Japan and Tacoma-Pierce County, Washington have participated in this exchange. Ninety-seven percent of them have gone on to college. These young men will become future leaders in their countries, and hopefully role models and mentors to the next generation.

1997

Asheville, North Carolina accepted the award for Best Overall Program (50,000-100,000). Asheville has sister city relationships with Karakol, Kyrgystan; San Cristobal de las Casas, Mexico; Vladikavkaz, Russia; and Saumur, France.

Attendees from Bakersfield, California accept the award for Best Overall Program (100,000-500,000). Bakersfield has sister city relationships with Wakayama, Japan; Partisan District of Minsk, Belarus; and Cixi, China.

Sister Cities International ANNUAL CONFERENCE

San Diego

July 30 – August 2, 1997
Town & Country Hotel

Delegates from Lynchburg, Virginia, sister city to Rueil-Malmaison, France, happily accept the award for Best First Year Program.

Youth Exchanges Change Lives
Grants Pass, Oregon – Rubtsovsk, Russian Federation

"I may say that at least one delegation member's life was changed due to that exchange. I mean myself. . . . I'd even say that I began to consider it a turning point, because now I perceive my life as 'before the exchange' and 'after it.' And I should say that I like the 'after' part better. . . . I wasn't very sociable, but during the exchange I met a lot of new people who were eager to communicate with me. This taught me to be more relaxed and open. I liked learning more about American culture and the American people as they are, and not as they are pictured in some books and media. Moreover, I managed to see my own culture through American people's eyes."
- Tanya Oskolkova, of Rubtsovsk, Russian Federation, remembering her experience as an exchange student in Grants Pass, Oregon in 1997. The two communities have been sister cities since 1990, and hosted a thematic youth exchange in 1997 with a grant from Sister Cities International. Tanya enjoys being an English language teacher today.

Kayla Turnbull welcomes 1997 Thematic Youth Exchange participant Alexei Volkov from Rubtsovsk, Russian Federation.

Russian students display folk attire during their visit to Grants Pass, Oregon for the 1997 Thematic Youth Exchange.

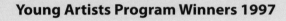

Eisenhower INTERNATIONAL Scholarship Fund

pportunity experience Travel reams

Sponsored by
SISTER CITIES INTERNATIONAL

By the time the 1997 Eisenhower International Golf Classic was held, funds from the prestigious tournament had enabled Sister Cities International to award more than 100 scholarships to international students coming to the United States.

"The Band Playing the Future"
Ikuyo Hirai, Fukui, Japan, sister city to
New Brunswick, New Jersey

Jeff Kriege (Honorable mention)

Young Artists Program Winners 1997

1st - Greg Badalian – Scottsdale, Arizona
2nd - Michaela Bergman – Apolda, Germany
(sister city to Rapid City, South Dakota)
3rd - Kate Earley – Steamboat Springs, Colorado
4th - Alyson Edie – Lincoln, Nebraska
5th - Marcella Gillenwater – Pocatello, Idaho
6th - Ikuyo Hirai – Fukui, Japan
(sister city to New Brunswick, New Jersey)
7th - Sachiko Hirayama – Yao, Japan
(sister city to Bellevue, Washington)
8th - Yuki Kimura – Utsunomiya, Japan
(sister city to Tulsa, Oklahoma)
9th - Christin Morgan – Tyler, Texas
10th - Jose Biaani Paxual – Oaxaca, Mexico
(sister city to Palo Alto, California)
11th- Lauren Rizzo – Toledo, Ohio
12th - Danielle Vardakas – Philadelphia, Pennsylvania
13th - Amy Werntz – Tyler, Texas
14th - Wu Yue – Beihai, China (sister city to Tulsa, Oklahoma)
Honorable Mention - Teresa Goss – Lexington, Kentucky
Honorable Mention - Jeff Kreige – Sacramento, California
Honorable Mention - Maria Hubkova – Bellevue, Washington

"Unity"
Christin Morgan, 18, Tyler, Texas
"I was trying to create a scene of unity where everything different is joined together. The baby is green to represent universal life."

"Mother Nature and I"
Wu Yue, 13, Beihai, China, sister city to Tulsa, Oklahoma
"Please don't forget to protect the eco-environment in the global community in which high technology advances by leaps and bounds. Leave us a lovely Mother Nature, an amicable and auspicious place covered with flowers, fruits and resounding with sweet sounds."

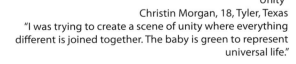

HIGHLITES OF "OPEN" HAPPENINGS IN 1997

OPEN

Organization Promoting Everlasting Neighbors

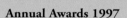

Annual Awards 1997

Best Overall Program
*Over 350,000: Jacksonville, Florida – sister city to Masan, Korea;
Yingkou, China; Murmansk, Russia; Nantes, France; and Bahia
Blanca, Argentina
100,000 – 350,000: Bakersfield, California – sister city to
Wakayama, Japan; Partisan District of Minsk, Belarus; and Cixi, China
50,000 – 100,000: Asheville, North Carolina – sister city to Karakol,
Kyrgystan; San Cristobal de las Casas, Mexico; Vladikavkaz, Russia;
and Saumur, France
Under 50,000:*

Best Overall Project
Denver, Colorado – sister city to Nairobi, Kenya

Special Achievement Awards

Education:
*Sonoma, California
Pocatello, Idaho
Fort Worth, Texas
Phoenix, Arizona
San Diego, California*

Health:
*Council Bluffs, Iowa
Louisville, Kentucky*

Environment:
*Aspen, Colorado
Philadelphia, Pennsylvania*

Volunteers of the Year
*Leo Blackburn (Portsmouth, Ohio)
Mary Higbie (Irving, Texas)*

Collaboration
*Redlands, California – sister city to Hino, Japan
Lexington, Kentucky – sister city to County Kildare, Ireland
Columbus, Ohio – sister city to Dresden, Germany*

Best First Year Program
*Lynchburg, Virginia – sister city to Rueil-Malmaison, France
Rochester, New York – sister city to Hamamatsu, Japan*

Diversity
*Wise, Virginia – sister city to Cesme, Turkey
Tacoma, Wisconsin – sister city to Kitakyushu, Japan
Albuquerque, New Mexico – sister city to Ashgabat, Turkmenistan*

Youth Leadership Development
*Riverside, California – sister city to Ensenada, Mexico
Atlanta, Georgia – sister city to Rio de Janeiro, Brazil; Montego Bay,
Jamaica; Newcastle Upon Tyne, England*

Did you know?

Four cities in Nevada are members of Sister Cities International. Elko is seeking a sister city. Fallon is paired with Vani, Georgia. Las Vegas has four sisters and is linked with An San, Republic of Korea; Angeles, Philippines; Huludao, China; and Phuket, Thailand. And finally, Reno is partnered with Guadalupe, Mexico; Hatzor, Israel; Nalchick, Russian Federation; Nanhai, China; San Sebastian, Spain; Taichung, Taiwan, China; Udonthani, Thailand and Wanganui, New Zealand.

Board of Directors 1997-98

President - Rodger Randle
President-Elect - Jim Amato
Chairman of the Board- Richard Neuheisel
Vice President - Launa Kowalski
Vice President - Ambassador Charles Nelson
Vice President - Ann Galloway
Vice President - Jane Tublin
Vice President - Thelma Press
Vice President - James Turner
Secretary - Henry Cole
Treasurer - Charles Stokke
Chairman of International Executive Board -
  Dr. George Hamm

Youth Member to the Board - Josh Lader
President of the Ambassador's Association -
  Janet Downey
State Coordinator Liaison - Priscilla Harris

Jerry Abramson
Don Brandes
Donna Briggs
Henry Cole

Dr. Stelle Feuers
John Henry Fullen
Nancy Huppert
David Lisk
Elena Lu
Sandra McCormick
Thomas Miner
Mary Palko
Carlton Parker
Dr. David Perez-Ginart
Mary Palko
Carlton Parker
Sharon Receveur
Shirley Rivens Smith
Brian Smith
Bonnie Talley
Peggy Wesp
Paula West
Dr. Charles Wheeler
Joseph Wilkinson
Betty Wilson
Louis Wozar

SISTER CITIES INTERNATIONAL ANNUAL CONFERENCE
July 30-August 1, Greater Miami & the Beaches, Florida
Theme: Cities: A Challenge for the New Millennium

THE FIFTH DECADE 1996-2006

1998

Roger Randle, Jim Amato and Chuck Stokke at the 1998 Conference in Miami.

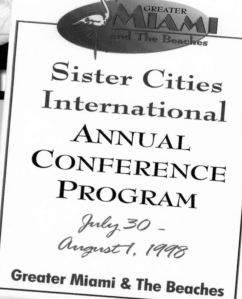

Sister Cities International ANNUAL CONFERENCE PROGRAM
July 30 - August 1, 1998
Greater Miami & The Beaches

"Sister Cities International plays an important role in understanding and improving the international changes taking place in our community. It assists our city's effort to achieve world-class status and brings local residents into the global economy."

- Mayor Jerry Abramson, Louisville, Kentucky, 1996

Did you know?

West Virginia has three members of Sister Cities International and two of them are linked with communities in the Russian Federation. The State of West Virginia is partnered with Respublika of Komi in the Russian Federation and Princeton is linked with Yoshkar Ola. Meanwhile, South Charleston is seeking a sister city. Who knows? Maybe they'll continue the Russian tradition in West Virginia.

Annual Awards 1998

Best Overall Program: Population
Oak Ridge, Tennessee
Lakeland, Florida
Tempe, Arizona
Fort Worth, Texas

Special Achievement Awards

Arts & Culture:
Kent, Washington
Virginia Beach, Virginia

Assistance & Relief:
Corvallis, Oregon

Economic Development:
San Antonio, Texas

Education:
Columbus, Ohio

Environment:
San Diego, California

Health & Public Safety:
La Crosse, Wisconsin

Municipal Cooperation:
Los Angeles, California

Technology & Communication:
Saline, Michigan

Volunteers of the Year
Evelyn Leonard of La Mirada, California
Takako T. Johnson of Orlando, Florida
Frank Wobst of Columbus, Ohio

Collaboration Award: Population
Vandalia, Ohio – sister city to Prestwick, Scotland
Portland, Oregon – sister city to Guadalajara, Mexico

Best Youth Program: Population
Grants Pass, Oregon
Fremont, California
Miami Beach, Florida
Phoenix, Arizona

NOD/AETNA Disability Award
Austin, Texas

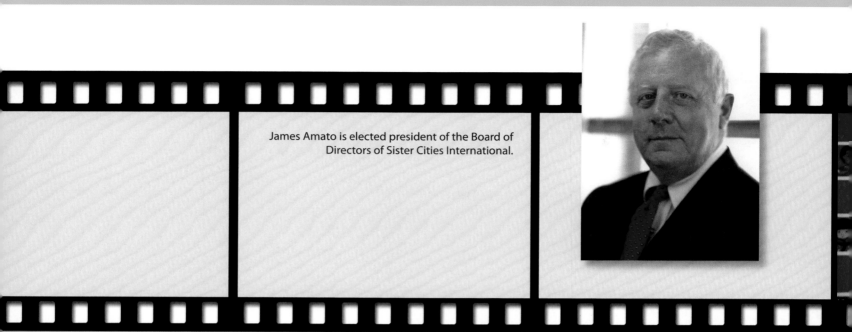

James Amato is elected president of the Board of Directors of Sister Cities International.

A Reel International Experience

Sarasota, Florida – Tel Mond, Israel - Perpignan, France - Vladimir, Russian Federation - Hamilton, Canada - Santo Domingo, Dominican Republic

Internationally, Sarasota, Florida, is known as a small town with great city amenities, but do teens share this perception? A resounding "yes" came in July 1998 when a Sister Cities Video Bootcamp arranged through Sarasota High School surpassed all expectations. Initially planned to encourage youth in Tel Mond, Israel to enter the field of cable communications, the camp extended to 20 participants from Tel Mond, Israel; Perpignan, France; Vladimir, Russia; Hamilton, Ontario, Canada; and Santo Domingo, Dominican Republic. Four area Sarasota High Schools joined together to produce a first class video showing how youngsters from other continents perceive Sarasota. The video showcased Sarasota to thousands of foreign viewers through media release in the community's five sister cities.

With the help of the Rotary Club of Sarasota Bay, businesses, private individuals, Sarasota Sister Cities, and the City of Sarasota; Sarasota High School was able to fund this intensive, hands-on introduction to video production and broadcast journalism. Curriculum for the intensive course included television reporting, writing, recording, and editing. Students met civic, educational, and business leaders and members of Sarasota's art community. They attended athletic events, the International Grand Prix, cultural presentations, and attractions while they produced a news video about Sarasota. More than 25 volunteers, including the assistant video director and six host families, worked together to plan the program, assist in the studio, and coordinate logistics, activities, and video shoots.

The course engendered close, new friendships and cultural interaction. Evaluations from students, host families, and those involved in the planning and implementation were glowingly positive. Many participants even suggested replicating this successful event in other sister cities. Two years later, Hamilton, Ontario (Canada) held a similar program with its own sister cities.

"Children of the Global Village," by Ruxandra Isai, La Mirada, California

SISTER CITIES INTERNATIONAL

1998
Young Artists Competition
Entry Form

Impressions of Unity
in a Global Neighborhood

Young Artists Program Winners 1998

1st - Buo-bao Huang – Taipei, Taiwan, China
2nd - Anna Slater – Kent, Washington
3rd - Cheryl Skelton – Suffolk, Virginia
4th - Christopher Neal – Philadelphia, Pennsylvania
5th - Ruxandra Isai – La Mirada, California
6th - Sandra Parrinello – Florence, Italy
7th - Carolyn Sun – Houston, Texas
8th - Katrinn-Mynam Laux-Franck – Schorndorf, Germany
9th - Marcella Gillenwater – Pocatello, Idaho
10th - Hikari Tachibana – Mercer Island, Washington
Honorable Mention- Cherline Victor – Lakeland, Florida
Honorable Mention - David Bush – St. Louis, Missouri

"Fragile Worlds" by Marcella Gillenwater, Pocatello, Idaho

"Unity" by Cheryl Skelton, Suffolk, Virginia

"Unity of Race" by Anna Slater, Kent, Washington

171

1999

"The men and women participating actively in the sister city program do more than talk about world understanding, they are contributing their ideas, resources and brotherhood to improve international understanding on a planet that grows smaller with each count-down."

- Edward R. Murrow

A Blossoming Friendship: 1999 Rose Garden Dedication
Pasadena, California and Xicheng District, China

Sharing art and culture have been part of Pasadena's sister city relationship with the Xicheng District in Beijing since it began in 1999. In 2004, Pasadena City held a naming ceremony for its Rose Garden to commemorate the fifth anniversary of their relationship. Cultural performances were an important part of the event. Middle school and high school students have corresponded with their sister city counterparts since 1998 and Xicheng sent hundreds of books on Chinese art, history, literature, cooking, medicine and culture to libraries in Pasadena.

Strings of Peace
Vandalia, Ohio and Prestwick, Scotland, United Kingdom

Wallace Galbraith, director of the Ayrshire Fiddle Orchestra from Scotland takes a gracious bow. The orchestra visited sister city Vandalia, Ohio in 1999 to play traditional Scots fiddle music, light classical works, and popular theme music. Two special instruments traveled with the group - the "Burns Fiddle" which is usually displayed at Culzean Castle, and the "Vandalia Violin" presented to the orchestra during its 1995 visit to Vandalia.

Sister Cities International®

Outstanding exchanges . . . innovative programming . . . citizen involvement . . . these are but a few of the ingredients that make up an excellent sister cities program. In an effort to honor and recognize both citizens and communities alike, Sister Cities International announces its . . .

1999
Annual Awards Program

D.C. – Dakar members and friends gather to honor H.E. Mary M. Kanya, Ambassador of Swaziland, and H.E. Makate Sheila Sisulu, Ambassador of South Africa at the Female African Ambassadors luncheon at Fort McNeir in 1999.

Annual Awards 1999

Best Overall Program
Over 300,000: Seattle, Washington
100,000-300,000: Lexington, Kentucky
Under 100,000: La Crosse, Wisconsin

Special Achievement Awards

Arts & Culture:
Montgomery, Ohio

Assistance & Relief:
Boyertown, Pennsylvania

Economic Development:
Lexington, Kentucky

Education:
San Antonio, Texas

Environment:
*no winner selected

Health & Public Safety:
Jacksonville, Florida

Municipal Cooperation:
Virginia Beach, Virginia
Cincinnati, Ohio

Technology & Communication:
Centerville, Ohio

Best First Year Affiliation
*no winner selected

Volunteer of the Year
Over 300,000: Tom McDonald of Portland, Oregon
100,000-300,000: Joan M. Hensler of Rochester, New York
Under 100,000: Sandra J. McCormick of La Crosse, Wisconsin

Collaboration Award
Over 300,000: Anchorage, Alabama
100,000-300,000: Louisville, Kentucky
Under 100,000: Oak Ridge, Tennessee

Best Youth Program:
Over 300,000: Indianapolis, Indiana
Under 100,000: Sarasota, Florida

NOD/AETNA Disability Award
Phoenix, Arizona
Corvallis, Oregon

President's Award
Henry M. Morozumi of Cincinnati, Ohio

Best Overall Web Site
Oak Ridge, Tennessee

Humanitarian Aid Sends a Warm Message of Friendship to a Sister City
Washington, D.C. and Dakar, Senegal

Over the past 25 years, the Washington, D.C. - Dakar, Senegal, sister city link has worked to improve lives. In 1987 a container and six crates of medical equipment, instruments, and literature were sent to Dakar. Donated by a local physician, the shipment was transported by the U.S. Navy, free of charge. Doctors and nurses from the National Institutes of Health traveled to Senegal in 1996 as part of Project Senegal to conduct health education. They worked in five cities and villages for ten days, achieving a major goal envisioned only a year earlier during the U.S. Africa Sister Cities Conference. The year 2000 brought a joint initiative with Africare to coordinate efforts to alleviate the impact of HIV-AIDS and provide health information for Ker Yaakaaru Jigeen Ni (House of Hope for Girls), a shelter for young women. In 2005 a delegation visited Dakar to discuss training for hospice and palliative care volunteers, especially for HIV-AIDS cases. The group toured health care units and pledged assistance in supplies for a maternity ward and seeds for a hospital garden which supplements to patient diets, and wheelchairs for the disabled. The warm message of friendship sent by Washington, D.C. to its sister city Dakar has improved daily life for many.

Board of Directors 1999-2000

President - James Amato
President-Elect - Charles Stokke
Chairman of the Board - Rodger Randle
Vice President - Jim Dailey
Vice President - Glenn Gray
Vice President - Nancy Huppert
Vice President - Mary Palko
Vice President - Thelma Press
Vice President - Brian Smith
Secretary - Paula West
Treasurer - Sandra McCormick

Youth Member to the Board - Nick Kissel
President of the Ambassador's Association - Janet Downey
State Coordinator Liaison - Kay Sargent

Jerry Abramson
Henry Cole
Nancy Eidam
Dr. Stelle Feuers
John Henry Fullen
Joshua Lader

David Lisk
Elena Lu
Charles Nelson
Richard Neuheisel
Dr. David Perez-Ginart
Dr. Thomas Ten Hoeve

Carmen Perkins, of Sydney, Australia, during the Parade of Nations in Little Rock in July 1999.

Enthusiastic delegates line up for the Parade of Nations behind the sign for the United Kingdom of Great Britain and Northern Ireland.

Young Artists Program Winners 1999

1st - Michele Lanan-Longmont, California
2nd - Shogo Shibata - Highland, California
3rd - Sarah Martin - St Charles, Montana
4th - Johannah Reimer - Fairfield, Iowa
5th - Beth Gramms - New Smyrna Beach, Florida
6th - Wang Peng - Kent, Washington
7th - Mary Clinkenbeard - Stillwater, Oklahoma
8th - Friederike Thaimm – Regensburg, Germany
(sister city to Tempe, Arizona)
9th - Courtney Clark - Ephrata, Pennsylvania

Samples of the outstanding work of the 2000 Young Artists Program winners.

2000

The Honorable Charles Stokke is elected president of the Board of Directors for Sister Cities International.

Annual Awards 2000

Best Overall Program
Over 300,000: Phoenix, Arizona
100,000-300,000: Lexington, Kentucky
Under 100,000: Freemont County, Colorado

Special Achievement Awards

Arts & Culture:
Miami Beach, Florida

Assistance & Relief:
Corvallis, Oregon

Economic Development:
Columbus, Ohio

Education:
Tempe, Arizona

Health & Public Safety:
La Crosse, Wisconsin
Riverside, California

Municipal Cooperation:
San Antonio, Texas

Technology & Communication:
Jacksonville, Florida

Best First Year Affiliation
Dothan, Alabama – sister city to Alajuela, Costa Rica

Volunteer of the Year
Mary Palko of Fort Worth, Texas

NOD/AETNA Disability Award
Phoenix, Arizona
Austin, Texas

Collaboration Award
Over 300,000: Cincinnati, Ohio
100,000-300,000: Louisville, Kentucky
Under 100,000 – Aspen, Colorado

Best Youth Program
Brighton, Colorado

President's Award
Pearl Lung Fu of Roanoke Valley, Virginia

Board of Directors 2000-2001

President - Charles Stokke
President-Elect - Glenn Gray
Vice President - Mary Palko
Vice President - Thelma Press
Vice President - John Henry Fullen
Vice President - Jim Dailey
Vice President - Brian Smith
Vice President - Nancy Huppert
Secretary - Paula West
Treasurer - Sandra McCormick

Youth Member to the Board - Nick Kissel
President of the Ambassador's Association -
 Janet Downey
State Coordinator Liaison - Hampton Rothwell

Hilde Berg
Jo Anna Edgerton
Nancy Eidam
Stelle Feuers
Ann Galloway
Jose Luis Garcia

Josh Lader
David Lisk
Ambassador Charles Nelson
Richard Neuheisel
Mary Palko
Gene Perez
Luis Quintana
Brian Smith
Tom Ten Hoeve

Wheelchair Basketball Exchange
Phoenix, Arizona – Hermosillo, Mexico

The Wheelchair Basketball Exchange and Disabilities Program in February 2000 brought a delegation from Hermosillo, Mexico to sister city Phoenix, Arizona. Events included: seminars for the delegation's rehabilitation doctors and therapists, discussions between architects and experts on disability issues, a tour of a ballpark highlighting accessibility features, and the donation of a new power wheelchair for a child in Hermosillo.

Tip off for the Hermosillo and Phoenix wheelchair basketball teams.

Tango Exchange: Dance Builds Friendship
Jacksonville, Florida – Bahia Blanca, Argentina

The Tango Exchange from Bahia Blanca, Argentina is an annual event that many Jacksonville residents look forward to. It began in 1995 during the second Sister Cities Week, when the Bahia Blanca delegation brought entertainers Sergio and Adriana Katz with them to perform during the celebration. They were so well received, that the Jacksonville Parks & Recreation Department sponsored their participation in the festival with grants for two years. After their first trip to Florida, Sergio and Adriana began teaching weekly classes in Bahia Blanca's City Hall for the Public. Their classes were so successful that they continued for a decade, teaching thousands of people to dance. In 2000, they brought the First Tango Ballet of Bahia Blanca to perform in Jacksonville, and each year, more requests pour in for their performances. They included a student who is blind in the troupe one year, and he inspired many disabled children in Jacksonville with his performance. In 2005 they were invited to perform at Walt Disney World's EPCOT Center.

"You have been working for years to multiply and strengthen the ties of understanding and friendship between two nations, who, by virtue of fate, have been playing the key role in the development of world politics. May your movement's goal of bringing the two countries' cities closer together find triumph."

- Mikhail S. Gorbachev

The Prince and I

As I practiced my curtsy with the other ladies, I wondered what I had gotten myself into by preparing to meet Prince Andrew, the Prince of Edinburgh. I was very nervous and it seemed to take forever for his tour of the new council building to finish so he could meet the guests. When he finally entered, Castlereagh Councilors Peter and Iris Robinson introduced me as their sister city exchange student from Kent, Washington. His Royal Highness asked me if I was enjoying Northern Ireland, what college I was attending, and what I thought was the biggest difference between the two places. I can't recall what my answers were because I was so astonished by how charming and handsome he was. He had a wonderful sense of humor and even pulled one over on the Castlereagh mayor. Prince Andrew was supposed to pull on a cord to unveil the dedication plaque for the new building. It even had a sign saying "pull," which he pointed out for everyone. But when the time came to pull the cord, it appeared to be stuck. Everyone's face fell until Prince Andrew began to laugh. The cord was not stuck, he thought it would be funny to pretend it was broken. After laughter filled the room, it was sadly time to say goodbye. As the Prince left, he paused to say hello to a group of schoolchildren outside. I was impressed by his sincerity and personal nature.
– Youth ambassador Kelly Meader, Kent-Castlereagh, Northern Ireland (United Kingdom)
Sister City Committee, Kent, Washington

Police and fire teams from Votkinsk, Russian Federation, visit their sister city, West Jordan, Utah.

Families in Voronezh, Russian Federation, receive medical supplies from their sister city, Charlotte, North Carolina.

Municipal Community Problem-Solving Grant Program

The Municipal and Community Problem-Solving Program provided partial funding and program development aid to U.S. cities and their partners in the Newly Independent States. The project began in 1997 and was funded by the Bureau of Educational and Cultural Affairs at the U.S. Department of State and administered by Sister Cities International.

During the first phase of the grant, the U.S. Department of State contributed $342,500 and local communities added an additional $500,000 in matching funds and in-kind donations. The first phase of the grant focused on critical issues for communities in the Newly Independent States after the breakup of the Union of Soviet Socialist Republics.

The program was so successful that a second phase began in 2000. It focused on municipal administration, business and economic development, social services, health care, community law enforcement, women's non-governmental organization development, and assistance for people with disabilities.

The "Secret City Partnerships" linked nuclear research and weapons production centers in the Russian Federation with similar communities in the United States. The project was designed to help previously-closed Russian communities transition to a democratic city government, enhance community development and establish a market economy.

Participating Communities – Municipal Community Problem-Solving Grant Program

Ukraine
"Meeting Challenges, Creating Opportunities [for people and children with disabilities]"
Corvallis, Oregon – Uzhgorod, Ukraine

"Political Campaign Management Institute [for women in Ukraine]"
Davis, California – Uman, Ukraine

"Young Women's Leadership Development"
Santa Rosa, California – Cherkasy, Ukraine

Russian Federation
"Evaluation of the Effects of Contamination on Public Health"
Albany, New York – Tula, Russian Federation

"Development of the Voronezh Rehabilitation and Training Center for People with Disabilities"
Charlotte, North Carolina – Voronezh, Russian Federation

"Tourism Development in Vladivostok"
Juneau, Alaska – Vladivostok, Russian Federation

"Solid Waste Management and Recycling Development"
Portland, Oregon – Khabarovsk, Russian Federation

"Partnership for Children"
Rochester, New York – Novgorod, Russian Federation

"Secret City" Partnerships
"Cooperation in Emergency Disaster Situations"
Appleton/Fox Cities, Wisconsin – Kurgan/Scshuchie, Russian Federation

"Establishment of a Rotary Club"
Livermore, California – Snezhinsk, Russian Federation

"Business & Economic Development"
Los Alamos, New Mexico – Sarov, Russian Federation

"Business & Economic Development"
Oak Ridge, Tennessee – Obninsk, Russian Federation

"Community Police and EMS Exchange and Training"
West Jordan, Utah – Votkinsk, Russian Federation

"Business & Economic Development"
Blount County/Maryville/Alcoa, Tennessee – Zheleznogorsk, Russian Federation

SISTER CITIES INTERNATIONAL ANNUAL CONFERENCE
JUNE 28-JULY 1, DENVER, COLORADO
THEME: A MILE HIGH FOR PEACE

Former Hostage and 11-Year-Old Genius Speak at Annual Conference in Denver
Two widely-publicized personalities, with similar interests in international peace and diplomacy, but with vast differences in their ages, were the keynote speakers for the Sister Cities International Annual Conference held in Denver, Colorado. The speakers were Dr. Thomas Sutherland, who was held hostage by terrorists in Lebanon for six years, and 11-year-old Gregory R. Smith, who recently completed his first year of college, and who has already established himself as a strong advocate of peace through quality education and the political participation of young people.

SISTER CITIES INTERNATIONAL

2000 Annual Conference
Denver, Colorado

"Uncles and Aunties" Program Brings Hope to Russian Orphans
Duluth, Minnesota – Petrozavodsk, Russia

Mayor Gary Doty helps his 11-year-old "niece" Nadia, try on a new pair of shoes. When the Duluth mayor first met Nadia while on a sister city visit to Petrozavodsk, Russia, she asked him to help the orphanage care for its many unwanted children who had little hope of ever being adopted. Doty and his wife Marcia went home to Minnesota and with the help of the Duluth Sister Cities Commission, they founded the "Aunties and Uncles" program to provide financial support to orphans ages 5-17 living in the four orphanages in Petrozavodsk. More than 150 people signed up right away and contributed $5 a month or $60 a year to help the children. "True understanding between people and nations is not something that can be brokered by officials or legislated by politicians. It begins with individual involvement," said Mayor Doty.

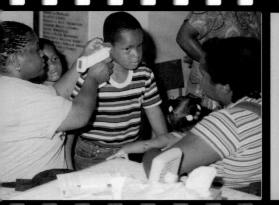

Healthcare That Builds Peace
Atlanta, Georgia – Montego Bay, Jamaica

Health professionals from Atlanta, Georgia visit Montego Bay, Jamaica in 2000 to conduct one of their twice-a-year healthcare clinics for under-privileged people in their sister city. It was their seventh annual healthcare mission and involved 45 nurses and doctors from throughout the United States. "They exemplify the epitome of volunteerism and find true reward in 'giving back' to their adopted community," said organizers when they applied for an Annual Award in 2000. Begun in 1972, the sister city relationship between Atlanta and Montego Bay is the second-oldest among Atlanta's 19 sister city relationships.

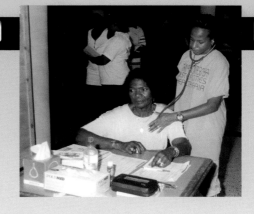

World peace can only be achieved when ideas and comprehension between people have more value than guns; when no human being considers himself owner of the absolute truth and exchanges his views with others; when borders between nations are considered permeable membranes instead of barrier walls. I am very pleased that these are shared values between Argentina's men and women and the Sister Cities International program."

- President Carlos Saul Menem, the Argentine Republic

The Stage is Set: Act 2000
'Peace Begins at Home'
2000

Young Artists Program Winners 2000

1st - Cheng Zhang, Beihai, China
(sister city to Tulsa, Okalahoma)

2nd - Zach Wagner – Red Wing, Minnesota

3rd - Sachiyo Kameda – Osaka, Japan
(sister city to Bellevue, Washington)

4th - Elizabeth Godwin – Boynton Beach, Florida
5th - Adriane McGillis – Lexington, Kentucky

6th - Don Wen – Tianjin, China
(sister city to Philadelphia, Pennsylvania)

7th - Saori Yasuhiko, Utsunomiya, Japan
(sister city to Tulsa, Okalahoma)

8th - Chang Hey – Incheon, Republic of Korea
(sister city to Anchorage, Alaska)

9th - Jennifer Pan – Sugarland, Texas

10th- Julia Yerofeeva – Nizhni Novgorod, Russia
(sister city to Philadelphia, Pennsylvania)

Honorable Mention - Michael Malone – Tyler, Texas

Honorable Mention - Zhang Jing Y'an – Zhenjiang, China
(sister city to Tempe, Arizona)

179

Supporting Sister City Relationships With Africa
Leonard Robinson, Jr. and Edna Mosley at the 9th Annual U.S. Africa Sister Cities Conference in Denver, Colorado.

"The past 36 years of involvement with Sister Cities International has afforded me the unique privilege and honor of working with and meeting hundreds of citizen diplomats. They have been responsible for the success of this 'grassroots' people-to-people city-to-city movement."

- Thelma Press, Vice President,
Board of Directors, Sister Cities International, 1996

President Clinton Donates Prize Money to Arlington – Aachen Sister Cities Program

Proclaiming the transatlantic alliance is vital to peace and stability between the United States and Europe, U.S. President Bill Clinton accepted the city of Aachen, Germany's prestigious Charlemagne Prize. The President commended Arlington, Virginia for fostering international understanding through its sister city relationship with Aachen, and presented his prize money to the Arlington-Aachen sister cities program. John McCracken, president of the Arlington program and Jim Rowland, chair of the Aachen committee, accepted the donation and personal congratulations from the President. At the time, Clinton became the first U.S. President and only the third American to receive the Charlemagne Prize. Arlington and Aachen have been sister cities since 1992.

President Clinton accepts the prestigious Charlemagne Prize.

Building New Bridges of Understanding
Portsmouth, New Hampshire - Severodvinsk, Russian Federation

Personal visits can help build understanding. "Until I visited Portsmouth, I did not fully understand the sincere desires of our American friends and colleagues to work together on a variety of projects crucial to both of us," said Alexander Beliaev, Mayor of Severodvinsk. The Portsmouth/Severodvinsk Connection is committed to enhancing relations and mutual understanding between the two communities through cooperative exchanges of people and ideas in the areas of education, social services, shipyard redevelopment, business, and culture. Portsmouth joined Sister Cities International in 2006 and we look forward to hearing more about their blossoming friendship.

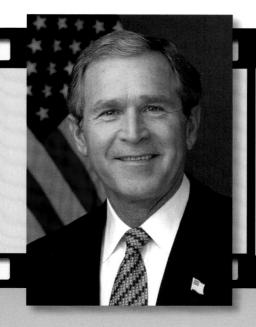

"For 45 years, Sister Cities International has been credited with establishing and strengthening partnerships between communities in the United States and similar communities internationally. Your organization fosters recognition that trust, cooperation, and peace between nations are built on understanding, and that real understanding comes from communication. I commend you for promoting the development of relationships among the leaders and citizens of different countries and cultures.

I also applaud the thousands of volunteers affiliated with your organization for their efforts on behalf of those in need. From humanitarian assistance to community development, you help give hope and comfort to countless individuals and communities throughout the world. I encourage Sister Cities International in its efforts to unite communities, build understanding, and promote peace across national and cultural barriers."

George W. Bush
July 17, 2001

Dick Oakland's devotion to the sister city movement inspired the Dick Oakland Award, which is given annually to a State Coordinator.

Tom Gittins talks to C-SPAN about the break-up of the Soviet Union and its impact on citizen diplomacy

Executive Director Carole Green and Drew Horgan, the Secretary-General of the International Union of Local Authorities, check out a publication from the National League of Cities.

Juanita Crabb helped Sister Cities International secure many grants.

Tim Honey worked in partnership with the Board of Directors to steer Sister Cities International through a time of transition and toward a promising future.

Executive Staff Leadership for the Sister City Movement

Sister Cities International was originally part of the National League of Cities from 1957-1967 and was known as the Town Affiliation Association of the United States, Inc. (TAA). At that time, the National League of Cities was known as the American Municipal Association, and the Association provided support to the growing sister city movement by donating office space and staff time. In 1967, after the number of town affiliations continued to climb, the TAA became an independent non-profit organization.

Alan Beals, John Slayton
Director of Town Affiliations, American Municipal Association
1957 - 1960

Richard Oakland
Director of Town Affiliations, American Municipal Association
1960 – 1967

Richard Oakland
Director of Membership Services, Town Affiliation Association of the U.S., Inc.
1967 – 1971

Tom Gittins
Executive Vice President, Town Affiliation Association of the U.S., Inc.
(the organization became known as Sister Cities International in 1974)
1971 – 1993

Carole Green
Executive Director, Sister Cities International
1993 - 1994

Juanita Crabb
Executive Director, Sister Cities International
1994 – 1999

Ned Benner
Acting Executive Director, Sister Cities International
March 1999 - July 2000

Tim Honey
Executive Director, Sister Cities International
2000 – Present

"Never doubt that a small group of thoughtful committed citizens can change the world. Indeed, it's the only thing that ever has."
– Margaret Mead

2001

Global Envoy Mary Palko, Fort Worth, Texas with Dick Neuheisel.

Mary Jean Eisenhower

The Global Envoy Program: Partners Spreading the Sister City Mission

The Global Envoy Program started in 2001 as a way to support having a Sister Cities International presence at global events. The envoys are asked to represent Sister Cities International at conferences, embassies, meetings and other events where a presence is important. They help spread the sister cities mission at functions the Sister Cities International staff are unable to attend. Global Envoy Sharon Receveur described her position as "…a good deal for Sister Cities International because the Global Envoys are volunteers who pay their own way when working on behalf of the sister city movement, and they also make significant monetary contributions to Sister Cities International." Sister city Global Envoys have attended meetings and conferences around the world and are relied on to inform municipal officials, conference delegates and others about the value of citizen diplomacy and the important inroads the sister cities movement is making in fostering international cooperation.

Global Envoy Sharon Receveur, Louisville, Kentucky (left) with Sherman Banks and Mary Jean Eisenhower in 2004.

Global Envoy Nancy Huppert, Rochester, New York (right).

Getting Past the "Hollywood" Mindset
Coventry, Rhode Island – Coventry, England

Norma Smith, director of "The Coventry Friendship Link", said the sister city relationship and exchanges it has facilitated have opened doors and minds to hundreds of people internationally. "[The exchange] gives everyone a better understanding of what each other is like," Smith said. "It allows for a better understanding of culture. Before meeting us our English friends saw only the Hollywood version of Americans and we too had preconceived notions of them. This is not only a way for individuals to meet internationally, locally people meet as well. It's opened up a whole new world to those who participate."

Executive Director Tim Honey, Mary Jean Eisenhower, President and Mrs.Chuck Stokke.

Memories of President Eisenhower

By Mary Jean Eisenhower, his granddaughter and CEO of People to People International

As one who loved him dearly, I can tell you my grandfather was not a glory seeker, he would be the first to say that his name isn't what makes the desire for peace worth pursuing – it is the unconditional love that he knew existed between global citizens, with no strings attached. It is the understanding, acceptance and chance at worldwide serenity that he knew could prevail; from the charter members of the President's People-to-People Program, to the youth of today, many of whom barely know his name.

Ike sleeps better knowing that global outreach in all corners of the earth is alive, well and making a difference. I can't help but think in some way that he does know that his passionately crafted organization is here and fervently working to restore the shield of peace, and dreams of man, to place the passage of bigotry, violence and war to the history books for good, and to close the cover.

He sleeps better knowing that we carry on the dream to live together, not as the same but as individual partners building global harmony in our communities, our states, our country, our planet. And, through face-to-face contact, we now celebrate the differences that used to frighten us.

Partnerships Breed Equality

"…the second key word about Sister Cities: partnership. The simplest way Sister Cities creates partnerships between two different municipalities, two different towns, two different counsels, one, the United States, the other elsewhere in the world and it brings those two together to do things together. That in itself is a partnership. And it also brings them together as equals because one day one town is the host, the next they are the guest, so that they have an equality in the relationship and they exchange one to the other. Of course, not everything is exactly the same and social and economic standing is not always the same, but they are doing things together, where the first one is the host, the other is the guest, and in that relationship there is no patronization. There is an equal respect for people. Inevitably, working together changes the way in which people see each other, and it breeds friendship, tolerance and understanding. That in itself is going to change the way in which people look at each other and change the way in which the cultures relate to each other."

— The Honorable David Trimble, former First Minister of Northern Ireland

Lou Wozar Dedication by Ethelda Singer

Ethelda Singer gave a heartwarming tribute to Lou Wozar at the Annual Awards Ceremony, saying, "Today I am here to tell you about a very special friend, Louis Wozar. And this is how I remember Lou …He was always a perfect gentleman. He was kind and caring. He listened attentively, and then acted in the best interests to further the growth and development of Sister Cities International. Lou Wozar was from Dayton, Ohio. He was the third president of Sister Cities International, elected in 1972 at the Annual Conference in Seattle, Washington…While Lou was president and then chairman of the board, he traveled to 78 countries. I, as the Western Regional vice president, had an opportunity to travel many times with him, and other executives of the board, to countries where we met with our counterparts to help, again, further the growth of sister cities and continue to affiliate sister cities throughout the world. They particularly loved Lou in China, because of his gentleness and dignity. And our young guides affectionately called him, "Mr. Wou-zar"… So to all of you, "Just remember this, the fundamental things apply, as time goes by …" for Sister Cities International, and we always remember Lou."

Annual Awards 2001

Best Overall Program
Over 300,000: Chicago, Illinois
100,000-300,000: Rochester, New York
50,000-100,000: Corvallis, Oregon
Under 50,000: Oak Ridge, Tennessee

Innovation
Arts & Culture:
Jacksonville, Florida

Economic Development:
Phoenix, Arizona

Education:
Tulsa, Oklahoma

Environment:
New Britain, Connecticut

Healthcare:
Atlanta, Georgia

Humanitarian Assistance:
Portland, Oregon

Municipal Cooperation:
Fredericksburg, Virginia

Public Safety:
San Clemente, California

Technology & Communication:
Cincinnati, Ohio

Youth:
Walker, Michigan

Volunteer of the Year
Richard and Barbara Bartholomew of Binghamton, New York
Larry Jones of Stillwater, Oklahoma
Betty Stewart of Merced, California

NOD/AETNA Disability Award
Fort Lauderdale, Florida
Phoenix, Arizona

President's Award
Martha and Bob Atherton

Welcoming a New Year
Roanoke, Virginia celebrates New Year's with a lot of fun. Roanoke is a sister city to Lijiang, China.

Health Festival Builds Friendships Among Physicians, Benefits Health Care for All
San Antonio, Texas – Kumamoto, Japan

Celebration of the annual Health Festival between the Bexar County Medical Association and the Kumamoto City Medical Association in October 2001. From the right: Dr. Toyota, Dr. Ortega, and Mr. Goto, Deputy Mayor of Kumamoto City.

The "Crazy Quilt" made by Palatine, Illinois for Fontenay-le-Comte, France.

"We in Australia are keenly aware of the importance of sister city relationships in bringing countries closer together through understanding and friendship. I wish Sister Cities International continuing success in the future."

— Prime Minister J.L. Hawke,
the Commonwealth of Australia

Exporting the Arts, Importing Culture
Lynchburg, Virginia – Rueil-Malmaison, France

Over the past decade the Lynchburg Sister City Program has fostered the development of international arts and cultural exchanges. Organizers have reaped the fruits of kinship and cross-cultural understanding through these programs. Among the city's international "exports" are young musicians in the Lynchburg City Schools String Orchestra, dancers from the Virginia School of the Arts, singers in the Jefferson Choral Society, as well as a number of local painters. "Imports" have included visual artists from France and culinary artists from France and Italy.

From the beginning, the cultural arts were identified as an area of mutual interest between Lynchburg and its sister city Rueil-Malmaison, France. On July 4, 1996, for the proclamation ceremony twinning the two cities, the Lynchburg City Schools String Orchestra, a hundred young musicians strong, traveled to Rueil to entertain in the city's open-air amphitheater, Le Conservatoire National de Région. This was a "first-time" trip for all the young musicians and for many of their parents and chaperones. The young people performed in concert as the audience waved small American flags provided by Rueil's mayor for the occasion. The stirring program included both French and American selections.

At the same time, nationally known Lynchburg watercolorist Annie Adams Robertson Massie and Lynchburg Mayor James Whitaker, presented Massie's painting "Easter Parade on Monument Avenue" to Mayor Jacques Baumel as Lynchburg's official gift to its first sister city. A delegation came from Rueil-Malmaison to Lynchburg in September 1996 to repeat the proclamation ceremony, which was held at Thomas Jefferson's summer home, Poplar Forest.

The mutual interest in arts and culture reached far beyond music and paintings to include the savory experiences of cross-cultural culinary exchange. Lynchburg delighted in hosting a succession of chefs and culinary experts. In 1997, Chef Chantel Merle of Entre Deux Mers Restaurant in Rueil-Malmaison prepared dinner in Lynchburg for 150 guests, and it proved to be a successful fundraiser. In 1999, Chef Melissa Close of Palladio Restaurant in Barboursville, Virginia, prepared a five-course dinner in Lynchburg for 165 guests. This "Palladio Cabaret" was a salute to Lynchburg's second sister city candidate: Vicenza, Italy. Florentine singer Francesco Ronchetti headlined the entertainment and the event raised funds for the program.

Frank Britt, member of Sister City of Lynchburg and Board Member for Sister Cities International, divulged, "We wanted to dovetail cultural and individual business exchanges and integrate them with Lynchburg's Sister City fundraising efforts. We invited restaurant owner/chef of Entre Deux Mers (Between Two Seas), Chantal Merle and her son Cedric to work with the chef at our country club in preparing a sit-down French dinner for 150 guests."

"The event was such a success that we had full media coverage and a sold-out crowd. People are still talking about the fundraising event!" said Britt. "Our chef in Lynchburg was then invited to Rueil-Malmaison to learn more about the preparation of French cuisine. This was a truly worthwhile exchange that can be done on an annual basis with many twinned communities."

Lynchburg successfully "exported" artists and cultural understanding, while also kindly "importing" and welcoming the artists from their sister cities abroad. Claudie Rouzevel, member of the city council with responsibility for Sister City Programs for Rueil-Malmaison, France, summed it up best when she said, "Rueil-Malmaison has 16 sister cities, but there are more activities with Lynchburg than any of the others, thanks to this wonderful Virginia community's enthusiasm for the arts."

SISTER CITIES INTERNATIONAL *News*

December 2001

Sister cities worldwide respond with heart and hope following U.S. tragedies

The sister cities network and their partner communities have responded and coped with the September 11 attacks in different and extraordinary ways, organizing blood drives, donating funds and posting letters of support to aid the healing process. Though all of our lives have been changed following September 11, one thing has remained constant both here and abroad: the mission and heart of sister city programs, which has never been more important.

Indeed, all of our lives have been affected by this tragedy—whether through the unfortunate loss of loved ones or the disappointment of canceled trips and postponed events. Yet despite the sadness and uncertainty, sister city communities worldwide have served as remarkable examples of love, friendship and respect, and remained determined to carry our mission

throughout the world. Sister Cities International (SCI) is proud to share just a few of these stories.

Tsuruoka, Japan, the sister city of **New Brunswick, New Jersey**, canceled a planned trip to visit New Brunswick, opting instead to raise money for the victims of September 11. According to Jane L. Tublin, state coordinator for New Jersey, the president of Tsuruoka City Council and other officials have rescheduled their trip for January 2002, at which time they will present their funds to the mayor, who will then forward the donations to various September 11 charities.

continued on page 4

Children in Kurgan School No. 27, drew pictures to illustrate friendship between the American and Russian people. Kurgan, Russia, is a sister city of Appleton/Fox Cities, Wisconsin.

New York finds support in sister cities abroad
See page 5

Friendship Through Education to link students worldwide

SCI is proud to announce its involvement in the Friendship Through Education (FTE) consortium, a new initiative launched by President Bush October 25, 2001, to help American schoolchildren expand their links with students in Islamic countries through letters, e-mails, art and other collaborative classroom projects.

SCI Executive Director Tim Honey and nine other members of the new

consortium joined the President at Thurgood Marshall Elementary School in Washington, D.C., to jumpstart the event.

The project commenced with the connection of elementary schools in Washington, D.C.; Arlington, Virginia; and New York City, New York—areas most directly affected by the September 11 attacks—to others in Bahrain, Pakistan and Egypt. The goal is to link an American school in every state with a school in a country with Islamic populations.

continued on page 5

President Bush (right) launched the Friendship Through Education project at Thurgood Marshall Elementary School in Washington, D.C.

On September 11, 2001, the world reeled in horror after terrorist attacks hit New York City and Washington, D.C. and took more than two thousand lives. With offices only three blocks from the White House, Sister Cities International shut down quickly and evacuated its staff. When the staff returned later that week, they found messages from around the globe expressing sympathy and outrage. And many sister city programs around the world received similar expressions of condolence.

In a twist of irony, the September newsletter was on its way to members carrying a cover photo of Mary Jean Eisenhower delivering an address at the 2001 conference honoring her grandfather, President Eisenhower, who first spelled out his vision of citizen diplomacy and inspired the birth of the people-to-people movement in a speech on September 11, 1956.

New York City's bonds with its sister cities grew closer. The government of Tokyo donated $5 million to the City of New York and another $5 million to New York State, while Tokyo Metropolitan Assembly members donated an additional $50,000 to New York City. Sister city Jerusalem sent 100 pounds of chocolate for rescue workers and made plans to send a trauma intervention team to assist in recovery. The Mayor of Rome withdrew his city's bid for the 2012 Olympics and urged that New York City be awarded the honor instead. The sister city linkage with London grew stronger, with a special service at St. Thomas attended by Prime Minister Tony Blair for the 300 British citizens still missing after the attacks on the World Trade Center. The name of the UKinNY festival honoring their sister city relationship, an event that was in the works for more than three years, was changed to UKwithNY to demonstrate their solidarity.

Many sister city members and supporters around the globe re-dedicated themselves to the sister city movement, renewing their promise to build a world of peace based on understanding. The five-year initiative, "Sister Cities United for International Peace and Friendship" was launched in response to the September 11th attacks.

"Like most of you, we watched yesterday in stunned disbelief the footage from the terrible catastrophes that hit New York City and Washington. Who could have ever imagined the collapse of both towers of the World Trade Center? An entire nation came to a standstill. We at the Union of Local Authorities in Israel would like to express our deep grief over what has happened. Our hearts and thoughts go out to all those who have become victims of these horrific attacks, from family members and loved ones to witnesses. We applaud the selfless heroism of the numerous rescue workers and volunteers across the country. We sincerely hope that the American nation will soon recover from the immense shock this tragedy has left behind. Be assured of our full support and assistance. May God protect us all from hatred and fanaticism. With our heartfelt support,"

— Avi Rabinovitch, Deputy Director General,
Union of Local Authorities in Israel

"It is hard for us to find the right words about what happened in New York and Washington three days ago. The imagination frightens us, that this could be the beginning of a renewed spiral of violence worldwide…Dialogue and understanding, not terror and violence, have to take place because the solidarity of all people is stronger than bombs and acts of terrorism. We do not have to give up our active engagement together for a better understanding of the people and a peaceful world."

— Volker Wendorff, Youth Officer,
City of Hanover, Germany, sister city to Kansas City, Missouri

"Dear friends: We are all in shock about the attacks in New York City and Washington D.C. Tuesday morning, September 11, the darkest day in American history. The Chinese people strongly condemn these inhuman atrocities by terrorists. I am writing to let you know that we are standing with you and sharing your sorrows at this difficult time of the American people.…What we have been working on together for years is to wage peace. We are all committed to this mission, and will continue to pursue this mission as best as we can. Now, more than ever, we need to continue our work of waging peace. With deep sympathy and firm support to the American people."

— An-Wei, President, The Edgar & Helen Snow Center, Xi'an, China

"I believe that what we in the City of Tacoma are doing in conjunction with our friends from around the United States and the World involved in Sister Cities programs is doing is most important for the promotion of World Peace. This drive for World Peace and understanding is more important today and in the future than ever before. I urge all Citizens of the City of Tacoma to come and join our sister cities programs and volunteer to help us to promote the similarities we all have to share with one another instead of focusing on the differences. United we stand, divided we fall."

— Tony Anderson, Board of Directors, Sister Cities International

Youth Exchange Programs Cancelled After 9-11, Find New Life
Madison, Mississippi – Solleftea, Sweden

Student exchange programs between Madison, Mississippi and Solleftea, Sweden were put on hold after the terrorist attacks on the United States in 2001. But the arrival of a new Swedish-American Chamber of Commerce in Mississippi has reignited fervor for student exchange, and organizers hope to see students benefit from the friendly ties. The two communities last exchanged students in 2000, and are now planning a visit to Sweden and a hosting trip in 2006. The student exchange program will help support their growing economic development project, say organizers, because with more Swedish businesses exploring the idea of working in the United States, the student exchange will build more understanding. "If we're going to continue to bring in Swedish businesses and families, we need to address how to help them here so they won't be quite so isolated when they arrive," said teacher Beth Kellogg.

Sister City Delegation in New York on 9-11 Forges New Ties to the U.S. Amid Tragedy
New Paltz, New York – Osa, Japan

I was at LaGuardia Airport with nine members of our delegation from Osa, Japan. We had just finished our official visit to our sister city, New Paltz Village, New York. At 4:30 a.m. on September 11, 2001, we had gathered at the village hall and said good-bye to our "sisters and brothers" who woke up early to see us off without knowing what would happen in several hours. They told us to come back soon and we said we would like to come back very soon and were hoping to come back in a year or so.

Our flight was scheduled at 9:12 a.m. After some of the passengers had boarded the plane, they returned to the waiting area running, and so did the captains and the flight attendants. The announcement told us to evacuate. There were many people outside and we heard the sirens of police cars and ambulances. Someone told me planes had crashed into the World Trade Center. We had to get out of this chaotic airport. But, no taxis or regular buses were available, and our friends' vans were long gone. Finally, I heard a man in a Connecticut Limo uniform yelling "Any passengers to Rye?" I did not know where Rye is, but I thought getting out of here was the first priority, so I asked if he could drive us out.

The bus got out of the airport but soon was caught in stopped traffic on a freeway. We could see smoke rising from lower Manhattan. The driver kept the radio on, and horrible facts were continuously announced. I was afraid a war might have started and would prevent us from coming back to Japan for a while or forever. I do not know how many hours we were on the bus stopped on the freeway before it started again. We were sad, nervous, worried and at a loss about what to do, but there was certainly a unity among us on the bus.

We ended up in Greenwich, Connecticut. We decided to get off the bus at a large hotel, even though there was no vacancy, since it was already evening. We put our names on the hotel's waiting list, put our baggage in the hall, called New Paltz, ate at a restaurant, and waited for the rescue team. It was after nine when four vehicles from our home away from home arrived. Friends in need are friends indeed! It was around midnight when we arrived at the Village Hall and some of our New Paltz friends were waiting for us. We were very glad to see them again so soon! We felt really at home in New Paltz.

Every year on September 11, we get together and remember that day. In September 2006, as the fifth anniversary of the day, we are planning to come back to New Paltz to show our gratitude to our friends in our sister city.

By Kiyoshi Yamauchi, from Osa, Japan, sister city to New Paltz, New York

We Stand United
We hold candles to express our sorrow at the horrific loss suffered by so many on September 11, 2001 and our solidarity with our many friends in the United States.

"The world is in a time of historic transition. No longer does ideology polarize nations and alienate people. We will continue to look to organizations like Sister Cities for help in presenting America to the world now eager to share and learn from our experience. It is a momentous task we share."

— Dr. Joseph Duffey, Director, U.S. Information Agency

President George W. Bush Praises Sister City Program

We Will Not Forget
Every year on September 11th, we commemorate the day and remember the lives lost and our friendship with the United States.

Sister Cities International Joins Friendship Through Education Initiative
The Friendship Through Education consortium was a new initiative launched by President George W. Bush in October 2001 to help American school children expand linkages with students in Islamic countries through letters, email messages, art and other collaborative classroom projects. Tim Honey, executive director for Sister Cities International and nine other members of the consortium joined the President at Thurgood Marshall Elementary School in Washington, D.C. to launch the program. President Bush said, "I think the best way…to handle the attacks of September 11 is to fight fear with friendship; is to fight fear with hope; is to remind people all around the world we have much more in common than people might think; that we share basic values – the importance of family, and the importance of faith, and the importance of friendship."

A Farewell from Friends
We bid goodbye to our friends in New Paltz, New York, not knowing that we would soon bear witness to the September 11th terrorist attacks on the United States as we tried to return to Japan.

Young Artists Program Winners 2001

1st – David Doria - Corpus Christi, Texas
2nd – Xu Jun – Quzhou, China (sister city to Red Wing, Minnesota)
3rd – Morgan Ng – San Jose, California
4th – Julie Riddle – St. Peters, Missouri
5th – Michelle Kubat – La Mirada, California
6th – Zhang Chenc – Beihai, China (sister city to Tulsa, Oklahoma)
7th – Miyuki Fujii – Osaka, Japan (sister city to Bellevue, Washington)
8th – Anna Adamkieicz – Torun, Poland (sister city to Philadelphia, Pennsylvania)
9th – Aleksandar Zafirovskl – Skopje, Macedonia (sister city to Tempe, Arizona)
10th – Tinne Leysen – Kasterlee, Belgium - (sister city to Fountain Hills, Arizona)
11th – Natalie Crawford – Tuscaloosa, Alabama

Honorable Mention – Morgan Brotherton – Lexington, Kentucky
Honorable Mention – Ashley Lynn Fink – Fountain Hills, Arizona
Honorable Mention – Victor Flores – Phoenix, Arizona
Honorable Mention – Wierke Quader – Tulsa, Oklahoma
Honorable Mention – Ok-Bee Hyun – Incheon, Republic of Korea (sister city to Anchorage, Alaska)

Micro-Grants That Build Communities
The Senegalese grant recipients with Chairperson Barbara Green, Louise Teneyck,and an interpreter.

You Are My Sister: Senegalese Women in Action Project
Prince George's County, Maryland – Ziguinchor, Senegal

The Women in Action Project organized in 2001 by the Senegal Friendship Committee sponsored businesswomen in Ziguinchor, Senegal – and the project is empowering women to do more with their lives and improve communities. Envisioned by Barbara Davis, who originally began doing micro-loans with women in Sierra Leone, the project built on the family-focused nature of many women who invested profits in better education for their children and family improvements. They awarded grants to five applicants in 2001, and "you are my sister" was heard often during the presentation ceremony. They provided $500 grants to these small African woman-owned businesses. They sewed clothes, sold wares, or marketed cashews. After the grantees repaid their micro-loans, funds were re-deployed to other women to help them with their businesses. The project has continued annually and in 2005, 40 applicants requested grants. Many women receiving grants took new pride in their businesses and the investment made in them by their sisters in the United States. The committee hopes to help even more women in the future.

Signing Up for a Brighter Future
Barbara Davis presents the agreement to be signed by the Coordinator, Mrs. Diallo, for the grant recipients.

2002

Emergency Preparedness Brings Communities Together

As part of the "Sister Cities United for International Peace & Friendship" initiative, the U.S. – Islamic Sister Cities Emergency Preparedness Exchange Program was funded by the U.S. Department of State's Bureau of Educational and Cultural Affairs. This program linked U.S. communities with sister cities in predominantly Islamic communities in Europe and Asia to address the common need for emergency preparedness training and knowledge. The four sister city partnerships selected to participate in the program were Arvada, Colorado - Kyzylorda, Kazakhstan; Fort Worth, Texas - Bandung, Indonesia; Houston, Texas - Baku, Azerbaijan; and Tucson, Arizona - Almaty, Kazakhstan. Through general training sessions, each community worked to increase and improve the overall medical and emergency response infrastructure available in emergency situations. From 2002 to 2004, these exchanges focused on providing emergency medical training, developing an emergency response plan, encouraging intercultural dialogue among leaders, donating medical supplies, and training citizens to respond to emergencies. They also participated in a number of conferences to share their progress, challenges, and outcomes.

Wheelchairs for Peace: Bringing Mobility to Thousands World-Wide

In 2002, Sister Cities International and the Wheelchair Foundation embarked on an initiative to distribute wheelchairs to sister city communities throughout the world. Through the Wheelchairs for Peace program, the Wheelchair Foundation committed to match funds raised by sister city programs to deliver wheelchairs to children and adults living with disabilities. As of February 2006, 22 sister city communities raised $525,000, which was matched dollar-for-dollar by the Wheelchair Foundation. This enabled the delivery of wheelchairs to sister city communities in Argentina, Armenia, Brazil, China, Ghana, Iraq, Israel, Kazakhstan, Lebanon, Macedonia, Mali, Mexico, Moldova, Peru, Poland, Portugal, Russia, South Africa, Swaziland, and Turkey. The first sister city community to sign up for the project was Fort Lauderdale, Florida. Since 2000, Greater Fort Lauderdale Sister Cities International has provided more than 7,000 wheelchairs to physically disabled people in their sister cities throughout the world. More than 100 million people around the world are in need of wheelchairs and go without because they cannot afford or do not have access to one. The Wheelchair Foundation has delivered nearly 430,000 wheelchairs to 145 countries.

Recipients of wheelchairs in China are ready to wheel into a new life, thanks to their sister city.

A little boy in Turkey smiles happily in his new wheelchair.

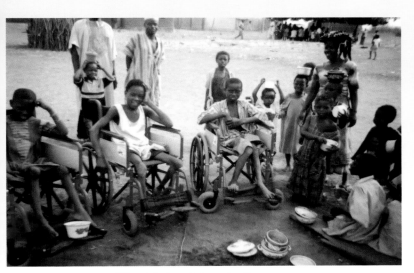

Wheelchair recipients in Ghana.

Founder of the Wheelchair Foundation, Ken Behring, with incoming President Glenn Gray. Behring received the President's Award for his work bringing mobility to thousands around the globe and in honor of the partnership through Wheelchairs for Peace that involves many sister city programs.

Pat Buchanan presents the first-ever Dick Oakland Award to Linda "Jay" Jackson, state coordinator for Alaska. The award was created to recognize outstanding work by state coordinators. Jay's work focused largely on humanitarian projects, with a special emphasis on Nepal.

Sister Cities United for International Peace and Friendship

SISTER CITIES INTERNATIONAL
Annual Conference

July 17 - 20, 2002 • Toledo, Ohio

In the Parade of Nations, this young lady represented Toledo's sister city relationship with Toledo, Spain. It is the earliest relationship recognized by Sister Cities International, and was signed in 1931.

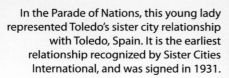

Seeds of Peace
Delegates enjoyed hearing from Seeds of Peace graduates about how the innovative program is building peace among youth. (Left to Right): Ariel Tal and Jamal Abu Zant from Seeds of Peace, moderator Mark Gerzon, and youth leaders Erica Althans-Smith and Jenna Borys from Longmont, Colorado.

Glenn Gray became President of the Board of Directors in 2002.

Annual Awards 2002

Best Overall Program
Over 300,000: Fort Worth, Texas and Phoenix, Arizona
100,000 - 300,000: Lexington, Kentucky

Innovation

Arts & Culture:
Palatine, Illinois

Economic Development:
Phoenix, Arizona

Education:
Tulsa, Oklahoma

Environment:
Bellevue, Washington

Healthcare:
Chicago, Illinois

Humanitarian Assistance:
Fort Lauderdale, Florida
Tacoma, Washington

Municipal Cooperation:
Denton, Texas

Sports:
Fredericksburg, Virginia

Technology & Communication:
Los Angeles, California

Youth Program:
Grand Rapids, Michigan

Volunteer of the Year
Amy Coury, Torrance, California

NOD/AETNA Disability Award
Austin, Texas
Phoenix, Arizona

Board of Directors 2001-2002

President – Glenn Gray
1st Vice President – Sherman Banks
2nd Vice President – Jo Anna Edgerton
3rd Vice President – Randy Avon
Secretary – Paula West
Treasurer – Thomas Ten Hoeve

Youth Member to the Board – Heather Jones
President of the Ambassador's Association – Lisa Marie Kowalski
State Coordinator Liaison – Pat Buchanan

Tony Anderson
John Henry Fullen
Jose Luis Garcia
Robert Heuermann
Mae Ferguson
Georgiana McLeod
Brian Propp
Luis A. Quintana
Mariela Ramirez
Kathleen Roche-Tansey
Brian Smith
Georgianne Thomas
Robert Utter
Jean Van Buskirk
Jane Wood

Police Exchanges Build Safer Communities
Puerto Vallarta, Mexico police officers participated in a law enforcement exchange with sister city Santa Barbara, California in 2002 and pause for a picture with long-time sister city volunteer Evie Treen.

Young Artists Program Winners 2002

1st - Johnny Lee Ivory, Jr. - Stuttgart, Germany (sister city to St. Louis, Missouri)
2nd - Amber Beamesderfer - Ephrata, Pennsylvania
3rd - Anna Pankratova - Khersok, Ukraine – (sister city to Kent, Washington)
4th - Aleksandar Zafirovski - Skopje, Macedonia (sister city to Tempe. Arizona)
5th - Huang Yang - Behai, China (sister city to Tulsa, Oklahoma)
6th - Soumalee (Molly) McNamara - Gilbert, Arizona
7th - Sarah Needham Stillwater, Oklahoma
8th- Francisco Magano - Modesto, California
9th - Bryan Jeitner - Philadelphia, Pennsylvania
10th - Jo Ko-Won Incheon, Republic of Korea (sister city to Philadelphia, Pennsylvania)

Honorable Mention - Asako Sugiyoma - Utsunomiya, Japan (sister city to Tulsa, Oklahoma)
Honorable Mention - Aurelie Charron - Aix-en-Provence, France (sister city to Philadelphia, Pennsylvania)
Honorable Mention - Jess Kelly - Red Wing, Minnesota

The Open World Program – Opening Doors for Communities

Since 2002, 52 communities have participated in the Open World Program by hosting or nominating delegates from Russia, Ukraine, Lithuania, and Uzbekistan. Programs address the theme of federalism and representation in government, as well as other topics such as economic development, education, health, youth, environment, rule of law, and women as leaders. The Open World Program is sponsored by the Open World Leadership Center, which believes that the principles of accountability, governance, and the role of citizenry in government are most effectively illustrated through direct interaction between participants and their U.S. professional counterparts. Sister Cities International and the Academy for Educational Development (AED) are partners in supporting the Open World Program, which enables Eurasian elected officials, political candidates, and emerging political and civic leaders to observe the U.S.democratic system firsthand. The program brings groups of four to five participants accompanied by a facilitator for ten-day theme-based visits to the United States. The visits usually begin with an orientation in Washington, D.C., followed by eight days in a local community. Participants are placed in homestays and attend professional and cultural events.

Open World delegates from sister city Izhevsk, Russian Federation, rode on top of a fire truck in the 4th of July Parade in 2003 in Salt Lake City, Utah. Appropriately, their visit was designed to explore federalism, and they were joined on the truck by Mayor Ross C. "Rocky" Anderson.

Mayor Charlie Roberts gets a heart check-up from the Open World delegation visiting from Kambarka, Russia. As they prepared to leave later that week, Kambarka Mayor Georgiy Kislov offered this toast, "To our dear friends," he said, "we've been here for a week, but feels like we've been here half our lives."

Wheelchair Marathon Program
Austin, Texas – Oita, Japan

Since 1994, the Austin-Oita Sister City Committee has sponsored a wheelchair athlete to compete in the International Wheelchair Marathon in Oita. The goal of the marathon is to promote the full participation of people with disabilities in society. In 2002, they chose Michael Weeden, 44, a quadriplegic wheelchair athlete, to travel to Japan to represent Austin. Pictured, Weeden and a rider from Barbados warm up before the race.

Telling the Sister City Story
Spokane, Washington – Nishinimoya, Japan
Sister cities keep coming up with new ways to tell their story. Spokane, Washington published this booklet about their community's relationship with Nishinimoya, Japan. It recounts more than 40 years of history. They became sister cities in 1962.

"The first sister city relationship that Japan ever established was with an American city in 1955. Thanks to the active cooperation of Sister Cities International, sister city affiliations have flourished between the United States and Japan. Fostering mutual understanding and respect among the peoples of the world has been high on the agenda of local government administrations throughout Japan. Indeed, I cannot think of a better way to attain these objectives than through the friendship formed by such international exchanges."

— Minister of Home Affairs Akira Fukita, the Government of Japan, 1996

SPOKANE–NISHINOMIYA
More Than 40 Years of Friendship

Sister City Mission: Develop, exchange and promote deeper understanding and respect through the sister city efforts.

Youth Exchange: Friendship is Universal
Oak Ridge, Tennessee – Naka, Japan
Getting to know each other and making new friends is part of every sister city exchange program.

True Texas Hospitality…Complete with Honorary Citizenship

Benbrook, Texas – Bled, Slovenia

In 2002, Bled Sister Cities International President Jerry Dunn welcomed nine youth and two chaperones from sister city Bled, Slovenia. The youth were granted honorary citizenship by Benbrook's mayor and stayed for two weeks as part of the Youth Ambassador Program. They developed teamwork and leadership on a ropes course during their stay, and experienced true Texas hospitality. They even rode a few bucking broncos.

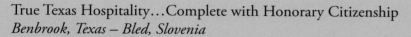

A Relationship Sketched Through History

This mural by San Antonio, Texas Randolph High School students and their art teacher showcases youthful eagerness to communicate our historic connections. Relationships with Las Palmas de Gran Canaria and Santa Cruz de Tenerife date back to San Antonio's 1731 founding by sixteen Canary Island families when life revolved around its first parish church, la Villa de San Fernando. The Canary Islands Government established a trade office in San Antonio in 1999. Now in its sixth year, it coordinates academic, cultural and trade relations supported by the Friends of the Canary Islands Foundation which underwrites engineering exchange students who commercialize wind and other technologies. Plans for San Antonio's 2006 celebration of the 275th anniversary of its founding as the Canary Islanders' first civic settlement in Texas are underway. San Fernando Cathedral, the oldest U.S. sanctuary in continuous use, will be the center of the festivities.

2003

Peace Pole: May Peace Prevail on Earth Corpus Christi, Texas

Visiting and local exchange students stop for a photo in 2003 by the newly-installed Peace Pole in Corpus Christi Sister City Park. Many sister city programs have erected peace poles as a way to educate students and the community about friendship-building abroad.

Archbishop Desmond Tutu Helps Launch Wheelchairs for Peace Project for Jacksonville

More than 200 people joined Jacksonville, Florida in welcoming Archbishop Desmond Tutu of South Africa and launching the Wheelchairs for Peace project on February 19, 2003 at the annual Jacksonville sister city meeting. "We can just imagine the smiles of joy...from the people who will benefit from your amazing bounty," said Archbishop Tutu. He and his wife, Leah, were honored for their efforts promoting peace worldwide, as well as their support helping Jacksonville form its sister cities partnership with Port Elizabeth, South Africa. The two have already engaged in educational, cultural, medical and municipal exchanges. Jacksonville raised funds to match an award it received from the Florida Department of State to send wheelchairs to Port Elizabeth and Bahia Blanca, Argentina through the Wheelchairs for Peace program. Tutu received the Nobel Peace Prize in 1984 for his work against apartheid in South Africa.

(Left to right) Sister Cities International board member Randy Avon, executive director Tim Honey, artist Tony Rodriguez, Leah Tutu, Archbishop Desmond Tutu, and Sister Cities International board member Jane Wood, helped launch Jacksonville's Wheelchairs for Peace project.

The fifty-member Orchestre and Chorus du Conservatoire de Sevres (France) visited their sister city, Mount Prospect, Illinois, in 2003. With the entire group aboard a fire truck, this photo captures the exuberance and zest for experiencing daily life in another country so treasured by sister city members the world over. In addition to musical performances, their trip also included a traditional Thanksgiving dinner (in October) with 400+ guests, as well as the opening of "The New Villas of Sevres" townhome development.

YOUR
COMMUNITY'S
PASSPORT TO
THE WORLD

SISTER
CITIES
INTERNATIONAL

World Peace Conference Brings Together the Secret Sisters
Mikhail Gorbachev Salutes Efforts Toward Peace

Fox Cities – Kurgan Sister Cities, Inc. and World Services of La Crosse, Inc. in conjunction with the Open World Leadership Center, brought together colleagues from the U.S. and Russia for a conference in Appleton, Wisconsin on October 1 – 3, 2003.

Themed "security through stability," the conference examined the crucial role grassroots-based community-to-community partnerships can play in reducing the threat posed by Cold War era weapons stockpiles. The keynote address was delivered by Mikhail Gorbachev, former president of the Soviet Union and recipient of the Nobel Peace Prize.

Gorbachev was greeted warmly by the delegates and told them, "Together with the governor of your state I would like to salute those Sister Cities. This is a wonderful example. If we work together as communities then I am sure that there will be less of a need for government decisions. The communities of Russia and of the US now are the communities based on the rule of law and they can do a great deal together. This is what civil society can do – this is how it can succeed. I would like to have more Sister Cities – to see more Sister Cities."

For the first time, the conference brought together the "secret cities," five sister city partnerships linking U.S. and Russian communities dealing with weapons of mass destruction. They discussed best practices and worked to strengthen collaborative programs in economic development, education, health care, the environment, civic development and federalism. As the culmination of the conference they launched Communities for International Development to continue their work.

WHALE BONES BRIDGE A FRIENDSHIP FROM ALASKA TO ENGLAND
ANCHORAGE, ALASKA – WHITBY, ENGLAND, UNITED KINGDOM

The town of Whitby had a problem – its historic whalebone arch and centerpiece of its waterfront, originally a gift from Norway in 1960, was beginning to rot. They looked to their sister city – Anchorage, Alaska – for help. Teaming up with the North Slope Borough, the Anchorage group found a whaling captain, Don Nungasak from Barrow, who was willing to donate a pair of bowhead jawbones for Whitby. It took more than a year of traveling, negotiation, fundraising for transit costs, and customs authorization, before the new jawbones of a bowhead whale arrived from Alaska. A dedication ceremony was held by a grateful community, and their sister city relationship continues to blossom. Pictured at right, the Alaska delegation joins Whitby's leaders under the arch at the dedication ceremony.

Far left: Sculptor Craig Shankles with a replica of "Stone and Steel #14."

Sculptor Craig Shankles works on the sculpture in Osa.

NEW PALTZ, NEW YORK – OSA, JAPAN

Sculpture Exchange Tightens Sister City Bonds, Involves Community

What does it take to build two sculptures on different continents? A lot! New Paltz sculptor Craig Shankles designed the twelve-foot-high "Stone and Steel #14" for Friendship Forest in New Paltz's sister city Osa, Japan. Another sculpture was built in New Paltz's Peace Park by Osa Professor Kasuhiko Kanayama titled "Odo Gorge." The 2003 sculpture exchange was envisioned by Elisabeth Clock. She said, "We now have a visible symbol of our friendship with our Sister City Osa, Japan. Halfway around the world in Japan, there is another sculpture that reflects the same friendship and understanding. The finished works create a significant symbol of friendship between our two communities, commemorating the efforts of the many people involved in organizing and producing this project."

Workmen in Osa help Craig Shankles put the sculpture in place.

Toyota Truck Plant in San Antonio Has Roots in Sister City Connection

"Toyota is coming to San Antonio" – was proclaimed on front-page headlines and TV news stories in February 2003. Toyota Motor Company selected San Antonio for its sixth North American assembly plant – an $800 million plant that will produce 150,000 full-size Tundra trucks per year, beginning in 2006. "This is big news for San Antonio – probably more than we realize right now," said Jose Luis Garcia, board member of Sister Cities International and Chief of Protocol for the City of San Antonio. But this type of economic windfall doesn't just happen overnight or by chance. Long-term global investments are nurtured by communities committed to a sister city relationship. Since the beginning of the sister city relationship in 1986, the City of San Antonio has had over 180 exchanges and programs with Kumamoto and new doors have been opened with other cities and prefectures in Japan. San Antonio's long-standing ties with Japan have served as a springboard to bringing several Japanese-owned companies to the city, including Colin Medical Instruments, makers of blood pressure monitoring equipment; Sony Semiconductor, Inc. (Sony's first U.S. chip manufacturing plant); and Takata Seat Belts.

Toyota Motor Corp. President Fujio Cho (left) and Texas Governor Rick Perry place a Toyota logo where San Antonio lies on the map of Texas. Photo by Jerry Lara/*Express-News*.

A delegate representing Prescott, Arizona accepts the Annual Award for an outstanding program in education. Tim Honey, executive director, is on his right, and Laverne Johnson with the U.S. Department of State and Glenn Gray, president of the Board of Directors are on his left.

The Parade of Nations featured signs representing every member country of Sister Cities International.

Delegates enjoyed the Parade of Nations.

Executive director Tim Honey greets arriving delegates.

200

Board of Directors 2003 – 2004

President - Glenn Gray
1st Vice President - Sherman Banks
2nd Vice President - Randy Avon
Secretary - Mae Ferguson
Treasurer - Thomas Ten Hoeve
Executive Committee, Open Seat - Jo Anna Edgerton
Executive Committee, Open Seat - Jane Wood
Youth Member to the Board - Jason Hibner

President of the Ambassador's Association – Paige Pearman
State Coordinator Liaison - Robert Bensing

Tony Anderson
Frank C. Britt
Pat Buchanan
Alan Chambers
Pat F. Fallin
Martha Fujita
Robert R. Heuermann, Jr.
Nancy Huppert
Georgiana McLeod
Brian Propp
Kathleen Roche-Tansey
Georgianne Thomas
Robert Utter
Jean Van Buskirk

Annual Awards 2003

Best Overall Program
Over 300,000: Chicago, Illinois
100,000-300,000: Sarasota, Florida
50,000-100,000: Corvallis, Oregon
25,000-50,000: Burlington, Vermont
Under 25,000 - Red Wing, Minnesota

Innovation
Arts & Culture:
Palm Desert, California

Economic Development:
Phoenix, Arizona

Education:
Prescott, Arizona

Environment:
Bellevue, Washington

Healthcare:
Oak Ridge, Tennessee

Humanitarian Assistance:
Chicago, Illinois

Municipal Cooperation:
Temecula, California

Public Safety:
Kansas City, Missouri

Sports:
Phoenix, Arizona

Technology & Communication:
Cincinnati, Ohio (Luizhou Committee)

Youth Program:
Fort Worth, Texas

Volunteer of the Year
Robert Chien, Kansas City, Missouri
Dana Kelly, Lakeland, Florida

NOD/AETNA Disability Award
Portland, Oregon
Sandy City, Utah

Sister City Leaders: Alan Chambers

Alan Chambers of Bangor, Northern Ireland is elected to the Board of Directors in 2003, becoming the first elected board member from outside the United States. Chambers commented, "Citizens of the smallest community, be it in Ireland or Pennsylvania, are totally dependent on each other to enjoy a satisfactory quality of life. We need farmers to grow our food, bakers to bake our bread, shopkeepers to sell us all that we need and teachers to educate our children…If we apply this concept to the world in which we live every country is interdependent on each other…In a world full of poverty, suffering and cruelty, I believe passionately that we all have a moral responsibility to do more than sit in front of our TV screens, watching the news and saying, "Isn't that awful?" Sister Cities International gives us all an opportunity and a basis through citizen diplomacy to make the world a safer and better place in which to raise a family…Governments can shuttle back and forth but our concept is people-to-people, one community at a time…Fifty years on, I am proud to be able to say that I am a part of this movement."

1st Place – Alieh Robinson, Kent, Washington

3rd Place – Hailey Rogge - Erie, Colorado

2nd Place – Charles Schwab, Port Orange, Volusia County, Florida

4th Place – Joel Goodrich, Winchester, Kentucky "This chalk pastel was inspired by the hands of a relief worker mixing milk to give starving children. It inspired me to think that those hands were touching the hearts of hundreds in one simple act of love," said Goodrich when asked about his piece, "Hands of Love."

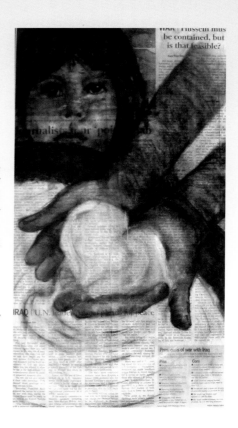

5th Place – Kristina Etson, Centerville, Ohio

6th Place – Kristin Mravec, Elkhart, Indiana

7th Place – Rachael Huston. Gastonia, North Carolina

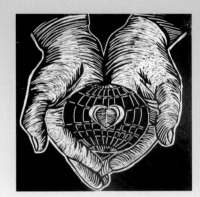

9th Place – Veronika Hanzlikova, Kladno, Czech Republic (sister city to Bellevue, Washington)

8th Place – Sarah Coppinger - Philadelphia, Pennsylvania This untitled entry used a digital medium. When asked what inspired her, she responded, "In my piece a hand is seen, which has within it different places and peoples. This hand is writing a letter: this is to show all creatures should communicate with each other. It is signed 'your friend,' which is to show that if we all share with each other, youths of every country will grow up to understand each other."

10th Place – Yuki Tokunaga, Yao, Japan (sister city to Bellevue, Washington). Titled "Perhaps Everyone's Ideas." Yuki Tokunaga said her inspiration lies in "my wish is that everyone would seek happiness for all, just as they seek their own happiness."

11th Place – Zhang Liang-liang - Quzhou, China (sister city to Red Wing, Minnesota)

Princess Anne Attends Signing for Newmarket and Lexington

With Her Royal Highness The Princess Royal, Princess Anne in attendance, Lexington, Kentucky Mayor Teresa Ann Isaac and Newmarket, England Mayor Linda Sherer signed a memorandum of intent on October 10, 2003. The signing ceremony for Lexington's fourth sister city coincided with Princess Anne's visit to see the Kentucky Horse Park's exhibition of "All the Queen's Horses."

"Apart from the creation of enduring relationships between cities, the vast majority of (sister city) affiliations are positive and foster such noble human values as compassion in the face of disaster, understanding between different nations/races and improvement of the quality of life through technical assistance and related programmes..."

— Sampson Nyaoke-Owuor, Kisumu, Kenya, sister city to Roanoke, Virginia

A FESTIVAL OF FRIENDSHIP:
INTERNATIONAL SISTER CITIES FESTIVAL
LAREDO, TEXAS

The ballet from sister city Monclova, Mexico performs during the festival.

The 2003 International Sister Cities Festival in Laredo, Texas opens with a ceremonial ribbon cutting. The annual event draws representatives from Laredo's fifteen sister cities around the globe.

This police exchange between Irvine, California and Hermosillo, Mexico helped both communities prepare for the future.

Portland, Oregon and Khabarovsk, Russia have conducted exchanges to improve infrastructure.

Sister Cities Network for Sustainable Development is Founded

Sister Cities International launched the Sister Cities Network for Sustainable Development in 2003. The network emerged to support the many sister city programs undertaking development projects around the world that reduce poverty and help communities plan for a better future.

Sustainable development refers to community and societal development that "meets the needs of the present without undermining the environment or social systems on which we depend for the future." The goals of the Network are threefold: (1) to increase the capacity of member communities to design and deliver effective programs that incorporate innovative solutions around the issues of sustainable development; (2) to educate members of the Network about the importance of sustainable development and the types of projects and programs that support a more sustainable world; and (3) to create and sustain long-term, mutually beneficial partnerships.

Since 2003, the Network has grown to include 45 U.S. communities partnered with 125 international communities, mostly in developing countries. Key partners, including PADCO | AECOM, Citrix Systems, Inc., Standard & Poor's, the Academy for Educational Development, Global

Giving, the World Bank Institute, The Africa Channel, Water for People, and UN-Habitat support and contribute to the success of the Network. The network has supported and managed more than 100 sustainable development grant projects for HIV/AIDS awareness and prevention, educational and technical exchanges, emergency preparedness, humanitarian assistance, environmental management and good governance. Membership in the network is free to members of Sister Cities International.

A firefighter exchange helped Tooele City, Utah and Kambarka, Russia develop professionally.

"This we know. The earth does not belong to man, man belongs to the earth. This we know. All things are connected like blood which unites one family. All things are connected. Whatever befalls the earth befalls the sons of the earth. Man did not weave the web of life; he is merely a strand in it. Whatever he does to the web, he does to himself."

— Chief Seattle, addressing the U.S. Congress 150 years ago

Children's Artwork Builds Sister City Links

The "Hands of Heritage Children's Art Project" featured 167 pieces of original artwork by middle schoolers from Sarasota, as well as Perpignan, France; Tel Mond, Israel; Treviso, Italy (sister city candidate); and Vladimir, Russian Federation. Wall murals, bright colors, and messages of peace helped Sarasota celebrate its 100th anniversary with gusto.

Did You Know?

In 1981, there were more than 740 U.S. cities, representing more than 85 million American people, affiliated with over 950 communities around the world in 77 other countries located on five continents.

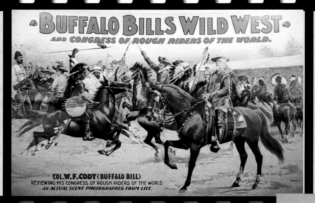

Handbills for Buffalo Bill's Wild West Show erroneously used the term West Cossack. The historical record was corrected when a new history book was published and when Cody, Wyoming signed a sister city agreement with Lanchkuti, Georgia.

The Truth Untold: Buffalo Bill
Cody, Wyoming; & Lanchkhuti, Georgia

On the same day in 2003 that Cody became a sister city to Lanchkhuti, Republic of Georgia, the truth came to light, "This is a story 111 years untold," said Bill McCall. The revelation concerned the nationality of the trick riders in Buffalo Bill's Wild West show in 1892-1910. For years, the trick horse riders traveling in the famous Wild West show were referred to as "Cossack horsemen." Promoters played up the angle that the saber-bearing riders appearing in the show were fierce warriors from the czarist Russian army. But a newly-published book showed that the "Cossacks" were actually trick riders from what is now the Republic of Georgia - a region with a long history of expert horsemanship. Historians at the Buffalo Bill museum changed signs and set the story straight. Bill McCall, a Cody native who worked as business consultant in the Republic of Georgia for more than a decade, helped connect Georgian researchers with the local museum and foster the sister city relationship between Cody and Lanchkhuti.

Four Legs for Boenjeres
A boy gets a new lease on life, thanks to a sister city's generosity

A young boy growing up in Somoto, Nicaragua named Boenjeres Gutierrez lost both his legs in a bus accident. Artificial legs were not an option for him, because his legs were amputated too high. A wheelchair was not practical either, since Gutierrez lived on a hill. He had to crawl to get around.

But thanks to sister city friends in California, now he can go to school and play with his friends. Shirley Olsen from Somoto's sister city, Merced, California, bought him a $50 donkey and a $25 saddle. The gift has given him something many people take for granted – mobility.

And Gutierrez is only one of many people being helped by their sister city. On one visit to Somoto, Olsen met a woman who had a Caesarian delivery without the use of any pain-relieving medications. Now, the Merced sister city program collects donations and recruits sponsors, including Rite-Aid and Wal-Mart. They also raise money selling Nicaraguan coffee.

Thanks to the efforts of many people in Merced, medication and educational scholarships are bringing hope to the Nicaraguan community. And Boenjeres Gutierrez hopes to qualify for one of the scholarships to continue his education.

Cristy Olson, part of a 10-person delegation from Merced, stands in the doorway with Boenjeres Gutierrez and his mothers and sisters at their home in Nicaragua.

Boenjeres Gutierrez on burro "Angelita."

206

2004

Islamic Peace and Friendship Initiative

The "Islamic Peace and Friendship Initiative" aims to increase people-to-people exchanges, intercultural communication and cooperation between the Islamic world and the United States. The Islamic Peace and Friendship Initiative includes:

• Youth Exchange and Study (YES) Program – A consortium of organizations led by AYUSA that organizes high school exchanges allowing students from predominantly Islamic countries to study in a U.S. high school for one academic year.

• U.S. – Iraq International Partners for Peace Program – A grant program funded by the U.S. Department of State to foster increased communication, cooperation and understanding between five U.S.-Iraq partners and to provide humanitarian assistance to the Iraqi communities.

• Wheelchairs for Peace Program – An initiative between Sister Cities International and the Wheelchair Foundation to provide wheelchairs to mobility-impaired individuals around the world, and including several predominantly Islamic countries such as Armenia, Iraq, Kazakhstan, Lebanon, Mali, and Turkey.

Since the launch of the "Sister Cities United for Peace and Friendship Initiative" in October 2001 and the introduction of the Islamic Peace and Friendship Initiative in 2004, Sister Cities International has seen a 33% increase in the number of U.S. communities with certified relationships with predominantly Islamic countries.

Additionally, the Islamic Initiative has fostered a number of meetings and summits in the last few years between Islamic and U.S. citizen diplomats focused on telling the remarkable stories of cooperation between U.S. and Islamic communities. Some of these citizen diplomats have joined together to form the Islamic Task Force, which works alongside the Board of Directors to further the goals of the program.

A MAYOR FOSTERS TIES TO THE MIDDLE EAST: DEARBORN, MICHIGAN – QANA, LEBANON

In October 2004, Mayor Michael A. Guido of Dearborn, Michigan led a sister city delegation to Lebanon. The group included city officials, Arab-American business leaders, and executive director Tim Honey. The 40-member delegation focused on economic and municipal government issues. They met with President Emil Lahoud, House Speaker Nabih Berri and mayors from throughout Lebanon. The group was inspired by these riders on horseback. Dearborn became a sister city to Qana, Lebanon in 1999 and Mayor Guido has encouraged several exchanges and programs that benefit both communities.

YES students meet with President Bush during a special event

YES: Youth Exchange and Study Program

Since 2003, Sister Cities International has participated in the Youth Exchange and Study (YES) program. The YES program was launched by the U.S. Department of State to build bridges of understanding between the U.S. and the Arab and Muslim world.

The YES program provides full scholarships to secondary school students from countries with significant Muslim populations to spend up to one academic year in the U.S. The students are required to conduct presentations on their home countries to student groups and are asked to give back to their host communities through service projects.

"The YES program is a dramatic project which affords future leaders from this crucial region an opportunity to discover first-hand the fundamental good of the American people and discover the common values shared by our respective cultures," said Craig Brown, Vice President for Government Affairs and Partnership Development at AYUSA, which helps manage part of the YES program through a consortium, with which Sister Cities International is involved.

Each spring, Sister Cities International hosts a leadership summit for the YES students in Boulder, Colorado. Interactive leadership workshops and team-building ropes courses challenge teens to grow and learn how to get along with others different from themselves. The summit has also helped them think about their experiences in the U.S. and how they can take lessons learned back to their home countries after their year in the U.S. ends.

"Programs like this help us engage Muslim and Arab communities and understand other cultures," said Tim Honey, executive director of Sister Cities International. "Every time exchange students go home from the YES program, they share what they learned and did in America. When a student from a Muslim or Arab country lives in our community for a year, we learn about their way of life and perspective too. It's diplomacy at its most basic level - people-to-people."

YES students pause for a picture with U.S. Senator Edward Kennedy before returning home after a year in the U.S.

This teambuilding activity during the Boulder Summit helps students learn how to work together as a group, and teaches them how to get along with people they may not always agree with.

If These Rocks Could Talk: A Solid Foundation for Cross-Cultural Understanding
Scottsbluff, Nebraska - Bamiyan, Bamiyan Province, Afghanistan

Two monuments keep watch. One is carved by the forces of nature, the other by human hands. One is a strategic lookout for Native American villagers and a gateway for Oregon Trail pioneers. The other is a silent sentinel marking the passage of the Spice Routes and the marches of Genghis Khan. For centuries, the Scotts Bluff National Monument and the Buddhas of Bamiyan provided shelter for two divergent agriculture communities, each shaped by their own history and culture. Recent world events provided the impetus to bring these two communities together as sisters.

For many, the September 11, 2001, attacks in New York and Washington, D.C., brought about feelings of fear, anger and confusion. They also prompted a need to find understanding. A group of people from the twin cites of Scottsbluff and Gering, Nebraska, contacted the Center for Afghanistan Studies at the University of Nebraska at Omaha (UNO) for guidance. The Center provided the network of assistance needed for Scottsbluff/Gering, Nebraska, and Bamiyan, Bamiyan Province, Afghanistan, to become Afghanistan's first official sister city partnership in May 2003.

It was meaningful, then, that September 11, 2005, marked the arrival of the sixth group of Afghan teachers to the Scottsbluff/Gering area through UNO's Afghan Teacher Education Program. Each group of twelve female teachers spent 4-5 days in the community studying educational processes. Scottsbluff/Gering hosted then-governor Mohammed Rahim Aliyar for a one-day economic, agricultural and government overview. Governor Aliyar hosted five representatives of Scottsbluff/Gering for a visit to Bamiyan in June 2004. The delegation met with Bamiyan leaders to discuss potential agriculture and health care partnerships. They continue to exchange political officials, medical personnel and, most importantly, knowledge and friendship.

"I Madonnari" Goes to Toba: Santa Barbara, California – Toba, Japan

In 2004, Santa Barbara sponsored an "I Madonnari" street painting festival in Toba, Japan. Based on a tradition that began in 16th century Italy, Santa Barbarans were excited to share this festival with their sister city friends. But the people in Toba weren't so sure – it took a lot of convincing to convey that the festival would not be just for children, and would not be graffiti. Everything was planned – and nine artists traveled to Toba with the mayor to put on a street painting extravaganza. Alas, their high hopes were dashed by downpours of rain. But their sister city friends tried very hard to cover the beautiful artwork with buckets, newspapers, tents and rugs to protect it. Even though the event was "washed out" literally, it forged a strong bond among the participants, and a new street festival is planned for Toba, and Santa Barbara is hoping to share this project with its other sister cities: Puerto Vallarta, Mexico; Dingle, Ireland; Palma de Mallorca, Spain; San Juan, Philippines; Weihai, China and Yalta, Ukraine.

Three generations of submarine families at a tree-planting ceremony in Ireland in August 2004.

From Enemies to Friends: One Man's Quest for Reconciliation
Torrance, California – Kashiwa, Japan

Akira Tsurukame, a travel agent living in Torrance, Calif., hosted a couple from Kashiwa, Japan during activities to honor the 30th anniversary of the Torrence-Kashiwa partnership. His guest, Hirakawa, was a Japanese Navy veteran who had been in the Japanese Imperial Navy during the Second World War. Tsurukame told Hirakawa that his father had also served in the Japanese Navy and was killed while serving aboard a submarine torpedoed by a British vessel. Tsurukame didn't know much more about his father as his father died when he was three years old.

Upon returning to Japan, Hirakawa sent Tsurukame information about his father that he obtained by researching naval records and talking to Imperial Navy Veterans. Tsurukame traveled to Japan to fill in missing pieces of his father's life by researching detailed military records and by talking to people who knew his father personally.

Eventually, Tsurukame found the daughter of a Dutch submariner whose ship was torpedoed by his father's ship before she was born. He also found the now 94-year-old commander of the British submarine who was living in a small town in Ireland. Tsurukame arranged for the submariner families to meet in Ireland. "We talked, ate and drank. We laughed and cried. Three families became one," Tsurukame said.

It was a moving meeting – as the children of three soldiers from opposing countries reconciled in the name of peace.

Inset: The delegation was led by Sherman Banks, president of the Board of Directors of Sister Cities International and Jack Lynch, deputy mayor of the City of Spokane. Other delegation members included: Cynthia Maka, assistant executive director, Sister Cities International; Kent Watkins, urban development representative, Sister Cities International, Fred Peterson, co-chair, U.S. – China Sister City Conference; Nancy Huppert, past-president, Board of Directors and Global Envoy, Sister Cities International; Earnest Williams, councilman, City of St. Petersburg, Florida; Claire McLeigh, director of international affairs, City of St. Petersburg, Florida; Lily Shelden, president of Gresham Sister City Association, Gresham, Oregon; Mimi Barker, Board of Directors, Sister Cities International, and Maura Lynch.

2004 Delegation to China Lays Groundwork for Conference, New Relationships

An eleven member Sister Cities International delegation went to China in 2004 for a ten day visit to build international understanding, trade and sister city relationships. The delegation also made plans for the Second United States - Sino Sister City Conference, scheduled for 2005 in Spokane, Washington. Stops on the trip included Beijing (sister city to Washington, D.C.), Changchun (sister city to Flint, Michigan and Little Rock, Arkansas), Jilin (sister city to Spokane, Washington), Xi'an (sister city to Kansas City, Missouri) and Shanghai (sister city to Chicago, Illinois and San Francisco, California). The delegation also visited several cities in China near Xi'an seeking sister cities.

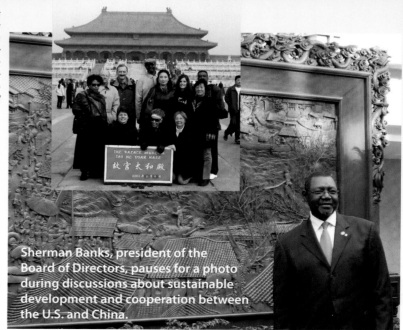

Sherman Banks, president of the Board of Directors, pauses for a photo during discussions about sustainable development and cooperation between the U.S. and China.

Soviet war veterans, now living in Cincinnati, stand for the "Star Spangled Banner," which opened the preview. Veterans include the three women closest to the camera in the front row.

'Under Fire' Documentary Sheds Light on an Unknown Story
Women veterans from Kharkiv, Ukraine share their story in Cincinnati, Ohio

World War II veterans from the former Soviet Union and the United States joined forces on Veterans Day 2004 to shed light on a little-known chapter in history.

Cincinnati hosted the premier of a documentary showing how thousands of women from their sister city, Kharkiv, Ukraine, fought in combat during the Second World War. The documentary featured interviews with some of the women who served.

"It's almost unknown to Americans that Soviet women served in combat," said Jan Sherbin of Cincinnati, Ohio. "It was very emotional to learn that and to see them as real people."

Before the film began, high school singers performed the Star Spangled Banner. Fifteen women, dubbed the "15 Singing Babushkas" because they were schoolgirls in the Soviet Union during the war but now live in Cincinnati, sang songs of war that they remembered from their childhoods.

"English speakers followed a translation and understood what a wrenching, melancholy experience the Soviet people suffered," Sherban wrote. The emotions ebbing out of the documentary were only enhanced by the singing, she said.

The evening closed with the choir and the 15 babushkas singing "God Bless America."

"The audience was inspired to join in spontaneously," Sherbin wrote. Roses were presented to the four World War II veterans from the Soviet Army and two veterans from the U.S. Army.

Soviet veteran Maria Tolokolnikova, featured in "Under Fire," describes leading the charge to capture a strategically important hill.

"I am keenly aware of the importance of the program carried out by Sister Cities International. The type of relationship it develops between peoples of different countries, the feeling of personal involvement it instills in the ordinary citizen, and the concrete results it produces through inter-community cooperation closely parallel the aims and efforts of the Organization of American States, which views Sister Cities International as an extremely valuable ally in its endeavor to build a better world in the Americas."

— Secretary General Alejandro Orfila, Organization of American States

Africa HIV/AIDS Prevention and Education

In 2003, the U.S. Department of State's Bureau of Educational and Cultural Affairs awarded a grant to Sister Cities International to create and support innovative HIV/AIDS education and prevention strategies. The grant included Amesbury, Massachusetts – Esabalu, Kenya; Newburyport, Massachusetts – Bura, Kenya; Lansing, Michigan – Akuapem South District, Ghana; Grand Rapids, Michigan – Ga District, Ghana; Hanover Park, Illinois – Cape Coast, Ghana; and Oakland, California – Sekondi Takoradi, Ghana. Each community pair received $20,000 to conduct exchanges and implement their plans. The program managers met for a leadership workshop where they learned to identify stakeholders, facilitate meetings, build consensus, write action plans and encourage community participation. Activities included study tours, peer education, training, awareness building, and economic development initiatives to support people affected by HIV/AIDS. They received additional support through a partnership with the Alliance of Mayors Initiative for Community Action on AIDS at the Local Level.

"A sister cities program, TRADE 2000, is one of the most valuable programs supported by the commercial office of the Embassy of the Republic of Hungary and is the most successful in bringing together Hungarian and U.S. business leaders for the purpose of developing new and productive relationships."

— Dr. Tibor Nemes, Commercial Counselor,
Embassy of the Republic of Hungary,
New York, New York

Millennium Development Goals City-to-City Challenge Pilot Program

The Millennium Development Goals City-to-City Challenge Pilot Program was designed to demonstrate the effectiveness of international cooperation in addressing the UN Millennium Development Goals (MDGs). Developed in conjunction with the World Bank Institute (WBI), this pilot program drew upon three sister city partnerships to further the principles of the MDGs as adopted at the United Nations Millennium Summit in September 2000. The three pairs of communities were Louisville, Kentucky -Tamale, Ghana; Chicago, Illinois-Casablanca, Morocco; and Boulder, Colorado-Dushanbe, Tajikistan. Each partnership chose a specific millennium development goal to focus on. Tamale and Louisville selected MDG 7 – Ensure Environmental Sustainability. They focused on providing safe drinking water and improved sanitation in Tamale and on educating citizens in both communities on the importance of the MDGs to their lives. Casablanca and Chicago selected MDG 2 – Achieve Universal Primary Education. They worked to increase the literacy rates of youth and young adults aged 15 to 24 in two disadvantaged neighborhoods. Boulder and Dushanbe chose MDG

8 - Develop a "Global Partnership for Development." Concentrating on their ongoing project, the construction and outfitting of an eco-friendly cyber café in Dushanbe, the pilot helped the two partners develop sustainable uses for the cyber café. Once constructed, the building will be a showcase of "green" architecture, with solar heat and natural light, low-water-use toilets, and other innovations.

PADEC students at the turtle village in Sangalkam in Senegal.

Genius Tournament Awards Ceremony in Dakar.

From Pen Pals to Education Partners
Washington, D.C. and Dakar, Senegal

In 1986, fifth grade students at the J.O. Wilson Elementary School in Washington, DC, prepared letters to present to Ambassador Falilou Kane of Dakar, Senegal. Little did they know how far these letters would go. Thanks to the letters and an article in Sister Cities International News, the Patte d'Oie English Club (PAD EC) school relationship was born. Since 1989, the D.C.-Dakar Capital Cities Friendship Council, Inc. (D.C. – Dakar) has visited the school, planted trees on the site, and lobbied the city of Dakar to support the school. Sister city organizers have donated computers, books, school supplies and monetary contributions each year for the program. These gifts have enabled the school to start a summer enrichment program and a cyber café. The program has grown from just 6 students to more than 200. No longer a seasonal program, it provides year-round computer classes, and offers a summer enrichment program. Several students from the program have become teachers and returned to teach computer science. In the beginning, the school only took students from Dakar. Now students from all parts of Senegal and beyond attend to learn computer skills. Each year the program hosts a Genius Tournament Award Ceremony. It's an academic competition for 30 teams from nine elementary schools. Students compete from November through May, with a final tournament in June. Who would have thought so much could come from a fifth-grade class project?!

213

Fort Worth Mayor Mike Moncreif dons the traditional dress of newly-signed sister city Mbabane, Swaziland at the World Welcoming Reception.

SISTER CITIES INTERNATIONAL
2004 ANNUAL CONFERENCE

PARTNERS AND PEACE

FORT WORTH, TEXAS

More than 200 youth attended the Youth Summit to develop further their leadership and cross-cultural communication skills.

The South African delegation lines up for the Parade of Nations.

The Ukrainian delegation takes a picture with Mary Jean Eisenhower (second from left)

Board of Directors 2004 – 2005

President - Sherman Banks
1st Vice President - Randy Avon
2nd Vice President - Mae Ferguson
Secretary - Pat Fallin
Treasurer - Robert Heuermann
Executive Committee, Open Seat - Brian Propp
Executive Committee, Open Seat - Jane Wood

Youth Member to the Board - Carly Keller
President of the Ambassador's Association - Paige Pearman
State Coordinator Liaison - Robert Bensing

Mimi Barker
Steve Beinke
Frank Britt
Pat Buchanan
Saïda Moussadaq
Alan Chambers
Jo Anna Edgerton
Martha Fujita
Nancy Huppert
Michael Hyatt
Georgiana McLeod
Rodger Randle
Kathleen Roche-Tansey
Bill Stafford
Georgianne Thomas

Sister City Leaders: Sherman Banks

Sherman Banks began his two-year term as President of the
Board of Directors in 2004.

Annual Awards 2004

Best Overall Program
Over 500,000: Fort Worth, Texas
300,000 to 500,000: Virginia Beach, Virginia
100,000 to 300,000: Laredo, Texas
100,000 to 300,000: Tempe, Arizona
50,000 to 100,000: Kent, Washington
Under 25,000: Great Neck Plaza, New York

Innovation
Arts & Culture:
Tacoma, Washington

Economic Development:
Louisville, Kentucky

Education:
Phoenix, Arizona

Environment:
Louisville, Kentucky

Healthcare:
Corvallis, Oregon

Humanitarian Assistance:
West Bend, Wisconsin

Municipal Cooperation:
Riverside, California

Public Safety:
Fort Worth, Texas

Technology & Communication:
Wichita, Kansas

Youth Program:
Fort Worth, Texas

Volunteer of the Year
Dr. Susan Herlin of Louisville, Kentucky

Award for Disability Advocacy
Benbrook, Texas

Central Asian Teens Tour USA Playing Soccer and Visit U.S. Sister Cities

The U.S. – Central Asia Friendship Tour brought boys ages 13-15 from Kazakhstan, Kyrgyzstan, Tajikistan and Uzbekistan to spend 3 weeks in the United States playing soccer, learning about American culture, living with host families and sharing about their home countries. The players visited areas with strong sister city programs. They visited Arlington, Virginia; Tucson, Arizona (sister city to Almaty, Kazakhstan); Boston, Massachusetts; Boulder, Colorado (sister city to Dushanbe, Tajikistan); Arvada, Colorado (sister city to Kyzylorda, Kazakhstan); and Colorado Springs, Colorado (sister city to Bishkek, Kyrgyzstan). The team's visit will contribute to cross-cultural understanding, say organizers. "We know that the best place to start breaking down barriers of misunderstanding among cultures and peoples is with the young. Their first flight on a plane and their first interaction with American[s] will leave an indelible mark, and we expect it will open the eyes of their newfound friends here," said Wendell Knox, president and CEO of Abt Associates. The tour is an extension of the Sport and Health Education Project sponsored by the U.S. Agency for International Development which organizes youth overseas in soccer and volleyball activities, computer and vocational training, and health education programs.

ECONOMIC DEVELOPMENT: THREE U.S. CITIES WITH GERMAN SISTERS TEAM UP
LOUISVILLE, KENTUCKY – INDIANAPOLIS, INDIANA – CINCINNATI, OHIO

Sister Cities of Louisville, Sister Cities of Indianapolis, and Sister Cities of Cincinnati formed a tri-city partnership to promote economic development between Germany and the United States. Each organization has a sister city in Germany (Mainz, Cologne and Munich, respectively), and the three partners wanted to encourage tourism and economic development in the tri-state region. They designed materials to help market the area, tabling materials for use in Germany at tourism events, and a website. In 2003, they participated in a Cologne Tourism Convention. They are working through a five-year plan and expanding their economic development opportunities.

So that they may see!

Medical Mission to Port Harcourt, Nigeria Has Lasting Impact

More than 5,000 people benefited from the Medical Mission organized by the Kansas City (Missouri) – Port Harcourt Sister City Committee. The mission studied the extent of eye diseases in Port Harcourt, and examined trauma management and surgical care at local hospitals. They also provided continuing health education to nurses, resident doctors and public health workers in ophthalmology, general and trauma surgeries, cardiovascular diseases and low vision/blind rehabilitation. Interestingly, the medical mission took place at a time when all government hospitals were closed and the Port Harcourt Teaching Hospital was shut down due to a labor dispute. Mobile operating vans from Pro-Health International saved the Mission by providing surgical units, generators, autoclaves, refrigerators, and equipment. The team saw more than 5,650 patients and provided medical consultations, eye operations, general surgeries, dental exams, low vision evaluation, blind rehabilitation/counseling and health education. Prescribed medications and eyeglasses were distributed. And although the team returned home, the medical mission and the local government have continued the project as a sustainable community economic development project. They are working on a training plan for local instructors, professionals and administrators in health education, transparency in government, cost-effective administration and community involvement. Their excellent track record in sponsorship and fundraising will ensure that this medical mission is the first of many to come!

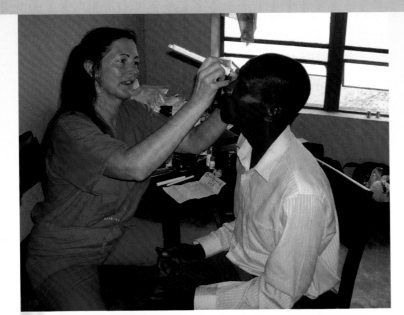

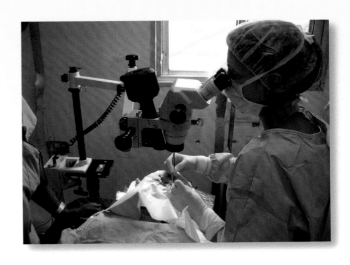

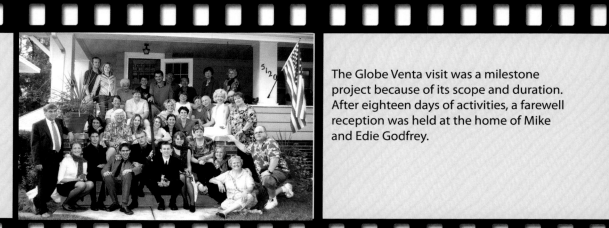

The Globe Venta visit was a milestone project because of its scope and duration. After eighteen days of activities, a farewell reception was held at the home of Mike and Edie Godfrey.

"Globe Venta:" A River Connects Lithuania to the World... and to the Heart

Omaha, Nebraska - Siauliai, Lithuania

"I had no idea how my life would change when I volunteered to escort the Shakespeare students of "Globe Venta," wrote Sue Mehaffey, of Omaha, Nebraska. The group of 8 students arrived in the summer of 2004 from Lithuania to perform a play, and Mehaffey was impressed by their poise and captivating personalities. "My life was so strongly touched by their visit, that I wanted my 21-year-old daughter, Sarah, to meet them." They traveled to Lithuania in July 2005, where they lived with the students' English teacher, attended their high school graduation, met their families, canoed and camped along the Jura River, visited the dunes at Nida, and swam in the Baltic Sea. "My intent, when I joined the Omaha Sister Cities Association several years ago, was to simply experience a variety of cultural differences," noted Mehaffey. "However, the spirit of Lithuanian history, language, traditions, and customs has become personally alive for me. I have a true family across the ocean...not by blood connections, but by heartfelt love."

Globe Venta takes a bow after their opening night performance. Pictured are Arvydas Rascikas, Vaidotas Jarasius, Evelina Bislyte, Arnas Bakavicius, Silvija Povilaityte (a professional actress of the Siauliai Drama Theatre), Dovile Gaubaite, Ruta Roikaite, Vaidas Gajauskas, and Akvile Rapseviciute.

Sue Mehaffey is greeted by her "Lithuanian kids" upon arriving in Kursenai, Lithuania.

Presented By:
City of Santa Fe Springs
Sister City Committee
Santa Fe Springs Thunder Baseball Team

BIENVENIDOS
MAYOS DE NAVOJOA,
SONORA, MEXICO

Lake Center Athletic Park
11641 Florence Avenue
Santa Fe Springs
August 5 - 8, 2004

Baseball Brings Communities Together
In 2004, Santa Fe Springs, California hosted the "Sister City Series." Baseball players from Mexico stayed with host families, played several games, and went on cultural field trips. Santa Fe Springs has been affiliated with Navojoa, Sonora, Mexico since 1964.

Amidst Tragedy and Unspeakable Sorrow – A Sister City Offers Comfort

Asheville, North Carolina – Vladikavkaz, Russian Federation

Tragedy may happen on the other side of the globe, but it can still hit close to home. In September 2004, members of Asheville Sister Cities were horrified to see on the news an indescribable horror – a school in Beslan, a small town close by their sister city Vladikavkaz, was assaulted by terrorists – the unfolding tragedy left dead 338 people, many of them schoolchildren. They reached out to their sister city and quickly organized a relief effort. Donations were used to buy humanitarian aid and medical supplies for families in Beslan as they struggled to put their lives together, and schoolchildren in Asheville sent cards and messages of condolence and support to the families. Vladikavkaz became the first of Asheville's three sister cities in 1990. When tragedy strikes a sister city partner, it can be very personal, but it can also spur us to action.

Constance Richards, chair of the Vladikavkaz Committee from Asheville Sister Cities, unfurls a banner from Table Rock Middle School seventh graders in Morganton, North Carolina, in the destroyed gymnasium of School # 1 in Beslan in the Russian Federation's Caucasus Mountains. The banner carries messages of condolence and support.

"Like Beslan and Vladikavkaz, Asheville is in the mountains. Our strength and our courage come from the mountains, but we gladly share them with others who come here for shelter or salvation. Many people are calling to find out what they can do or how they can send their well wishes to the families of Beslan, who have suffered so much from this terrible event. Like the events of September 11, 2001 in America, we understand that you have suffered just as much as we."

— A letter written to the bereaved community by Asheville Sister Cities president, Carroll Hughes

Comforting the Smallest Victims
Artist Vadim Bora, honorary member of Asheville Sister Cities and a native of North Ossetia, visits with the smallest victims of the attack on School #1 in Beslan. Bora was born in Beslan and now lives in Asheville.

219

Sister Cities
International
Young Artists
Competition
2004

SISTER
CITIES
INTERNATIONAL

**Coming Together to
Build a Better World**

Tracey Collett's
2004 YAP entry

Young Artists Program Winners 2004

1st – Alana Purcell – Los Angeles, California
2nd – Bryce Corbett – Corpus Christi, Texas
3rd – Davin Singh – Tulsa, Oklahoma
4th – Hyun Jin Yoo – Palo Alto, California
5th – Nichole Phillips – Ephrata, Pennsylvania
6th – Qin Lue – Beihai, Guangxi, China (sister city to Tulsa, Oklahoma)
7th – Raul Martinez – Fort Worth, Texas
8th – Terry Morton – Morayshire, Scotland (sister city to Houston, Texas)
9th – Tracey Collett – Lexington, Kentucky
10th – Whitney Schieltz – Vandalia, Ohio

1st Place – Alana Purcell, Los Angeles, California

4th Place – Hyun Jin Yoo, Palo Alto, California

\Whitney Schieltz,
from Vandalia, Ohio,
submitted this entry

220

5th Place – Nichole Phillips, Ephrata, Pennsylvania

8th Place – Terry Morton, Morayshire, Scotland (sister city to Houston, Texas)

10th Place – Whitney Schieltz, Vandalia, Ohio

Showcase of Young Artists: Transforms Communities and Lives
Beihai, China – Tulsa, Oklahoma

For a community in China named Beihai – the Showcase of Young Artists program brought joy and goodwill. It all started with a young girl named Qin Lue who created, "Coming Together to Build a Better World" for the showcase, and her artwork was sent to sister city Tulsa, Oklahoma. Impressed with her talent and interpretation of the theme, the committee in Tulsa sent the award on to the international competition – where it received high honors. Beihai held a large event to celebrate Qin Lue's achievement and present the award of $300 from Sister Cities International. The award was worth nearly a year's income for her family. Multiply that gesture of friendship and goodwill thousands of times over – and you understand the power within the sister city movement. We are truly about promoting peace through mutual respect and understanding – one individual, one community at a time.

Children of the world celebrate peace in Qin Lue's artwork titled, "Coming Together to Build a Better World."

Qin Lue talks to the crowd in Beihai about her artwork and its message of peace.

2005

International Partners for Peace Builds Ties Between the U.S. and Iraq

Sister Cities International responded to members' requests for a way to work with programs in conflict-ridden areas with the International Partners program in 2004. Distinct from long-term sister city relationships, these partnerships allow communities to undertake collaborative projects focused on specific issues for six months to 24 months. The need for understanding and cooperation in Iraq led to the creation of five U.S.-Iraq partnerships as International Partners for Peace with the hopeful intentions of fostering increased communication, cooperation, and understanding between Americans and Iraqis. These partnerships include: Dallas, Texas – Kirkuk, Iraq; Denver Regional Council of Governments – Baghdad, Iraq; Philadelphia, Pennsylvania – Mosul, Iraq; Tempe, Arizona – Hillah, Iraq; and Tucson, Arizona – Sulaymaniyah, Iraq. This initiative was supported by the U.S. Department of State and matched many times over by corporate and individual donations in the participating sister cities.

Craigavon and LaGrange produced a book highlighting their sister city relationship.

Sisters With Pictures
Craigavon, Northern Ireland – LaGrange, Georgia

2006 will mark the 10th Anniversary of the sister city relationship between Craigavon, Northern Ireland and LaGrange, Georgia. After attending the 1998 Annual Conference, Craigavon became the first international member of Sister Cities International. Craigavon sent the Honorable David Trimble, First Minister to Northern Ireland, to the 2000 Annual Conference held in Atlanta, Georgia just 70 miles from their sister city. Working jointly with its sister city, they published a book about the history of the two communities. Each community sent an artist and photographer to spend time in their sister city and capture on canvas and film their perceptions. Other initiatives have included exchange visits by drama troupes; youth orchestras and bands; folk groups and music ensembles; civic delegations; trade delegations and sister libraries.

FRIENDSHIP IN ART AND CULTURE: CHULA VISTA, CALIFORNIA – ODAWARA, JAPAN

The Friends of Odawara [Japan] participate annually in the Festival of the Arts in Chula Vista, California. "I am proud of our ever-growing relationship with our friends in Odawara and our second sister city, Cebu City, Phillipines. Our world truly is becoming closer and in a tighter-knit environment," said deputy mayor Patty Davis. "The more we can learn about our fellow brothers and sisters abroad, the more enriched socially, culturally, and economically we all can become."

A Leaping Gazelle Arrives in Detroit
Sculptor Marshall Fredericks (left) joins Detroit Chief Executive Assistant Fred Martin and Toyota, Japan Mayor Takashi Nishiyama to dedicate the "Leaping Gazelle" statue at Detroit's Belle Isle Park in 1985. Toyota, Japan is one of Detroit's five sister cities.

Gilbert Takes a Bride
Smallest Community Recognized by Sister Cities International Find Sister City Bonds

Becoming involved in Sister Cities International is big news, especially in one of the smallest towns in Arkansas. In 2005 Gilbert, Arkansas paired up with Bride on the Isle of Man in the United Kingdom – they were the smallest communities ever recognized by Sister Cities International. Although Gilbert has a population of only 28 people, and Bride has just over 300, they have big plans for their sister city relationship. Already twenty sets of pen pal relationships are set up, and elementary and secondary classes are learning about people from another culture. "Our schools are bridging the gap over the ocean through the means of Sister Cities International," said Ruth Andre, a fourth grade teacher in Arkansas. In October 2005 Bill and Bonnie Baker made a two week trip to the Isle of Man serving as ambassadors for the city of Gilbert. They met with commissioners, the local Methodist church and visited the schools. "Bride is the smallest parish with a local government on Isle of Man and Gilbert is the smallest municipality in the state of Arkansas so we consider this an ideal match!" said Bill Baker, co-chair of Gilbert's Sister City Committee. It is with great pride and anticipation of the wonderful exchanges to come that Gilbert and Bride on the Isle of Man link together. No matter how small the population or effort, it all builds world peace.

Innovative Online Fundraising: The Wave of the Future

Funds to improve water quality and sanitation in Axum, Ethiopia are being raised online by sister city Denver, Colorado through www.SupportSisterCities.org, a new fundraising website launched in 2005 for the 50th Anniversary of the sister city movement. The secure website allows local sister city programs to post information about a project and raise funds for it online.

Festivals Draw Together Sister Cities
Springfield, Missouri – Isesaki, Japan – Tlaquepaque, Mexico

Festivals are an important part of the relationship between Springfield, Missouri and its two sister cities: Isesaki, Japan and Tlaquepaque, Mexico. The annual Fall Festival features visitors from Isesaki. ArtsFiesta is held in the Spring with a mariachi band from Mexico.

Parading for Peace
One of the highlights is the parade of school children who walk through the Garden during opening ceremonies. Their headbands are made by volunteers from the Sister Cities Association.

223

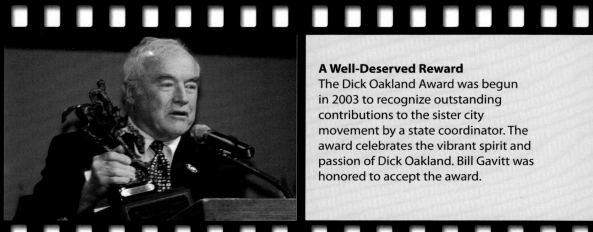

A Well-Deserved Reward
The Dick Oakland Award was begun in 2003 to recognize outstanding contributions to the sister city movement by a state coordinator. The award celebrates the vibrant spirit and passion of Dick Oakland. Bill Gavitt was honored to accept the award.

Pulling for Home
The dragon boat racers gave their all, and drew thousands to the riverbanks to watch the festivities.

Sherman Banks, President of the Board of Directors, welcomes delegates to the opening ceremony in Spokane.

Delegates arriving in Spokane found a warm welcome and plenty of help navigating the community.

Board of Directors 2005 – 2006

President - Sherman Banks
1st Vice President - Mae Ferguson
2nd Vice President - Pat Fallin
Secretary - Kathleen Roche-Tansey
Treasurer - Michael Hyatt
Executive Committee, Open Seat - Alan Chambers
Executive Committee, Open Seat - Jane Wood

Youth Member to the Board - Luigi Campos
President of the Ambassador's Association - Heather Jones

State Coordinator Liaison - Ann Geiger

Mimi Barker
Frederick Blanton
Steve Beinke
Enda Brennan
Frank Britt
Pat Buchanan
Honorable Brad Cole
Jo Anna Edgerton
Martha Fujita (Resigned before term ended)
Nancy Huppert
Georgiana McLeod
Saïda Moussadaq
Eddy Remy
Bill Stafford
Jean Van Buskirk

Sister City Leaders: Mae Ferguson

Mae Ferguson was chosen as president-elect for the Board of Directors and assumes the presidency in 2006. She is the second woman to serve on the Board of Directors in this role.

Annual Awards 2005

Best Overall Program
Over 500,000: Phoenix, Arizona
100,000 to 300,000: Lexington, Kentucky
25,000 to 50,000: Tooele City, Utah
Under 25,000: New Ulm, Minnesota

Innovation
Arts & Culture:
Under 100,000 – Cincinnati, Ohio

Humanitarian Assistance:
Under 100,000 – Palm Desert, California
Over 100,000 – Fort Worth, Texas

Sustainable Development:
Over 100,000 – Phoenix, Arizona

Youth & Education:
Under 100,000 – Boyertown, Pennsylvania
Over 100,000 – San Diego, California

Volunteer of the Year
Jane Neuheisel of Tempe, Arizona

Award for Disability Advocacy
Phoenix, Arizona

Michalska Marika, hailing from Plock, Poland, sister city of Fort Wayne, Indiana, submitted a painting called "Connecting Global Villages." It represents the hemispheres as people with eyes, hands, nose and mouth. Each hemisphere reaches out to the other and their eyes meet in compassion and understanding.

Young Artists Program Winners 2005

1st – Giovanna Bittar – Cartagena, Columbia (sister city to Coral Gables, Florida)
2nd – Qin Lue – Beihai, Guangxi, China (sister city to Tulsa, Oklahoma)
3rd – Zhai Tianlei – Beijing, China (sister city to New York, New York)
4th – Leyla Mozayen – Gastonia, North Carolina
5th – Austin Spitz – Daytona Beach, Florida
6th – Raul Martinez – Fort Worth, Texas
7th – Allison Phillips – Sierra Vista, Arizona
8th – Shou Yi – Leshan, China (sister city to Gilbert, Arizona)
9th – Alex Chychkova – Rice Lake, Wisconsin
10th – Brigitte Lapiner – Miami Beach, Florida
11th – Afton Geyer – Stillwater, Oklahoma
12th – Michalska Marika – Plock, Poland

Qin Lue is from Beihai, Guangxi, China, and sister city of Tulsa, Oklahoma, and is a second year winner. The work offers a mirage of light pastels in her paintings of doves, flowers, trees, international landmarks and children circling together. Doves, the traditional symbol of peace, are the focal point of her painting.

Raul Martinez from Fort Worth, Texas, portrays agile hands sewing threads through the globe and tying countries together. This colored pencil drawing entitled, "We need to get closer," plays on the symbolism of hands and their potential to work and build a new world in which we work together.

Sample of artwork submitted for the Young Artists Program.

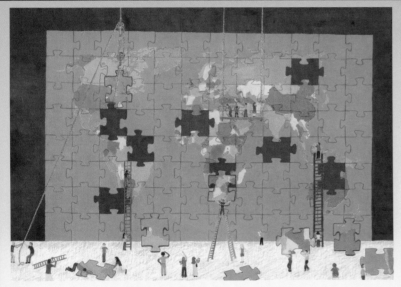

Davin Singh, Tulsa, Oklahoma, 2004 Young Artists Program Winner

"The Showcase of Young Artists helps young people develop valuable life skills and express their hopes for a more peaceful world," said Tim Honey, executive director. "Thousands of youth participate annually in this program and use their creativity to promote better understanding and cultural awareness."

CELEBRATING A 25TH ANNIVERSARY: SAN FRANCISCO, CALIFORNIA – SHANGHAI, CHINA
SENATOR FEINSTEIN AND MAYOR GAVIN NEWSOM LEAD DELEGATION

Senator Dianne Feinstein co-led a 50-member delegation to China with San Francisco Mayor Gavin Newsom to Beijing, Shanghai and Hong Kong to celebrate the 25th anniversary of the sister city relationship between San Francisco and Shanghai. As Mayor of San Francisco at the time, Feinstein brokered the arrangement, which was the first sister city relationship between the U.S. and China. Her efforts helped pave the way for many U.S. communities to initiate sister city relationships with China. Senator Feinstein told the *San Francisco Chronicle*, "I happen to believe in people-to-people diplomacy. I think over the years that if you have good people-to-people interaction, it has a huge dividend for foreign policy." While in Shanghai, Mayor Newsom signed an agreement to continue business internships between the two sister cities that will nurture economic development and friendly relations.

SECOND SINO-U.S.
SISTER CITIES CONFERENCE
SPOKANE · WASHINGTON
中美友城

The closing banquet celebrated Chinese culture and featured traditional dancers.

Second Sino – U.S. Sister Cities Conference

The Second Sino - U.S. Sister Cities Conference was held in Spokane, Washington with 300 participants representing 35 sister city partnerships. It was the first time the event has been held in the U.S. and as part of the Sister Cities International Annual Conference. The conference was open to communities with sister city partners in China, Taiwan or Singapore. The Boeing Company donated funds to support the event.

Delegates enjoyed learning more about how to expand sister city partnerships between the United States and China, Taiwan, and Singapore. This delegate from Jilin is also enjoying the lobby in the Davenport Hotel. Photo by Reta West.

Trilateral Trade and Technology Summits: An American Collaboration
Summits bring together Calgary, Monterrey, and San Antonio

Sister cities are stronger when they work together. San Antonio, Texas created a forum to promote and advance trade and the technology industry in 2001 with the help of Calgary, Canada and its sister city, Monterrey, Mexico. The summits have been held in each of the three cities. Each focused on a different area of emerging technology related to commerce, education and government. Companies shared solutions for customs and immigration issues, exploring how they can work to foster trade. Lloyd Brink, chair of San Antonio Trilateral Trade and Technology noted, "We are reminded daily of the prominent role that technology plays in the international trade arena."

The summits have helped all three participating communities develop new business ties. "The summits are a collaborative effort intended to broaden business practices and match-making opportunities throughout North America," wrote José Luis García, San Antonio's chief of protocol and Sister Cities International honorary board member.

Participants at the first community summit in Spokane, Washington included 2005 conference delegates and many people from the local community.

Blending Cultures Through Music: Symphony of the Americas
Fort Lauderdale, Florida and Cap-Haitien, Haiti

Music is a universal language, and thanks to a sister city project, a symphony orchestra performed for the first time in more than fifty years in Cap Haitien, Haiti. The event faced many financial and logistical obstacles. No major airlines flew to Cap Haitien, and travel advisories against Americans traveling dissuaded some. And the orchestra's musical instruments were delicate and sensitive to heat. Even with these challenges, supporters in Fort Lauderdale, Florida raised more than $35,000 in corporate sponsorships and $22,000 from a benefit concert. Meanwhile, organizers in Haiti set up the concert schedule and raised funds to cover the orchestra's expenses there. It was the first time a native Cap Haitien maestro conducted a European symphony orchestra. Nicol Levy, who was invited to conduct the orchestra by the American maestro, arranged two traditional Haitian songs for the violin, viola, cello and string bass and included six drums in the background. "When local drummers joined them on stage and performed the original pieces arranged by Maestro Levy for the Symphony, it was a blend so flawless that any cultural or class divisions melted into the notes," wrote organizers. The musicians later said that they were so touched by the appreciation of the local Haitians, noting that they had never felt as drawn into the audience in any other country. The orchestra performed in Cap Haitien six times. After the last performance, the musicians and natives of Cap Haitien carried seedlings up the mountainside to plant hundreds of trees on a deforested hillside. Organizers said, "If there was a lesson to learn, it is from the people who made what seems impossible clearly visible, and then actual."

Symphony concert in the Labadie, Haitian church.

Symphony musicians plant citrus trees alongside Labadie residents after the concert.

Symphony of the Americas musicians and Cap Haitien students enjoy talking together about music.

A FRIENDSHIP TAKES FLIGHT: THE MONARCH BUTTERFLY PRESERVATION PROJECT
KANSAS CITY, MISSOURI - MORELIA, MEXICO

The monarch butterfly is a trademark of Morelia, Mexico. The largest sanctuary of these lovely butterflies is in Angangeo and the Kansas City Morelia Committee is making strides to protect this butterfly and its habitat. During a 2001 visit, they learned how these orange and black butterflies travel in the spring from central Mexico through the United States to Canada and in the fall from Canada through the United States to central Mexico. Typically, the monarch butterfly has a life expectancy of 5-6 weeks – but monarchs returning to Mexico live 4-6 months – a phenomenon of nature that repeats annually. In 2005, Vico Gutiérrez, a pilot from Mexico, flew the same path as the butterflies on their migration, and filmed with his crew a documentary on their habitats. They stopped at the University of Kansas and met Professor "Chip" Taylor, founder of the "Monarch Watch" program. Based on his recommendations, the Morelia Sister City Committee plans to build a way station for the monarch butterflies in Kansas City to nourish them while they migrate. The committee also plans to support the "Monarch Watch" project by tagging butterflies for research. The projects are designed to raise awareness in the United States, Mexico and Canada about the monarch butterfly and preserving this special creature's habitat. The Morelia Sister City Committee commitment to preserving this delicate creature is a true friend gesture to their sister city and our world.

Three Brides and Seven Weddings on Two Continents
Omaha, Nebraska - Siauliai, Lithuania

When the University of Nebraska and Siauliai University became "sister universities" in 1997, they thought they'd exchange just faculty and students – no one was expecting wedding vows. Three happy couples married in 2005. Due to the many transatlantic friends and family, the couples each had more than one ceremony to celebrate their nuptials. All of the brides were from Omaha's sister city, Siauliai, Lithuania. Pictured are: Peter and Jurgita Vonk, Nick and Agne Stakenaite, and Ruben and Agne Reizgeviciute (clockwise from left).

Helping Hands across the Globe: Hurricane Relief
Hanamaki, Japan and Hot Springs, Arkansas Help Survivors

After Hurricanes Katrina and Rita struck the United States and unleashed devastation, tiny Hot Springs, Arkansas was filled with evacuees. In Japan, Ichiro Fudai in Hanamaki City's International Relations office organized and directed a grassroots effort to help their sister city. A special hurricane recovery fund was established by the sister city programs. They collected and distributed food, clothing, toiletries, gas cards and children's items. They offered job fairs, social services, and medical assistance. The entire community, including churches, pitched in to help the survivors. The Sasami Daini Elementary School, the Hanamaki Junior High School and the Hanamaki Higashi School contributed funds, and a total of $2,732.96 was collected and distributed to meet the needs of local youth attending schools in Hot Springs. More than 3,000 people in Hanamaki, which has a population of 73,000, contributed to the fund. "The citizens of Hanamaki have truly set an example of friendship in action," said Hot Springs Mayor Mike Bush upon receiving the donations. "We may never know how many students and their families will receive help and hope at a very difficult time in their lives, thanks to the kindness and compassion of our sister city."

A Japanese student presents a check for donations to the hurricane relief fund to Ichiro Fudai in Hanamaki City's International Relations office.

THE PORTLAND-SAPPORO SISTER CITY ASSOCIATION.

The sister city program injected an international flair to Irvine Valley College Foundation's "Astounding Inventions" program in 2005. They brought six talented young innovators to Irving from Tsukuba, Hermosillo and Taoyuan to be part of the event. The students stayed with local families and created projects like the Chinese Revolving Lantern, which used heat to create visual effects, and the Eco-Fly, a photovoltaically recharged helicopter.

ASTOUNDING INVENTIONS: GLOBAL STEPS IN LEARNING

The "Vibrating Coin Bank" was a crowd-pleaser at the "Astounding Inventions" program for young middle school inventors. Created by Koji Sasaki, age 12, of Tsukuba, Japan, sister city to Irving, California. Sasaki's bank separates coins by denomination using sized compartments and vibration.

This innovative brochure featuring a ninja and a baseball player made people think twice about the Portland, Oregon – Sapporo, Japan sister city program.

Burlington, Arad and Bethlehem sent teens to the Seeds of Peace camp in Maine to build reconciliation through their sister city partnership.

Three-Way Sister City Relationship Builds Reconciliation
Burlington, Vermont – Arad, Israel – Bethlehem, Palestinian Authority

Burlington first developed sister city relationships with Bethlehem and Arad in 1991. They have nurtured understanding and awareness that supports a peaceful resolution of conflict in the region. In 2002, they organized a fundraising drive to provide humanitarian aid to Bethlehem, held cultural and secondary school exchanges, and hosted dialogues on conditions in the Middle East. Burlingtonians picked olives in a Palestinian town near Bethlehem and worked in the Aida Refugee Camp and Lutheran congregations raised thousands of dollars to help the Christmas Church in Bethlehem rebuild its destroyed structure. They received a grant from the U.S. State Department's Peace Partners program to promote technological and cooperative solutions to water scarcity in the Middle East.

BOOSTING SOCIO-ECONOMIC RELATIONS
ST. LOUIS COUNTY, MISSOURI – BOGOR, INDONESIA

St. Louis County Executive Charlie A. Dooley and Diani Budiarto, mayor of Bogor, Indonesia, are shown signing an agreement on September 12, 2005 to strengthen socio-economic relations between the two metropolitan areas by encouraging more affiliations among businesses, universities, governments and not-for-profit enterprises. They are with, from left, Robert R. Heuermann, Jr., Executive Director of the St. Louis Center for International Relations; Joe Passanise, President, St. Louis-Bogor Sister Cities Committee; former Missouri Governor Bob Holden; and Alex Soetjipto, Board Chairman, St. Louis-Bogor Sister Cities Committee.

Students from Nagaoka, Japan visit Fort Worth, Texas as part of a student exchange between the sister cities. The cities began their relationship in 1987. The student exchange is one of their longest running programs – going strong since 1990.

Partnerships With Afghanistan
San Diego, California - Jalalabad, Afghanistan

Jalalabad Mayor Arselai with five students from Afghanistan studying in high school in San Diego under a U.S. Department of State-sponsored program. The students sang the Afghanistan National Anthem at the beginning of the meeting between the Mayors of Jalalabad and San Diego, celebrating the signing of a truly unique sister city partnership.

A Birthday Gift That Changes Lives
Santa Fe Springs, California – Navojoa, Mexico

During a visit to Navojoa, Mexico to mark the 40th anniversary of their sister city relationship in 2005, a delegation from Santa Fe Springs, California witnessed firsthand the dire needs of the community's disabled population. They were moved by the sight of a mother carrying her adult son because she could not afford a wheelchair. A van was donated by the city and retrofitted with a wheelchair lift and twenty wheelchairs were donated. The Firemen's Association loaded up the van and drove it to Navojoa in time for a Special Olympics event.

People from throughout Santa Fe Springs, California donated funds to help disabled citizens in Navojoa, Mexico. City officials said that they were very proud of the community's heartfelt response.

The Firemen's Association was an important part of the fundraising drive to provide a van and wheelchairs for sister city Navojoa, Mexico.

Cyber Sister Cities
Fort Lauderdale, Florida – Agogo, Ghana

As the first "Cyber Sister Cities," Fort Lauderdale, Florida and Agogo, Ghana are working with Citrix Systems Inc. to give technology access and training to rural Ghanaians. With Citrix's commitment of technology, time and funding, underserved communities will have the information and communication access that offers improved health care, education, and economic opportunities. More than just donating computers, this initiative plugs entire Ghanaian communities into the information age. It teaches officials, students, and business people how to maximize their use of technology using the latest software applications. "The connectivity and skills which the Information and Communications Technology Center can provide will transform Agogo's educational, health and commercial possibilities! For the first time we will see the world and the world will see us!" said Nana Akoukou Sarpong, paramount chief of the traditional area of Ashante-Agogo. With partners the United Nations, the World Bank Institute, the Digital Development Partnership, and Sister Cities International, Citrix aims to bring information and communications technology to underserved communities and to use it as a driver for local economic development. The launch of the Agogo Information and Communications Technology Access and Training Center on April 13 is the first step toward realizing this goal.

BRINGING THE WORLD TOGETHER THROUGH SPORTS
FORT WORTH, TEXAS – REGGIO, ITALY

The Olimpiade Del Tricolore is a program that takes place every four years in Fort Worth's Italian sister city, Reggio Emilia. The initiative promotes healthy competition among youth sport teams from all over the world by conveying a tangible message of peace and brotherhood to the world. In August 2005, 173 Fort Worth student athletes, coaches and parents headed to Italy – the only representatives from the United States among 23 countries attending. Team USA contended against teams from Croatia, Poland, Spain, Moldova, Germany, Hungary, Sweden and the Czech Republic. The Olimpiade was first held in 1997 as a celebration of the birth of the "First Tricolore", the Italian national flag. They brought home 14 gold medals. The games demonstrate the depth of friendship between Reggio Emilia and Fort Worth.

Athletes from the Fort Worth women's swim team smile for the camera while in Italy.

Exchange students between Kaibara, Japan and Kent, Washington have enjoyed friendship for 40 years.

Friends for Life: Forty Years of High School Exchange Students
Kent, Washington – Kaibara, Japan

In 1965 two small cities began a sister city program with the commitment to exchange a high school student each year. Forty years later, the exchanges between Kent, Washington and Kaibara, Japan are thriving. Sixty-five students have participated in the program, staying with host families and learning the culture, language and traditions of their sister city. Although their communities have changed over the years, with Kent growing from 15,000 to 85,000 residents, and Kaibara merging with five cities to form a new community of 80,000 called Tamba, the communities foster a tight sister city bond. During a 2005 assembly at Kaibara High School in Japan, Gary Thomas, the second Kent exchange student to study in Kaibara, was in the crowd. With greying hair, a face just beginning to wrinkle, and a twinkle in his eye, Gary spoke about his year at Kaibara High School and how it gave direction to his life. Today, he is a very successful attorney practicing international law in Tokyo. As Thomas spoke, Kaibara High School student Yuka Kawai listened and knew that she would be the next student to travel to the United States and attend a Kent High School. At that same moment, Danielle Tuttle of Kent was traveling to Japan to begin her school year at Kaibara. For Gary – his experience was almost 40 years ago, and for Yuka and Danielle – theirs was just beginning

ケント市・柏原高校

高校生交流４０周年を祝して

今日、２００５年４月１９日、ここに *Jim White* ケント市長ご夫妻出席のもと、ケント市の高校と柏原高校との交流４０周年を祝す。末永い発展を願って。

On April 19, 2005, this monument was built to commemorate the fortieth anniversary of the sister school affiliation and good friendship between the City of Kent and Kaibara Senior High School. Present at the ceremony were the Honorable Jim White, Mayor, City of Kent, Washington, and his wife, Edna, to help honor this event.

柏原高校国際親善委員会

Three-Way Relationships Yield Benefits
Noblesville, Indiana – Nova Prata, Brazil – Cittadella, Italy

Many communities are exploring new ways to collaborate and work together. A three-way sister city relationship can be one way to foster new ties and communication. "I met again with their mayor [in Brazil] and told him that Sister Cities International had experimented with some tri-lateral arrangements, where two cities already linked find a third city willing to link with the original cities, forming a tri-lateral arrangement. He was very interested, and with the permission of our Noblesville mayor, I would try to find a city in the Veneto region of Italy to partner with both of us," remembered Indiana state coordinator Henry Cole. His efforts resulted in success three years later - pictured here (left to right) after signing a tri-lateral agreement in 2005: Mayor Vitor Pletsch of Nova Prata, Brazil; Vice Mayor Giuseppe Pan of Cittadella, Italy; and Councilwoman Mary Sue Rowland of Noblesville, Indiana.

Sister States Sports Exchange: Lacrosse makes friends and bridges cultures
The Towsontowne Recreational Council Boys and Girls lacrosse teams, parents, coaches and chaperones smile for a delegation photo at Kamakura in Kanagawa Prefecture, Japan in 2005.

Festival Highlights and Inspires Sister Cities Far and Near
Honolulu, Hawaii

In 2005, the Maui County Sister Cities Festival hosted a celebration of world peace with representatives from sister cities in Chile, China, Guam, Japan, Philippines and Peru. Maui County's economic development coordinator told the *Maui News* that the first-time festival was a successful event and that it will "definitely" come again next year. "It's better than I imagined it would be," Lynn Araki-Regan said as she looked out at the crowd. The festival opened with a peace pole dedication and closed with "A Celebration of Peace in the World" concert. Corazon J. Ruiz-Abad, the mayor of the municipality of Sarrat in Ilocos Norte, the Philippines, told the Maui News that the festival was a chance to enjoy Maui and invite residents to visit. "This will make our ties stronger in the area of tourism," Ruiz-Abad said. The establishment of a sister city relationship was a natural fit, because many of Maui's pioneer farm workers in pineapple and sugar cane immigrated from Sarrat. Many friendships were renewed through the festival.

Maui County SISTER CITIES FESTIVAL 2005 — June 8-11, 2005

Sponsored by:
County of Maui - Office of Economic Development
Hawaii Tourism Authority
Maui Visitors Bureau

HAWAII TOURISM AUTHORITY

MAUI the Magic Isles
MAUI • MOLOKAI • LANA'I

ニューオーリンズ日本庭園協会

The Japanese Garden Society of New Orleans presents

"An Island Garden of Friendship in City Park"

A Garden of Friendship: A Dream Realized, and Not Forgotten
New Orleans, Louisiana – Matsue, Japan

"Our garden will serve as a strong bond of friendship between New Orleans and its sister city of Matsue, Japan and sister port of Kushiro, Japan. It will stand as a unique tribute to Lafcadio Hearn, the journalist and Japanese folklore author credited with first establishing the common bond between cities," wrote the Japanese Garden Society of New Orleans in a brochure about their project. Founded in 1985, the society pledged to create a public space for all New Orleanians that celebrates the city's friendship with Matsue – a garden called "Yakumo Nihon Teien." Plans to build a beautiful Japanese garden were underway and a master plan announced in 1995. The official groundbreaking for the garden was held in 2003 and organizers soon saw their dream becoming a reality – with plants and walkways emerging. Although Hurricanes Katrina and Rita spared Yakumo Nihon Teien, the storms and resulting flooding decimated New Orleans. In spite of the many challenges they face, the committee is moving forward with determination.

2006

Mimi Barker, a member of the Board of Directors, distributes cookies to children and their families during a distribution of wheelchairs.

"Partnership and Peace Tour – Morocco" Builds Goodwill

During the Partnership & Peace Tour – Morocco, 45 delegates extended a hand in friendship to the people in Morocco. Led by Mary Jean Eisenhower, granddaughter of President Dwight D. Eisenhower and CEO of People-to-People International, and Sherman Banks, President of the Sister Cities International Board of Directors, the delegates visited Rabat, Meknes, Fez, Marrakech, Essaouira and Casablanca.

The participants visited extraordinary Moroccan architectural treasures, tasted Moroccan cuisine, stayed in a former castle, and enjoyed the warmth and kindness of the local people. They held meetings with several key officials seeking to set up new sister city ties and strengthen existing linkages.

More than 80 wheelchairs, purchased with donations from throughout the United States, were distributed to needy residents of Rabat and Fez during the trip. Eighty more wheelchairs were distributed in Marrakech and Casablanca in May 2006. As part of the humanitarian initiative, a group of delegates also visited an orphanage in Meknes.

As part of the 50th Anniversary of the citizen diplomacy movement in 2006, the U.S. delegation, in collaboration with the Casablanca-Chicago Sister City Association and the city of Casablanca, held a conference in Casablanca with 150 attendees titled, "Reaching Out to Your Global Neighbors Through Citizen Diplomacy: Promoting Islamic - U.S. Relationships."

Sherman Banks and Mary Jean Eisenhower admire a large photograph of President Dwight D. Eisenhower, who founded the people-to-people movement.

"If you think the first years of the sister cities program moved fast – just wait!"

— *Vice President Ann Galloway,*
40th Anniversary Magazine, Sister Cities International

THE SEPTEMBER CONCERT: BUILDING SUPPORT FOR A PEACEFUL WORLD
FILLING THE WORLD WITH MUSIC ON SEPTEMBER 11, 2006

Sister Cities International is recruiting 50 member communities to hold a concert on September 11, 2006 and be part of the 50th Anniversary of the sister city movement.

September 11th carries special meaning for the sister city movement in the United States, because President Eisenhower delivered his famous speech during the White House Summit on Citizen Diplomacy calling for people-to-people ties on September 11, 1956. His call to peace and global understanding is as relevant today as it was 50 years ago. We seek to honor President Eisenhower's memory and vision, as well as the memory of those lost to violence and intolerance, through joining The September Concert Foundation in holding a series of free concerts around the globe. Fill the world with music on September 11, 2006.

THE SEPTEMBER
Concert

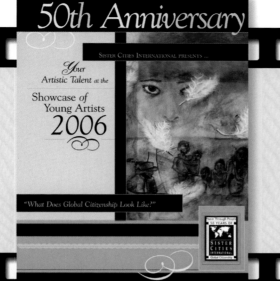

Sister Cities/Sister Schools
Opening up Classrooms to Let the World In!

Sister Cities International and the International Education and Resource Network (iEARN) joined efforts to bring global learning and cooperation into classrooms worldwide. Teachers and administrators in Sister Cities International's 2,500 member communities became eligible for partial scholarships to access iEARN's global learning resources and tools. "Through the Internet, students and teachers have the opportunity to go beyond international simulations and engage directly with students in other countries," said iEARN-USA director, Edwin Gragert. "Students have the opportunity to both learn and teach through direct interaction, enabling them to gain knowledge about new topics and the ability to work with other cultures. These are important 21st century skills." The program not only creates globally literate young people but it also makes it easier and more attractive for teachers to introduce international elements into lesson plans.

The 50th Anniversary: Community Summits Lay Groundwork

People came together and they spoke up. They said we believe in the power of citizen diplomacy and formulated action strategies to better integrate citizen diplomacy within communities and nations. These are the resounding results of nearly 50 successful Community Summits on Citizen Diplomacy held across the United States in late 2005 and 2006 as part of the 50th Anniversary of the sister city movement. Each summit brought a diverse group of people together to share ideas, develop action plans, and create networks. Ideas and priority action items from participants will guide discussion at the National Summit on Citizen Diplomacy being held in July 2006 during the 50th Anniversary Conference, and will be used to compile the "International Report on the Future of Citizen Diplomacy" that will be shared with the U.S. Congress.

Tulsa, Oklahoma organized a large community summit involving its sister cities from across the globe.

A Fond Farewell
The Ziguinchor, Senegal grant recipients bid farewell to the delegates from Prince George's County, Maryland at the airport.

Sister Cities International 50th Anniversary Conference

With 1,200 delegates from across the United States and around the globe, the 50th Anniversary Conference in Washington, D.C. celebrates the past, while building for the future of the citizen diplomacy movement. Delegates are visiting Capitol Hill to talk to decision-makers and legislators about sister city programs and to honor sister city volunteers and local government leaders. The Best Practices Showcase shares new ideas and profiles exceptional sister city programs, while the Mayor's Roundtable on Globalization and Local Economic Development inspires and informs community leaders. Held in conjunction with the conference, the National Summit on Citizen Diplomacy charts a course for citizen diplomacy in the future. The closing gala recognizes the most outstanding leaders in the citizen diplomacy movement today and inspires delegates to a renewed commitment and dedication to the sister city movement.

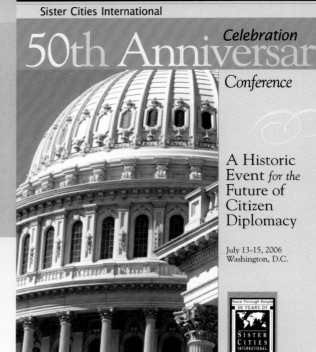

Sister Cities International

50th Anniversary *Celebration Conference*

A Historic Event *for the* Future of Citizen Diplomacy

July 13-15, 2006
Washington, D.C.

50th Anniversary Initiatives

50th Anniversary Conference
International Youth Summit on Global Citizenship
Annual Awards and 50th Anniversary Award
Showcase of Young Artists
Community Summits on Citizen Diplomacy
National Summit on Citizen Diplomacy
Islamic Peace & Friendship Initiative
Wheelchairs for Peace
Sister Cities/Sister Schools
Sister Cities September Concerts
Hewlett Packard Youth Global Citizenship Survey
50th Anniversary Local Government Leadership Circle
50th Anniversary Circle of Distinguished Volunteers
50th Anniversary Commemorative Book

Join the 50th Anniversary Celebration!
SISTER CITIES INTERNATIONAL

Annual Awards and 50th Anniversary Award

Sister Cities International unveiled a new award in 2006– the 50th Anniversary Award – to recognize sustainable sister city programs. More than 70 communities applied for recognition in 2006.

Sister Cities International
ANNUAL AWARDS PROGRAM
50th Anniversary

Peace Through People
50 YEARS OF
SISTER CITIES INTERNATIONAL.
Global Citizenship

for OUTSTANDING ACHIEVEMENT IN GLOBAL CITIZENSHIP
2006

INTERNATIONAL YOUTH SUMMIT ON GLOBAL CITIZENSHIP
JULY 11-16, 2006 – WASHINGTON, D.C.

Sister city youth delegates from around the world are taking part in the International Youth Summit on Global Citizenship being held July 11-16 in Washington, D.C. Held concurrently with the 50th Anniversary Conference, the Summit prepares youth to become effective global citizens in the 21st century. During the Summit, youth are building global leadership skills, advocate for citizen diplomacy issues on Capitol Hill, participate in discussions focused on peace and citizen diplomacy, visit Washington-based international non-profit agencies to learn about international engagement and careers, attend an Embassy reception and meet diplomatic officials, earn college credit, and make lifelong friendships. This extraordinary opportunity for young people from around the globe leads to greater international understanding and cooperation and raises awareness of the important contributions youth can make in addressing pressing community and global issues.

Sustained involvement of youth is critical to the long-term success of sister city programs. Workshops like this one developing leadership skills empower young people to be global leaders.

50th Anniversary Conference Partners

Sister Cities International's 50th Anniversary Celebration wishes to thank the companies, organizations and individuals who are sponsoring events at the 50th Conference.

GOLD PARTNERS

Citrix Systems, Inc.
Harrison Middleton University
Hewlett-Packard Company
International Council of Shopping Centers
PADCOIAECOM
United Airlines

SILVER PARTNERS

American Express
Greater Fort Lauderdale Sister Cities International
The George Washington University
ICMA Retirement Corporation
Sister Cities Foundation
Tropos Networks

BRONZE PARTNERS

Abercrombie and Kent Egypt
The Africa Channel
Black & Veatch
The Boeing Company
Chicago Sister Cities International Program, Inc
& Milan Program
Close Up Foundation
Fort Worth Sister Cities International
City of Hollywood, Florida
Hyatt Regency Washington on Capitol Hill
India Tourism Council
International Mayors Communication Centre
Japan National Tourist Organization, New York
City of Kansas City, Missouri
Laureate International Universities
Open World Leadership Center/aed
Marilyn Porter
St. Louis Center for International Relations
St. Louis Sister Cities
Standard & Poor's/McGraw-Hill
Starbucks Coffee Company
Stone Garden Vineyards
Tempe Sister City Corporation
Toyota Motor Sales U.S.A.
UBS
U.S. India Business Council
Wheelchair Foundation
World Bank Institute

FRIENDS

Raja Abderahim
AYUSA
CH2M HILL
City of Dearborn, Michigan
Ann Galloway
Margaret C. Honey
City of Laredo, Texas
McDonald's Corporation
Sister City Program of the City of New York, Inc.
NYC & Company
Palmea Ltd.
People to People Ambassador Programs
Phoenix Sister Cities Commission, Inc.
City of Sendai, Japan
City of St. Petersburg, Florida
Steppingstone LLC
Taj Hotels Resorts and Palaces
Dorothy Zammit

EMBASSY HOSTS

Embassy of the People's Republic of China
Embassy of the Arab Republic of Egypt
Embassy of Hungary
Embassy of India
Embassy of Italy
Embassy of Japan
Organization of American States
Embassy of the Russian Federation
Embassy of the Republic of South Africa

50th Anniversary Community Partners

WE ARE GRATEFUL TO THESE MUNICIPALITIES AND INDIVIDUALS WHO HAVE JOINED WITH
SISTER CITIES INTERNATIONAL IN HELPING PRODUCE A HISTORIC 50TH ANNIVERSARY PROGRAM.

BAY COUNTY SISTER CITIES
BLOUNT COUNTY SISTER CITY ORGANIZATION
CITY OF BOSTON, MASSACHUSETTS
CARSON SISTER CITIES ASSOCIATION
COVINGTON & BURLING
CITY OF FORT LAUDERDALE, FLORIDA
JEANNIE & DAVID FOSTER
CITY OF HAMPTON, VIRGINIA
ANN M. HEINZ
CITY OF HOLLYWOOD, FLORIDA
OLIVER & RACHEL HOLMES
IMALGAM, INC.
JOHN C. & MARY T. HONEY
JACKSONVILLE SISTER CITIES ASSOCIATION
SISTER CITIES OF JASPER
CITY OF KANSAS CITY, MISSOURI
KANSAS CITY INTERNATIONAL AFFAIRS & TRADE OFFICE
KETTERING, OHIO SISTER CITY COMMITTEE
OFFICE OF THE SECRETARY OF STATE OF MARYLAND
CITY OF NORTH LITTLE ROCK, ARKANSAS
PALM DESERT SISTER CITIES
PHOENIX SISTER CITIES COMMISSION
SEATTLE SISTER CITIES
BRIAN R. SMITH
CHARLES & LUELLA STOKKE
TEMPE SISTER CITIES ORGANIZATION
JAMES R. TURNER
SISTER CITIES OF VANDALIA
CITY OF VIRGINIA BEACH, VIRGINIA

OUR THANKS TO OUR GLOBAL ENVOYS, WHO REPRESENT SISTER CITIES INTERNATIONAL
AT MEETINGS AND CONFERENCES AROUND THE GLOBE

NANCY HUPPERT
MARY PALKO
SHARON RECEVEUR

Sister Cities International 50th Anniversary
Local Government Leadership Circle

JERRY E. ABRAMSON
MAYOR
NOMINATED BY LOUISVILLE, KY

JAMES G. AMATO
FORMER MAYOR
NOMINATED BY LEXINGTON, KENTUCKY

ANATOLI ANATOLYEVICH RAZZHIVIN
ASSISTANT TO THE MAYOR
NOMINATED BY WEST JORDAN, UTAH

JOHN ANDERSON
FORMER MAYOR
NOMINATED BY TACOMA, WASHINGTON

CALVIN J. ANTHONY
FORMER MAYOR
NOMINATED BY STILLWATER, OKLAHOMA

DR. ROBERT K. ANTOZZI
DIRECTOR OF PARKS & RECREATION
NOMINATED BY FREDERICKSBURG, VIRGINIA

B. GENE AURAND
FORMER COUNCIL MEMBER
NOMINATED BY NEWBURGH, INDIANA

ED AUSTIN
FORMER MAYOR
NOMINATED BY JACKSONVILLE, FLORIDA

MARY AXE
NOMINATED BY BOULDER, COLORADO

BILL BAARSMA
MAYOR
NOMINATED BY TACOMA, WASHINGTON

SCOTTY BAESLER
FORMER MAYOR
NOMINATED BY LEXINGTON, KENTUCKY

DOROTHY F. BAILEY
COUNCIL MEMBER
NOMINATED BY PRINCE GEORGE'S COUNTY,
MARYLAND

VIKTOR V. BALAKIN
MAYOR
NOMINATED BY WEST JORDAN, UTAH

FRANK J. BARCELLS
FORMER MAYOR
NOMINATED BY SANTA CLARA, CALIFORNIA

LOU BARLETTA
MAYOR
NOMINATED BY HAZLETON, PENNSYLVANIA

KAY BARNES
MAYOR
NOMINATED BY KANSAS CITY, MISSOURI

KENNETH BARR
FORMER MAYOR
NOMINATED BY FORT WORTH, TEXAS

TONY BENAVIDES
MAYOR
NOMINATED BY LANSING, MICHIGAN

RICHARD L. BERKLEY
FORMER MAYOR
NOMINATED BY KANSAS CITY, MISSOURI

PEGGY BILSTEN
COUNCIL MEMBER
NOMINATED BY PHOENIX, ARIZONA

MARTY BLUM
MAYOR
NOMINATED BY SANTA BARBARA, CALIFORNIA

BOB BOLEN
FORMER MAYOR
NOMINATED BY FORT WORTH, TEXAS

MARVIN S. BOLINGER
FORMER CITY MANAGER
NOMINATED BY FREDERICKSBURG, VIRGINIA

ELAINE E. BROWN
COUNCIL MEMBER
NOMINATED BY JACKSONVILLE, FLORIDA

CATHIE BROWN
MAYOR
NOMINATED BY LIVERMORE, CALIFORNIA

LEE P. BROWN
FORMER MAYOR
NOMINATED BY HOUSTON, TEXAS

BRENDA BRUMFIELD-ROSS
NOMINATED BY VALLEJO, CALIFORNIA

JAMES M. CAHILL
MAYOR
NOMINATED BY NEW BRUNSWICK, NEW JERSEY

DOMINIC J. CASERTA
COUNCIL MEMBER
NOMINATED BY SANTA CLARA, CALIFORNIA

PETER CLAVELLE
MAYOR
NOMINATED BY BURLINGTON, VERMONT

EMANUEL CLEAVER
CONGRESSMAN
NOMINATED BY KANSAS CITY, MISSOURI

ESTHER B. CLENOTT
COMMISSIONER
NOMINATED BY PORTLAND, MAINE

CAROLEE CONKLIN
COUNCIL MEMBER
NOMINATED BY ROCHESTER, NEW YORK

BONNIE SUE COOPER
COUNCIL MEMBER
NOMINATED BY KANSAS CITY, MISSOURI

MELODY COOPER
NOMINATED BY CORPUS CHRISTI, TEXAS

RICHARD C. CRAWFORD
FORMER MAYOR
NOMINATED BY TULSA, OKLAHOMA

BUFORD CRITES
MAYOR
NOMINATED BY PALM DESERT, CALIFORNIA

FRANK E. CURRAN
FORMER MAYOR
NOMINATED BY SAN DIEGO, CALIFORNIA

WAYNE CURRY
COUNTY EXECUTIVE
NOMINATED BY PRINCE GEORGE'S COUNTY,
MARYLAND

LAD DANIELS
COUNCIL MEMBER
NOMINATED BY JACKSONVILLE, FLORIDA

WENDY DAVIS
COUNCIL MEMBER
NOMINATED BY FORT WORTH, TEXAS

PEGGY DEELY
COUNCIL MEMBER
NOMINATED BY PHOENIX, ARIZONA

E. DANA DICKENS
FORMER MAYOR
NOMINATED BY SUFFOLK, VIRGINIA

TERRY DOPSON
FORMER PARKS & RECREATION DIRECTOR
NOMINATED BY KANSAS CITY, MISSOURI

ALVIN P. DUPONT
FORMER MAYOR
NOMINATED BY TUSCALOOSA, ALABAMA

Sister Cities International 50th Anniversary
Circle of Distinguished Volunteers

SUREKA ACHARAYA
BRUCE F. ADAMS
RACHAEL ADONIS
JOHN AKIN
ANNMARIE ALANIZ
ROBY ALBOUY
DON ALEXANDER
CRAIG ALLEN
GREG AMOS
JENNIFER L. ANDELIN
KAREN ANDERSON
SANDI ANDERSON
TONY ANDERSON
ALAN ARAKAWA
IVAN ARBUTHNOT
JOE ARCE
THERESA ARGENTO
AL ARMENTI
STEPHANIE ARNOLD DE VERGES
KITSI ATKINSON
JIM BADZIN
K. BALASUNDRAM
SUSAN BALLEW
PEGGY BANGHAM
SANDI BANKS
RICHARD & BARBARA BARTHOLOMEW
JOANNA BARTOS
KIMBERLY BAYLOR
LOIS BEATTIE
BEVERLY BECK
WOLFGANG BECKER
GLORIA BECKWITH
LEONARD BELL
MARY BELL
FRANK BELTRAN
GAIL BENNETT
HUGH BENNETT
GLORIA BESSENBACHER
JOE BESSENBACHER
DAVID BETTEZ
ARNOLD BIEBER
ROBERT BISHOP
JANET BOLTON
KITTY BONISKE
SHERRY BORGREN
JOSEPH BORICH
VLADIMIR BOROVANSKY
YOKO MINE BOUCHER
BECKY BOWMAN
JAKE BOWSER, M.D.
JANA BOYD
PHILADELPHIA BOYS CHOIR & CHORALE
PATRICK R. BRADY
JOAN BROGAN
TED BROIDA
JOHN BROWN
KENNETH BROWN
RETA L. BRUDD
PAT BUCHANAN
JULIE C. BUCKINGHAM
DAVE BUEHLER
HERBERT BURE

NORMAN BURKHART
ARDATH BURKS
TOM BURNS
KEN BUSBY
CAROL BUTLER
HOPE BYRNES
VICKI CABOT
DAVE CADORET
SAM CAMPANA
JEAN A. CAPPELINO
WARREN & PAT CARLSON
SUZANNE CARRELL
PATRICIA CARRILLO-IÑIGUEZ
JOY CARTER
FRANK A. CASA
JOAN CAULFIELD
ANGELA CESAL
JOHN CHANG
DAVID CHANGE
SHEILA CHATFIELD RADJUNAS
NINA CHEREPANOVA
BOB CHIEN
DR. ALFONSO CHISCANO
DOROTHY CHRISTIAN
WEN CHYI CHIU
STANLEY CIESIELSKI
IVAN C. CLARE
PENELOPE CLARK
GAY CLARKSON
DR. EDNA K. CLAUNCH
SHARON CLAY
DOUGLAS S. COLEMAN
DRUE COMBS
JOYESE CONNELL SNEED
LISA CONYERS
WALTER COOPER
MARTI CORREA DE GARCIA
HENRY COWAN
JOYCE COX
SHARON CRAIN
PETE & WANDA CRAVEN
GORDON CRESSWELL
VIRGINIA CRESSWELL
LISA CROSS
MICHAEL HARRISON CURD
GLORIA CURTIS
JOHN DABEET
GENEVIEVE D'AMATO FIORE
TINA DANIELS
DONNA DARBY
ESTHER DAVIES
WILLIE DAVIS
RICHARD DAVIS, JR.
DEBBIE DAWSON
KARINJO DEJORE
DR. V. PRABHO DHALLA
HARKEET DHILLON
CLAYTON DOBSON
RICHARD DONKERVOET
KATHERINE DOPLER
JIM DOUGHERTY
RICHARD DOYLE
SHARON DOYLE

SUE DULANEY
DEBBIE L. DUNCAN
SYLVIA DUNCAN
PATRICIA DURAND
ROY DURBIN
DR. SHEILA DWIGHT
STEVE W. EBERLE
MARTINA ECKERT
MARY ANN EDMOND
MARY EGAN
NANCY EIDAM
ABDELWAHAB ELABD
CHARLES ELLINGER
JAN ELLINGER
MONTGOMERY ELMER
DIANE E. ELTON
DIANE J. ERICKSON
HARRY S. ERICKSON
RUTH ERICKSON
DEAN ESSLINGER
STEVE EVANS
PAT F. FALLIN
RITTER FAMILY
SARA FARTRO
MATTHEW P. FERNANDEZ
KAROLINA FERO
JANA FIALOVA
FUMIKO FISHER
GAIL B. FISHER
LYNN FISSELL
RICHARD & NANCY FITTS
PAUL FLANAGAN
JUDY FLASKERUD
ANN FONTAINE
WILLIAM R. FORBES
CLYDE FORBES
ELIZABETH A. FORBES
ROBERT FREDERICKS
SCOTT E. FREDRICKSON
ROSELYN FREEDMAN BAUM
ELINORE FRESH
EDIE & OTTO FUCHS
MITSUYO FUDAKA
JUVEN GARCIA
OSCAR SA. GARCIA
WIL GAUGHAN
MARY GAVIGAN
WILLIAM F. GAVITT, JR.
HARRY GEE
JOSEPH GERSITZ
KAY GIANOPULOS
SUSAN GIANOPULOS
JUDY M. GLEN
BOB & MARIANNE GOFONIA
ROXANA GOIN
RALPH GOITIA
VENIAMIN GOLDFARB
ANATOLI GORBUNOV
MIKHAIL GORDON
SHEA GORDON-FETZTOFF
BRIAN GOUGH
ERIN GRAFFY
CAROLYN GRAY

DOLORES L. GREEN
KATIE GREENE
JANE GRIFFITH
ROBERT GRIFFITH
JOSE GUADALUPE MARTINEZ QUINTERO
ROSE GUNJI
NOE GUTIERREZ
MARTIN GUZMAN
TSEGAYE HAILU
JESSIE HALVERSON
HIROYUKI HAMADA
MIZUKI HAMADA
MAYME HAMBY
GABE HAMDA
HELEN O. HAMILTON
WILLIAM HAMILTON
JUDITH A. HANSEN
SHINICHI HARA
OTTAWA HARRIS
PRISCILLA HARRIS
ROBERT HARRIS
DARRYL HARSMAN
PETER HASLUND
WILLIAM HENDRICKSON
STEVE HENDRICKSON
SUZANNE HENDRICKSON
JOAN M. HENSLER
PAUL HENSON
SUSAN J. HERLIN
MAGGIE HERNANDEZ
MARCIA HERONEMUS PATE
PATRICK P. HERVY
MARY E. HIGBIE
MATTHIAS HILGER
ALICE HILL
MARGARET HILL
JANE HIROHAMA
ELAINE HLAWEK
ROBERT A. HLAWEK
RUTH HODGES SMITH
DAVE HOFFMAN
MIKE HONG
JAMES HORVATH
E.T. HOULIHAN III
DAVID W. HUBLY
JEAN MARIE HUNG
GARY & KAREN HUNTER
NANCY M. HUPPERT
DEB HUTTON
MICHAEL S. HYATT
PATRICIA HYDE MATT
MARCELINO INES
MARILYN JACOBSEN
BOB JAMESON
JOHN L. JANG, PH.D.
LEE JOHNSON
PEGGY JOHNSON
WILLIAM A. JOHNSON, JR.
KAYO JONES
LARRY D. JONES
PAM JUSTICE
TONY KAO
DANIEL KARIN

YORIKO KASAI
JOHN KAVANAUGH
SUSAN KEIPP
CARLY KELLER
VERONICA KELLY
PAUL J. KENNEDY
ANNA KHRAMOVA
SHUNG KIM
YOUNG KIM
DALE KINNEAR
HY KLIMAN
LESLIE KNOX
THOMAS KODOMOTO
AL KOHLER
TRAUTE KOHLER
MIKHAIL KOLESNIKOV
JOE KOSAI
ESTHER KOZINETS
RABBI ROBERT L. KRAVITZ, D.D.
GLEN KREBS
LILLIAN KUMATA
KEN KURTZ
WILMA KUSY
TAKAYUKI KUWABARA
ROGER LAHATTON
FRANK LAMB
DOUG LANGHAM
GUY LAROCHE
MARY LARSEN
PHILIP A. LAURO
MICHAEL LEACH
JACK LEE
JOHN LEE
PEG LEISZ
RUTH ANN LEWELLEN
SARAH LIEBSCHUTZ
BOB LIESER
MARIKO LINDSEY
DAVID K. LISK
EDNA LOCKHART
GAYLE LONG
GERALD LORCH
DEAN LOVE
JUNE LOVE
SYLVIA LOVELY
KENNETH LUCKMANN
GEORGE MA
STEPHEN MACKINNON
JUDY MACULSAY
LEONARD J. MAHONY
MARSHA A. MALLORY-BENNETT
JAMES M. MALOUFF III
STEPHEN MANIS
LYDIE S. MANN
THOMAS P. MANN
RICK MARSI
CHERIE MARTIN
RAQUEL MARTINEZ
PATRICIA MASTBAUM
TERRY MATHEWS-DESANT
ANNA MARIA MATTEI, PH.D
ROSE M. MAYES
NUCCIA MCCORMICK
JON MCGRAW
ALANA MCIALWAIN
RAY MCLAUGHLIN
NORA MCMARTIN
PRESTON MCMURRY
PAT MCNALLY
REGULA A. MEIER
ALICIA A. MERRIAM
MARY JO MEUSER
ROBERT MEYER
MARIA MIKHALEVA
BONNIE MILENTHAL
LYNN RUSSELL MILLER

MARSHALL MILLER
ZELMA MILLMAN
BETTY MILLS
JOHN C. MILLS
TZU MING YANG
GEOFFREY S. MITCHELL
NAOKO MITSUI SHIRANE
JOANNA MOLDOW
AUGUST MOLNAR
OLGA MONROY
AMEAL MOORE
DR. VINCENT MOSES
RICHARD A. MOSHER
EDNA MOSLEY
JOHN MOSLEY
VIRGINIA S. MUELLER
ROY MURAOKA
TATYANA MURZIN
CHAR MUSSER
CHRIS NADERER
MARY JANE NAISMITH
HIROSHI NAKAZAWA, M.D.
MICHELLE NARDI
JAMES J. NASON
REGINA NELMS
MARESE NEPHEW
DICK NEUHEISEL
JANE NEUHEISEL
DEBORAH NEUHEISEL SMITH
MARCUS NEWTON
JEANNETTE NICHOLS
MILLER NICHOLS
DOLLY OGATA
MARLENE O'HAYRE
WALTER O'HAYRE
KIKKO OKAJIMA MURRAY
LEN OLENDER
MARYLOU OLIVAREZ MASON
ROSE OLIVERS
NANCY J. OLSON
SIL ONTIVEROS
PATRICIA O'REILLY
SANDY ORIJI
ROSEMARY ORTEGA
JOHN OVERDORFF
POLLY M. OWENS
CLARK PAGE
MARY PALKO
LINDA PARRISH
MARCIA PAYNE
BILL PEDERSON
MICHAEL PENDER, SR.
BRUCE PENNINGTON
HELGA PENNINGTON
LARISA PERMYAKOVA
RICK PESCATORE
BOB PESHALL
ELLEN PETERSEN
CYNTHIA PETREE
DOROTHY PICHNER
JERRY PIES
JANET D. PIKE
ROSALBA PISATURO
WILLIAM & MAGDALEN POFF
SLOBODAN POPOVIC
BOB PORTISS
SONIA POSPICHAL
AUSTIN POTENZA
LOWELL PRANGE
THELMA PRESS
LEE PRESTON
TATYANA PRISLONOVA
WOJCIECH & MARIA PRZEZDZIECKI
DOLORES PUENTE STRAND
WELLS PURMONT
RON QUESADA

CHRIS QUIGLEY
PEGGY RADOUMIS
ANA RAMON GARCIA
ANDREW RATERMANN
NATALIA K. REBROVA
SHARON RECEVEUR
KISHORI REDDY
KENNETH W. REEVES III
RUTH REICHMANN, PH.D.
CATHRYN RENDER
JAMES F. REYNOLDS
KENNETH L. RICHARDS
PHILIP A. ROBBINS
JANNA ROBERTS
GABRIELLE ROBINSON
BEATRICE RODRIGUEZ
CELESTE ROGERS
MARGARET ROSE
ELKE ROSEMANN-BADER
LINDA ROSENBLUTH
DOROTHY H. ROTH
DR. ROBERT FRANK ROTH
LEAH ROTTMAN
LEONARD I. ROVNER, PH.D.
MIKE ROWKOWSKY
MARY RUSSO
BARBARA RYON
TALGAT SALAKHOV
RICHARD SALLQUIST
MARIA J. SANTOS
MICHEL SARDA
KAY SARGENT
SYLVIA B. SASS
KAREN SCHAFER
GARY L. SCHEPF
JEANA K. SCHIEFFER
MILO & ELAINE SCHIEFFER
PHYLLIS SCHIEFFER
WOLFGANG SCHMIDT
ANGELIKA SCHMIDT-LANGE
HELEN SCHOLOSSBERG COHEN
TODD SCHWALLIE
SHERLA A. SCHYLING
ANALY SCORSONE
TIM SEAR
SUE SEARCY
MARY JEAN SEARS
KEN & CAROL SEIDBERG
BAMBI SHEN
CHUAN SHENG LIU
SVETLANA SHVYKINA
KIMIKO SIDE
MARIA SILVA
PAMELA SLAUGHTER
DONALD L. SMITH
HOKE L. SMITH
CHRISTINA SMITH WILLIAMS
MARY SMYTHE PARLANTI
CLYDE SODEN
ABIO-TONA SOKARI
FAUSTINO SOTO
JOE SPRACALE
JAMES A. SPROGGS
GERRIT STEENBLIK
DON STOLL
MELANIE STUART
DAN SUNDARESAN
TAL SUNG KIM
DR. ROBERT J. SWART
BERNARD L SZYMCZAK
MASAKO TAKIGUCHI
SUSIE TATTERSHALL
MICHAEL TAYLOR
WENDY TAYLOR
AKBARALI THOBHANI
GEORGIANNE THOMAS

LORAINE THOMAS
MILDRED THOMAS
TERESA THOMAS
DORIS THOMPSON
FRANKLIN D. THOMPSON
VIRGINIA THOMPSON
TEDDIE THROM
PAT TOMASEK
JOHN TOUSSIANT
SUSAN TOUSSIANT
EVIE TREEN
DIANE TRIFILETTI
JOHN J. TRIFILETTI
KAREN TROMP
CHARLES TSUI
ROBERT TUBLIN
WILLIAM DAVID TUBLIN
ESLUN TUCKER
LAWRENCE UEBNER
SHIGEKO Y. UPPULURI
PAUL VALACH
OFELIA VALDEZ-YEAGER
MAURICE VAN ACKERON
ALICE M. VAZQUEZ
JEANETTE VILLA
JANIECE VOHLAND
TOM & GLORIA VONASEK
MIYO WAGNER
TAKAKO WAKITA
JIM WALSH
PATRICIA WALSH
GEORGE WARBIZKY
ALAN M. WARNE
BERYL WARNER WILLIAMS
DANNY WEHR
SHEILA WEINBACH
MASAKO WEINTRAUB
MARILYN WELD
MIKE WELLS
THOMAS W. WELSH
GEORGENE WERLE
GEDEON WERNER
SAL WERTHEIM
JAIME WESOLOWSKI
PAULA WEST
PHYLLIS C. WHITLEY
MICHAEL WIDENER
DAVID WIENER
ARNIE WILLIAMS
DECKER WILLIAMS
DICK WILLIAMSON
MOLLIE WILLIFORD
ALAN M. WILNER
SANDY WOLFE TOMLINSON
EMILY WOOD
JANE R. WOOD
MICHAEL WOOD
SARAH WOODARD
GERALD WOODWARD
CAROL WORISCHECK
LARRY WRIGHT
PEGGY E. WRIGHT
SADIE WRIGHT
MILLIE WUGER
JO XIAOXUAN
ELAINE Y. YAMAGATA
NASUKO YAMAGUCHI
AL YEE
JOHN YEE
JOSEPH E. ZAYTOUN
WEI-BIN ZENG
SERGEY & IRINA ZHUPLATOV
ERROL ZIMMERMAN
GERI ZITARIUK

Sister Cities International Gala
Celebrating 50 Years of Global Citizenship

Award Honorees

EISENHOWER LEGACY AWARD FOR GLOBAL CITIZENSHIP - MARY JEAN EISENHOWER, PRESIDENT AND CEO, PEOPLE TO PEOPLE INTERNATIONAL

HUMANITARIAN PARTNERSHIP AWARD - KENNETH BEHRING, FOUNDER AND CHAIRMAN, WHEELCHAIR FOUNDATION

CORPORATE GLOBAL RESPONSIBILITY AWARD - CITRIX SYSTEMS, INC. - MARK TEMPLETON, CEO

GLOBAL YOUTH LEADERSHIP AWARD - YOUTH EXCHANGE AND STUDY PROGRAM (YES) STUDENTS- ACCEPTING THE AWARD ON BEHALF OF ALL YES STUDENTS WILL BE SEHRISH KHAN FROM PAKISTAN; HADEEL BAYOUMI, PALESTINIAN CITIZEN OF ISRAEL; MAYA ALKATEB FROM SYRIA; AND LAITH JAWAD FROM JORDAN.

DISTINGUISHED LEADERSHIP AWARD - AMBASSADOR ANDREW YOUNG

Annual Awards 2006

BEST OVERALL PROGRAM
OVER 500,000 – SAN ANTONIO, TEXAS
300,000 TO 500,000 – TULSA, OKLAHOMA
100,000 TO 300,000 – MAUI COUNTY, HAWAII
50,000 TO 100,000 – KENT, WASHINGTON
25,000 TO 50,000 – CORAL GABLES, FLORIDA
UNDER 25,000 – SCOTTSBLUFF, NEBRASKA

INNOVATION
ARTS & CULTURE
UNDER 100,000 – FISHERS, INDIANA
OVER 100,000 – OMAHA, NEBRASKA

HUMANITARIAN ASSISTANCE
UNDER 100,000 – ASHEVILLE, NORTH CAROLINA
OVER 100,000 – DENVER, COLORADO

SUSTAINABLE DEVELOPMENT
UNDER 100,000 – AMESBURY, MASSACHUSETTS
OVER 100,000 – LOUISVILLE, KENTUCKY

YOUTH & EDUCATION
UNDER 100,000 – COLUMBIA, MARYLAND
OVER 100,000 – NEW YORK, NEW YORK

VOLUNTEER OF THE YEAR
ELAINE YAMAGATA, FORT WORTH, TEXAS

50TH ANNIVERSARY AWARD
HOMER, ALASKA
MESA, ARIZONA
PHOENIX, ARIZONA
TEMPE, ARIZONA
PALM DESERT, CALIFORNIA
RIVERSIDE, CALIFORNIA
SAN FRANCISCO, CALIFORNIA
CLEARWATER, FLORIDA
JACKSONVILLE, FLORIDA
FORT WAYNE, INDIANA
BALTIMORE, MARYLAND
KANSAS CITY, MISSOURI
TEWKSBURY, NEW JERSEY
OMAHA, NEBRASKA
CARY, NORTH CAROLINA
CINCINNATI, OHIO
CLEVELAND, OHIO
CORVALLIS, OREGON
FORT WORTH, TEXAS
HOUSTON, TEXAS
RICE LAKE, WISCONSIN